Leave the Dishes
in the Sink

Leave the Dishes
in the Sink

Adventures of an Activist
in Conservative Utah

Alison Comish Thorne

UTAH STATE UNIVERSITY PRESS
Logan, Utah

Copyright © 2002 Utah State University Press

Utah State University Press
Logan, Utah 84322-7800

Manufactured in the United States of America
Printed on acid-free paper

08 07 06 05 04 03 02   1 2 3 4 5 6 7

Library of Congress Cataloging-in-Publication Data

Thorne, Alison Comish.
   Leave the dishes in the sink : adventures of an activist in
conservative Utah / Alison Comish Thorne.
      p. cm.
Includes bibliographical references and index.
   ISBN 0-87421-439-4 (acid-free paper)
   1. Thorne, Alison Comish. 2. College teachers—Utah—Biography.
3. Women college teachers—Utah—Biography. 4. Feminism and education—
Utah. I. Title.
   LA2317.T488 2002
   378.1'2'092—dc21

                    2002006674

To Wynne Thorne

Contents

Illustrations

Foreword

F. Ross Peterson

Alison Comish Thorne is literally one of Utah's finest treasures. In the tradition of Esther Peterson, Alice Louise Reynolds, Ione S. Bennion, Lucybeth Cardon Rampton, Juanita Brooks, and many other liberal Utah women, Alison is a bundle of enthusiasm who has never lacked for causes. She decided to write her memoirs as a statement about how individuals can and do make a difference. Her story also chronicles how difficult it is to make positive change in a conservative culture that mixes religion, values, and politics. Another major contribution of this volume is Alison's view of education in the twentieth century, especially at land-grant colleges. Her professional educational career led her to many places, where she crossed paths with some of the finest minds in economics and sociology. In this memoir she successfully weaves local issues into national trends and creates a fantastically clear view of her expansive world. As the wife of a world-famous agronomist; a mother of five children, three of whom are also academics, a social activist and a scholar, Alison is delightfully ahead of her time.

The daughter of a Utah State University graduate who became a professor at Oregon State University when it was presided over by a former Utah State University president, William Jasper Kerr, Alison has spent her entire life in a university environment. From Corvallis, Oregon, she moved to Brigham Young University in Provo, Utah, at a time when academic freedom was fiercely debated at the Church of Jesus Christ of Latter-day Saints–owned campus. Anxious to continue her education, she moved to Ames, Iowa, and obtained a master's degree at Iowa State University. She then moved on to the University of Chicago for special training before completing a Ph.D. At Chicago, she enjoyed the numerous famous intellectuals who taught and visited the campus. Alison also enjoyed teaching Sunday school with a young English graduate student from the Ogden, Utah, area, Fawn McKay. After a sojourn in Chicago, she returned to Ames and finished her Ph.D. in economics. She is the first female awarded a doctorate in economics at Iowa State University.

She then married a fellow graduate student, Wynne Thorne, whom she had met at church. As they embarked on professional careers shortly before World War II, they discovered that most universities had nepotism laws that forbade both spouses being employed by the same university. So, although she had Ph.D. in hand, Alison did not really work in her discipline for over a quarter of a century. Although the Thornes eventually taught at Texas A&M, Wisconsin, and finally Utah State University, Alison did not teach regularly until the late 1960s. While raising five children, she had enough to do, but her head never left academia and her heart never abandoned liberal efforts toward inclusiveness.

She became a champion for the oppressed and downtrodden. With her friends from university women's groups, she sought to right wrongs. When they saw or felt injustice, they responded with action. She and her great friend Ione Bennion, who lost her job as dean of women at Utah State because of nepotism, fought battles in behalf of unwed mothers, the disabled, and the elderly.

The story of Alison Thorne is a chronicle of how she chose to serve. She certainly was determined to do so, and her home, university, community, and church became better because of her commitment. As an advocate of civil rights, an opponent of the Vietnam War, an avid supporter of the Equal Rights Amendment, and an elected school board member, Alison remained consistent to her ideals and values. Her activities in these movements put her at odds with the church of her youth, and her disillusionment provides another example of why talented and brilliant individuals sometimes feel their voices are dismissed for political reasons. Alison boldly and passionately explains her journey away from the Church of Jesus Christ of Latter-day Saints. While her husband served the university and his profession, she carved her own destiny through empathy and compassion. They became a dynamic team who graced Cache Valley, Utah, for over six decades.

I have known Alison for over forty years and have learned much from her. She is constantly suggesting methods and ways to improve education. We serve on a committee set up by Ione Bennion, before her death, that encourages teachers to incorporate democratic principles in the curriculum. Alison sits on the front row of every session and takes voluminous notes and then questions the presenter with a certainty of conviction. While nearing ninety years of age, her quick walking pace, trademark short-trimmed hair, and razor-sharp mind serve her well. Her children's lives are a testament to the depth of her convictions. There is much to say for doing good and creating conscience.

The words of her autobiography provide a wonderful journey through the twentieth century. Many years ago, Alison, Alta Fife (the folklorist and widow of Austin Fife), and Ione Bennion attended nearly every Utah State University cultural function as a trio. In honor of Austin, I referred to them as the "true" three Nephites, those Book of Mormon disciples who would live forever. Alison is the last of the three who is still with us, but they all live because of their many contributions. This autobiography ensures a place for Alison and her friends in the history of a university and a community and also adds significantly to understanding the women who made higher education work in a land-grant setting. There is no end to service.

Introduction

I came to Logan, Utah, in 1939, with my husband Wynne Thorne, when he joined the agronomy faculty at Utah State Agricultural College, now Utah State University. Although I had recently earned my own Ph.D. in consumption economics, the administration did not want both husband and wife on the faculty; so I was a housewife, or full time homemaker as the home economists put it, and I added volunteer community work.

The culture of Cache Valley at that time encouraged homemakers to be perfect housekeepers and, in canning season, to bottle over three hundred quarts of peaches, pears, and tomatoes, not to mention jams, jellies, and pickles. Frankly I didn't go for perfect housekeeping, and I didn't always meet the quota of three hundred quarts, but I bottled, although I thought other things were more important.

I was seeking to make wise choices on how best to use my time, energy, and Wynne's income to create the level of living that we wanted. That's one aspect of consumption economics. Some aspects of the consumption of goods and services are outside the market system, including unpaid household production and governmental services such as safe water, schools, libraries, and good roads. Much of the giving and receiving of community services is outside the market system. Consumption economics is also concerned with the distribution of wealth and income, including the gap between rich and poor. During the Great Depression of the 1930s, and the War on Poverty of the 1960s, consumption economics was especially important, but it has remained significant no matter how the general economy performs. By the end of the twentieth century, consumption economics had become interdisciplinary and was known as family and consumer economics (or sciences).

Parallel to the growth of consumption economics were changes in the lives of women. Women entered the labor force in increasing numbers. Even mothers of young children were wage earners because families needed more than the male provider. The proportion of single parent families rose, and women began to ask questions about why men's wages were higher than women's for the same work, and why men dominated in economic and political affairs. In the late 1960s second wave feminism was born, and the women's movement would broaden throughout the rest of the century.

I grew up in Oregon with a father who helped found consumption economics. My academic experience as daughter, graduate student, and then wife of an academic took place at the land grant colleges and universities of Oregon, Iowa, Wisconsin, Texas, and Utah, with most of my years being spent in Utah.

In these pages I describe daily life in land grant universities, including free buttermilk spigots during the Great Depression, graduate work in the 1930s, and how careers were built, often with women's help. I seek also to make visible the work that women do at home and for the broader community, work that has rarely been recognized. Four major themes emerge:

- A local perspective on larger history. For example, I trace the grassroots activities of women's clubs in Oregon and Utah, and the ways in which some of them mobilized as the second wave of feminism emerged in the late 1960s and early 1970s. I also show how national movements— the 1960s war on poverty, the movement against the war in Vietnam, the ecology or environmental movement—took shape in northern Utah.

- Mobilization for social change on behalf of liberal causes, from efforts to get a sewage disposal system and adequate libraries in the 1950s, to funding migrant programs in the 1960s, and the introduction of women's studies into Utah State University's curriculum in the 1970s. Some of these activities were primarily local; at other times they linked with national initiatives and resources, as in the war on poverty.

- My ambivalent and changing relationship with the Mormon Church, from early years in Oregon as part of a Mormon minority facing prejudice, to the warmth of the LDS branch when I was a graduate student at Iowa State, to my subsequent decades living in Utah where the LDS Church dominates. My husband and I are fifth generation Mormons, descended from pioneers who crossed the plains to settle Utah, Arizona, and Idaho. I describe our ultimate disillusionment with the authoritarianism of the church. By now my children and I think of ourselves as ethnic Mormons although we are no longer church members.

- Finally this book portrays our family's cross-generational mobility out of subsistence farming and into urban, professional lives. My mother grew up on a small farm in Snowflake, Arizona, and at age nineteen married out of that rural life. My father grew up on a farm in Cove, on the Utah-Idaho border. My husband Wynne Thorne grew up on a farm in Perry, near Brigham City. Both my father and my husband graduated from Utah Agricultural College in Logan, Utah, and then went on to graduate work and academic careers.

Over the decades I balanced aspects of my life, which many people at the time regarded as contradictory. I was wife of an academic administrator, mother of five children, and yet, in spite of a late start, achieved an academic career of my own. I was a wife-mother and a feminist too, in spite of a strand of contemporary feminism that said family and feminism are incompatible. I was among the individuals who made feminism respectable on our university campus. Throughout my adult life I did community work, believing it vital to social justice. Most remarkable of all—in spite of living in conservative Cache Valley, Utah, for over sixty years—I remained a liberal.

My definition of a liberal is one who cares about social justice and who believes in equal opportunity and that the protections of the United States Constitution should apply to everyone on an equal basis. I had the good fortune of working with Calvin Rampton when he was governor of Utah (1964–1976). He once said, "I'm a liberal, and I ran the state rather well for twelve years." He also observed that our former United States senator, Frank Moss, was a liberal who served Utah well for eighteen years.[1]

At a crucial moment in 1971, Senator Moss and Governor Rampton helped me keep a Northern Utah community program from going down the drain.

My narration is not an exact historical chronicle, and these are not merely memoirs. I reach backward and forward in time, seeking to understand what happened. So I have chosen to call these accounts adventures, but they represent my perspective on—and experience of—historical American social change in the twentieth century, especially as it affected women.

Lewis Mumford once wrote that we should try to live life twice "as we encounter it day by day . . . Lacking this second life, we neither carry over consciously what is valuable from the past, nor successfully dominate the future; we fail to bring to it the energy and insight we have potentially acquired in the act of living: rather, we let ourselves be carried along by the tide, bobbing helplessly up and down like a corked bottle, with a message inside that may never come to shore."[2]

In a way I have lived my life twice, because after leaving home at age eighteen, I wrote regularly to my family. These letters, weekly as a student, later every three weeks, written over more than seven decades are one source of this book. I may be many things but I'm certainly not a corked bottle.

1 Growing Up in the 1920s

Corvallis, Oregon, was a pleasant town to grow up in. It was small. Many streets were unpaved roads with wild morning glories along edges and sometimes down the center. Sidewalks were mostly board walks. It was easy to lose a nickel between the cracks, if you were lucky enough to have a nickel. When barefoot, you got slivers in your feet. The vacant lots often had a blooming rose bush, wild blackberries, and what we called marguerites, a white daisy-type flower with a yellow center. Elaine, my sister, and I gathered them by the armful. I had been born in 1914, and she came along two years later. A neighbor once took a picture of the two of us. I was five and Elaine was three, and we were in our Sunday white dresses, standing in the vacant lot holding marguerites. But that wasn't the first picture. Earlier our neighbor, trying out her camera, snapped a picture of us in our everyday clothes as we stood on the board walk looking like ragamuffins. Mama, much upset, dashed out to ask for another picture after she got us properly cleaned up. We did not own a camera.

Houses in Corvallis were mostly frame. Only rich people had brick homes, or so we thought. Wood was universally burned for fuel, and we used it in the kitchen stove. We had no central heating, but there was a pot bellied stove in the living room. Our father bought cords of green slab wood in four-foot lengths, which were stacked in the yard until dry; whereupon the man who sawed wood came, and the whine of his saw spread throughout the neighborhood. Our father then used a wooden wheelbarrow to deposit the chunks in the woodshed.

My early years were spent in Corvallis because my father, Newel H. Comish, had joined the faculty of Oregon Agricultural College (OAC) in 1915. He taught economics-and-sociology, a phrase I learned to spill out as one word when asked, "What does your father do?"

The lower campus of Oregon Agricultural College was not far from our house. It had winding walks, and at the bottom was the Lady of the Fountain, a Grecian statue in a circular pool among shady trees. In summer, the traveling Chautauqua speakers would come and pitch their big tent in an open area of the lower campus. Our mother bought tickets and took Elaine and me. It was usually hot and breathless in the tent, and small children crawled among the legs of audience and wooden folding chairs. There we got our first experience of lectures and operetta. I can still remember the Mikado, with slant-eyed maidens singing about marrying Yum-Yum.

Going west from the lower campus and slightly uphill, one came to the administration building, beyond which was an open quadrangle with a white bandstand. The agricultural building was across the west end of that quadrangle. We used to walk there to buy ice cream. Beyond the buildings were the college barns, where Papa took us to learn about cows, sheep, pigs and horses, and about the parts of wagons and harnesses, so that we would not disgrace him when we visited our many aunts, uncles, and cousins living on farms on the Utah-Idaho border, where he grew up. Three times in my youth we visited Snowflake, Arizona, where Louise Larson, our mother, had grown up. Our last visit as a family was in 1930, and Grandpa and Grandma's home looked the same as earlier—they used coal oil lamps, they drew water from a well, and a path along the garden led to the outhouse. Grandpa Alof Larson was known as a fine farmer, but his acreage was so small, it was mostly subsistence farming.

Oregon Agricultural College, like other land grant institutions, had orderly experimental farm plots, a damp smell of growing plants in greenhouses and soils labs, and a head house with an inevitably dusty smell and look. I would one day marry a soil scientist and come to know such places well. Ice cream could be bought at the college dairy, and there was free buttermilk from a spigot, a help to poverty stricken students trying to get through college on a shoestring. It seemed that most students were poor. Later I would see free buttermilk spigots at the land grant institutions of Utah, Iowa, and Wisconsin. In the fall, "ag" students made and sold cider, real cider, which if kept a few days became hard—we called it apple jack—a transformation impossible with the insipid pasteurized apple juice that came later.

At Oregon Agricultural College, as at several other agricultural colleges, the students were called Aggies. As a small child I regarded the college students with awe. On Wednesdays the freshmen wore special attire: the men wore green beanie caps, and the women wore a green ribbon across the forehead and around the head, just above the round poof of hair over each ear. "Rats" made of hair combings were inside the poofs to keep them round. The college students went canoeing on Mary's River. For homecoming, they built a giant wooden framework that became a giant bonfire, to cheer their team on to football victory. College students liked music and played songs such as "Three O'Clock in the Morning" on Victrolas.

In 1920 I entered first grade in North School in Corvallis, a school later renamed Franklin School. It was a two-story, square, frame building, that somehow had been cut in half vertically and then moved in two parts from some earlier location and put back together again. It had very high ceilings. At the start of each morning, an eighth grade girl pounded out "Stars and Stripes Forever" on the piano in the lower hall, as girls and boys in separate lines marched in orderly manner into the building, past a framed portrait of Miss Willard on the wall. We knew she was a famous person and had done good deeds connected somehow with education.

When I was in the fifth grade, my mother became president of the Parent-Teacher Association, and when she sent me with a written message about official matters, I was allowed into the building ahead of the rest of the children. Such honor! Later she was president of the Corvallis PTA Council, when it was very new. My mother was also involved in carrying petitions to set aside a piece of land near the school for a small park. And she supported the public library when it was newly opened in a white frame house a few blocks from us. I was always checking out books, including all of the volumes of the *Book of Knowledge*. My mother also served as a judge of elections at voting time, on behalf of Democrats. All these activities were considered suitable for wives and mothers, but were not deemed anywhere near as important as what my father did. It took the feminist movement of the 1970s to make me realize the extent of my mother's civic activities and their influence on me.

My mother's membership in the College Folk Club and in the Women's Club were also considered appropriate for a woman in her position. The Folk Club included all women in any way connected with the college—women faculty, wives of faculty, secretaries, and even women relatives living in faculty homes. Actually, the college president's wife, Leonora Hamilton Kerr (Mrs. William Jasper Kerr) created the Folk Club. The Women's Club, on the other hand, was primarily for town women, but interested faculty wives could belong. Members dressed up for meetings, and spoke of each other as Mrs. or Miss, rarely using first names.

Home economics was an important part of Oregon Agricultural College. As a child I knew which was Snell Hall, and I heard the name

Dr. Margaret Snell. Years later I learned that OAC was the fourth oldest land grant institution continuously offering work in home economics, earlier called household economy or domestic science. In 1889 Dr. Margaret Snell, who held a degree in medicine from Boston University, was hired to teach household economy and hygiene to women students at OAC. The board of regents had hesitated over appointing her because she did not have a certificate from a school of cookery, but finally decided that her physician's qualifications (relevant for teaching hygiene and sanitation) outweighed this lack. Snell returned to Boston for quick training in cookery. At OAC, her laboratory included "a small wood-burning stove, a few saucepans, and a sewing machine or two."[1] Snell, by the way, wore loose dresses and flat heeled shoes rather than the fashionable wasp waist and corsets of the time.

When I was a high school student, I took a foods class from Lura Keiser who had trained under Snell at OAC. She told us that in the early days of the college, the shape of each saucepan was painted on the wall of the cooking laboratory to show where the pan was to be hung. We also learned from Miss Keiser that most women students were so poor they owned only two dresses; they wore one all week to class, and each evening they changed to the second dress for dinner because it was proper to change. The following week they reversed the order of the two dresses.

There were not many women faculty in the 1920s, and I think my mother knew most of them socially. She saw them at Folk Club and visited with them at all-faculty functions. I recall as a child standing beside Mama on the sidewalk near the campus, shifting my weight from one foot to another, silently, while she passed the time of day with Dean Ava B. Milam or with A. Grace Johnson, both in home economics. Something I noticed about home economists was that none of them had husbands. Only one had children, and she was a widow, Sara Prentiss, whose son Donald went through grade school with me. It seemed strange to me that most home economists were teaching about homemaking but did not themselves have husbands, and rarely had children.[2]

I was aware that my mother valued the information she received from home economists, much of it through the extension service. On warm afternoons in the early summer of 1923, when Mama was expecting her third child, Elaine and I would walk with her over to the college where she attended lectures given by a visiting doctor, Caroline O. Hedger. Elaine and I played in the shade of a large hedge outside the building, waiting for Mama to emerge, whereupon we walked sedately home, one on each side of her as she had taught us, because in this way we helped "conceal her condition from the eyes of the gazing public." Her dark cape was also concealing.

During the First World War, Dr. Hedger had gone to Belgium as representative of Chicago women's clubs, which had special concern for children and sought to help control a typhoid epidemic. Ava Milam arranged for Hedger to spend six different summers at the Oregon campus to discuss health habits of children. Early on, my mother had been terribly underweight and tense, and when she met Hedger for the first time, asked her advice. Hedger surmised that Mama needed eye-glasses and told her to go to Portland to get a really good medical eye examination. So Mama and Papa had gone to Portland on the train, and she secured eyeglasses that solved the problem. No wonder she attended Hedger's lectures every chance she got.

In her autobiography Milam wrote that Hedger reminded her a good deal of Margaret Snell—"Tall, large, but not overweight. An advocate of hygienic living, she wore men's shoes and decried the shoes decreed by fashion for women's wear."[3] Were Hedger and Snell part of first wave of feminism? It seems to me they were, though I doubt they used the term. Fifty years later I read early extension records of Utah Agricultural College to find out the nature of early pro-grams of farmers' institutes and homemakers' conferences. Caroline Hedger was a visiting speaker at these Utah conferences in the 1920s, just as she was at OAC. There was a circuit of agricultural colleges that she and other professionals visited.

The Utah Agricultural College records also mention a health score card for children. I know that Elaine and I were scored on a health card. And there is a suggestion that a home-constructed trapeze is good exercise for children. I still remember when Mama hung a trapeze made of two ropes and a section of broom handle on the back porch for us. We became quite adept on it. Faculty families had as much access to extension service information as farm families of the state.

After our baby brother, Newel William, was born in 1923 (having sur-prised an unsuspecting public), he was raised according to government bulletins put out by the United States Children's Bureau. The bulletin *Infant Care* emphasized establishing good habits in the baby. Keep him on a rigid schedule, it said. Feed him every four hours and pick him up to soothe his crying only if there is a physical cause, such as wet diapers or a pin sticking in him. Mama was unaware of the behavioral assump-tions of this bulletin and the history behind it. She followed the four hour schedule, but defied the bulletin by rocking and cuddling her baby whenever she wanted. She took Newel to the well baby clinic, one of thousands established across the country by the Sheppard-Towner Act.[4]

At this time intelligence quotient tests were being used in the schools, and our parents were pleased when we did well on them. In fact, when she was in second grade, Elaine was placed on the school stage at an evening PTA meeting and given an IQ test as a demonstration. The audience laughed when, replying to the question of where pork came from, she said "cows." As I watched I suspected that Elaine was being exploited, but this incident shows the enthusiasm of Oregon schools for "advanced" educational ideas. The idea that IQ tests support social mobility and justify inequities would come later.

My parents were "upwardly mobile," to use a term from sociology, but they never used such a term. They both had grown up on small subsistence farms, and now they were in the academic world. In his autobiography my father tells how he acquired the habit of correct speech. In 1905, at age seventeen, he drove by horse and wagon the twenty miles from the family farm in Cove, Utah, to Logan, where he found lodgings and entered a high school level class of 115 students. On that day he began six years of education, first at Brigham Young College in town and then at Utah Agricultural College on the hill. The 1911 Utah Agricultural College yearbook, *The Buzzer*, shows Newel Comish as a senior, a debater, and president of the Ethical Society (ten male members), which he organized because there was no course on ethics at the college, and he wanted to know about ideas of right and wrong. The society had speakers and did reading.

Newel Comish was the youngest in the family and the only one to complete college. Many years later he wrote of that experience:

> I grew up in an environment in which anything but the King's English was spoken. Everyone said, among other provincialisms: "It ain't so." "They was comin' home." "I have went to town." "We had saw him in the morning." "They was theirselves to blame" . . . My English habits were atrocious. I didn't know what was grammatically right and wrong. To me, a good course in grammar was a God-send . . . Yet it consumed considerable time to overcome bad English habits. I broke them largely by correcting an incorrect sentence by immediately repeating a correct one; and by thinking carefully before speaking. This latter device slowed my speech, but the results in time paid dividends. Indeed, by the time I received my Bachelor's degree, I could speak and

write effectively and usually correctly. In fact, I even headed the
English department in the Snowflake Stake Academy for two
years after graduating from college.[5]

While teaching at the Snowflake Stake Academy, a Mormon high
school, he fell in love with Louise Larson, his brightest student, and
they married in 1913, soon after her graduation. Louise had always
spoken good English because her mother, May Hunt Larson, had been
trained to teach and came of a line of women school teachers. Louise's
great-grandparents, Louisa Barnes Pratt and Addison Pratt, firm in the
Church of Jesus Christ of Latter-day Saints, kept journals that were
published by a later generation.[6]

Newel and Louise Comish lived in Chicago and then in Madison
while he pursued graduate work in economics, first at the University of
Chicago and then at the University of Wisconsin, where he completed
his master's degree. Many of his professors were Progressives, and when
he took the position at Oregon Agricultural College in 1915, Oregon was
known politically as a Progressive state because of its legislation.

The Progressive Movement

The Progressive movement, at its height from 1900 to 1915, tackled
problems such as tariffs, unjust taxes, monopolies, and graft. Its most
durable aspect was social legislation, much of which was passed from
the late nineteenth century through the 1920s. Progressives asserted that
government has a wide and pervasive responsibility for the welfare of
its citizens, and for the poor and powerless among them. In the presidential election of 1912, Woodrow Wilson and Theodore Roosevelt, both
running on Progressive platforms, garnered almost 70 percent of the
popular vote.[7]

As an undergraduate in Utah, Newel Comish had already indicated
interest in the Progressive movement by his comments on the proposed
federal income tax, which was a debate question, and in organizing the
Ethical Society. At the University of Chicago, he took a course in ethics
from the famous James H. Tufts, and a course in trade unionism from
Robert Hoxie. In moving to the University of Wisconsin, he became a
student of Richard T. Ely, economist, and E. A. Ross, sociologist, both
known as Progressives. The state of Wisconsin had a Progressive repu-
tation, thanks in large part to the LaFollettes and the famed economist,
John R. Commons.

Oregon was also a Progressive state with legislation such as the initiative and referendum, and recall. The Oregon law limiting the working day for women to ten hours was upheld by the United States Supreme Court in 1908, and Oregon's law for a ten hour day for both men and women was upheld in 1917.

My mother, too, was part of the Progressive movement as a member of women's clubs that supported the United States Children's Bureau and various social programs. The bureau, women's clubs, parent-teacher associations, civic groups, and trade unions provided impetus for the Sheppard-Towner Act, which existed from 1922 to 1929, and made possible prenatal and well baby clinics across the nation. The bureau focused especially on rural areas where women were isolated and lacked medical care, and here the extension service of the land grant colleges played an important part. The Children's Bureau sent out thousands of copies of *Infant Care* and although it was based on John Watson's behaviorist ideas, the bureau did a great deal of good.[8]

I inherited my sense of social justice from my parents, whose beliefs were influenced by the Progressive movement.

Our Pattern of Living

The president of Oregon Agricultural College, William Jasper Kerr, was a former president of Utah Agricultural College. In Utah, Kerr practiced polygamy, as did most Mormon men who held church leadership positions, but upon accepting the appointment in Oregon, he left the LDS church and brought only one wife to Corvallis. His polygamist past was a well kept secret. Kerr promptly joined the Presbyterian church and many of the OAC faculty did likewise, for reasons of status. When my father arrived in Corvallis to take up his new position, Kerr said to him, "I expect you to keep the Mormon missionaries off my doorstep," and Papa did.

Prejudice against Mormons was unbelievably strong, and our folks carefully told us, "If anyone asks what church you belong to, never say Mormon. Instead, say the Church of Jesus Christ of Latter-Day Saints, and they won't know what church it is. If people find out we are Mormons, Papa will lose his job at the college." Our parents were fourth-generation Mormons, descended from forebears who had crossed the plains under grueling conditions. Snowflake and Cove, the towns where they grew up, were almost entirely Mormon.

In Corvallis, if there were enough families, the tiny LDS branch held Sunday school. For a time we met in the upstairs of the city fire hall, and

I remember mothers clutching their young, afraid they would fall down the hole around the fire pole and break their necks. I recall that the water of the sacrament was passed in one drinking glass, with each member turning the glass a bit, trying to stay clear of other people's germs. In my earliest years there were not enough LDS members to hold Sunday school, and our mother took Elaine and me to the Evangelical church because it was near. Later we changed to the Congregational Church because it was "more thriving." Mama wrote in the family record book that I took part in children's programs "seeming not to have any sense of stage fright."

Mama taught me to read in the Wheeler *Primer* when I was three-and-a-half years old, and she taught me to write cursive when I was five. In Oregon schools each grade was divided into low and high sections. I entered first low when I was six, and was skipped to first high. In third low I came down with whooping cough, and Mama taught me so well while I was home that I was skipped to third high. I also skipped fourth low.[9] Fortunately, I was tall for my age, and most people didn't know how young I was.

As for upward mobility, the first year my parents lived in Corvallis, Papa hired a boy to put the firewood into the woodshed, believing that a professor should not do such menial work. However, after a time this seemed absurd, so he did it himself.

I suppose ours was the isolated nuclear family of which sociologists write. By becoming an academic, my father had left numerous relatives—all farmers—and my mother had left hers. There were letters and occasional visits, but mostly we led our own life miles away from relatives. My mother told us that she had been homesick in Corvallis until she made her first trip back to Snowflake, taking me (age three) and Elaine (age one) on the train. On our return she decided life in Corvallis was pretty good after all, and was not homesick again.

We were self-sufficient in the sense that, when our values clashed with those of other people, my folks would say, "We don't believe in keeping up with the Joneses. We decide for ourselves what is important," words which I found myself repeating years later to my own offspring.

In 1920 Mama took a college course in typing, at my father's suggestion. She typed at home on a portable which she held on her lap. She also took a course in economics from my father because he was writing a book and needed her help. In our upstairs bedroom, Elaine and I often fell asleep to the sound of Mama typing downstairs as she worked away on the manuscript, *The Standard of Living*, published in April 1923. It was a landmark book in the new field of consumption economics. Other important books were Hazel Kyrk's *A Theory of Consumption* and Elizabeth E. Hoyt's *The Consumption of Wealth*.[10]

Mama also took swimming classes at the college. The arid climate of Snowflake was not conducive to female swimming although boys all over the West swam naked in irrigation canals. Mama's ambition was to swim in every river of Oregon, clad in a swimming suit, and over the years we children swam with her in the Willamette, the Rogue, and the McKenzie rivers. When she chose spots in the mountains, the waters were terribly cold. Papa hated cold water, so he regularly swam in the college swimming pool.

My mother would have liked to take more college classes but there was little encouragement for wives to attend regular classes, and there was just too much housework and rearing of children to be done. Mama did a lot of housework in our home, even though Elaine and I helped. Laundry was hard work. Mama washed on a washboard and used a hand wringer, and then hung the clothes outdoors except when it rained (which was often in Corvallis), in which case she hung them on the back porch and across the kitchen. She heated water on the kitchen stove in the large, oval boiler and punched the clothes with a stick worn smooth from lots of punching to keep the clothes under the boiling water. Once when the side of the boiler sprang a tiny leak, she filled the hole with a bit of rag, and it held. She made starch but bought bottled bluing. She ironed with sad irons on the kitchen table on top of sheets folded square, which became satisfactorily smooth from the pressure.

When Mama got her first electric iron—it cost five dollars; what a wonderful thing it was!—the heavy sad irons were used only on cold nights when she heated them, wrapped them in newspaper, and put them at the foot of our bed in the chilly upstairs room where Elaine and I slept. How heavenly those warm sheets felt! If Mama forgot to heat the sad irons, she simply lifted up a stove lid and wrapped it in news-paper. I sometimes wondered why the stove lid didn't come unwrapped and leave soot in the sheets, but it never did.

After Newel was born, Mama decided that the sheets, towels, dish-towels, shirts, and cotton underwear would go to the local laundry, to come back as wet wash which we then hung and dried at home. We did the baby's diapers every day by hand, using the hand wringer. My father, as an economist, did not feel that investing in a washing machine was economical, but Mama said her back could not stand the washboard anymore.

As for cooking, for years we used a wood stove whose oven lacked a thermometer. Mama would wave her hand through the oven and know whether it was hot enough for bread, pie, or cake. Later we got an electric stove, but its oven was never satisfactory from the children's point of view. We liked the old wood stove because on cold winter mornings when we came downstairs to dress, we sat on a mail order catalog laid on the warm ledge, from which we could see the coals.

For years Papa refused to buy a refrigerator because the mark-up was so high that he was not going to let any retailer make that much profit off him. This suspicion of undue profit led him to organize the Cooperative Managers' Association at Oregon Agricultural College, through which fraternities and sororities bought wholesale all the items they needed, including groceries, fuel, and furniture.[11] Naturally the local merchants were incensed at this wholesale buying out of town and tried to break the contract. Papa was always very careful never to buy anything outside of the association, not so much as a loaf of bread, and we children were warned not to do so either. The director of the association sometimes came to our house to confer with Papa, and if the weather was good they would go for a long walk to discuss strategy to counteract local attempts to break up the association. If it rained, they secluded themselves in the front room behind closed doors.

Mama did a lot of canning, especially peaches and pears. Elaine's hand was small enough to put peach and pear halves into the Mason quart jars, a job Newel later inherited. We did tomatoes and pickled beets but never had a pressure cooker, so we didn't do other vegetables or meat. What Mama really enjoyed was sewing, and the fact that it saved money was also a big incentive. And yet her treadle sewing machine was not off-limits for play. It was a sturdy machine, with a wooden cover, rounded on the corners. As small children we were allowed to take off the cover and turn it upside down to make a boat. Sometimes we tried putting a roller skate under each end, hoping to paddle ourselves around the dining room table on the linoleum. As we grew up, Elaine and I learned to sew, and by ages eight and ten had each pieced a quilt top.

For her sewing, Mama brought home tiny samples of material from the stores to help decide what she wanted to buy. Some of these she tested. By burning a piece that was supposed to be wool, she noticed carefully whether it swelled and oozed; if so, she was satisfied it was really wool. She also burned silk; if it left a residue, it was "weighted" and therefore suspect. When she wrote her once-a-month letter home to her own mother in Snowflake, she would include a small sample of the material she was sewing.

Although I have sewed very little in my life, I still carry in my memory information I never learned in college: the names of all kinds of fabrics and patterns, such as muslin, percale, calico, gingham, nainsook, dimity, marquisette, organdy, taffeta, silk, satin, pongee silk, shantung, chiffon, crepe de chine, velvet, broadcloth, pique, sateen, cretonne, seersucker, challis, serge, cashmere, gabardine, damask, corduroy, poplin, sateen, dotted Swiss, cheese cloth, flannel, worsted, and monks cloth. There were paisley pattern, herring bone weave, and twill. And all of this before artificial fibers. I remember our excitement when rayon was invented, and Mama made a rayon dress for each of us. Mine was deep red-orange in color.

Mama made all our dresses, some of our underwear, and all our coats. I did not have a "boughten" coat until I reached high school. Used garments got taken apart to be re-used. How often I sat with a piece of an old coat being taken apart, pinned to my dress at the knee of my brown cotton stocking while I pulled on one edge of a sewed seam and cut the stitching with a razor blade, being careful not to cut the material.

When we were quite young, Mama made summer coats for Elaine and me out of an old graduation robe of Papa's—wonderful black, thin wool. We wore those coats on pleasant evenings when the family walked downtown to the movies, taking the diagonal walk past the white courthouse of Benton County. Walking home afterwards, arm-in-arm in the dark, Elaine and I were tired, and took turns closing our eyes for a block while the other kept awake and guided the legs. I am happy to report that the Benton County Courthouse still stands today, in regal splendor.

My parents were frugal. Papa was determined to save enough for their old age so they would not have to live with their children. Elaine and I used to wish for a larger wardrobe. We got tired of having just two school dresses, one for a week and a change for the next week, and then repeat. We felt we were no better off than Lura Keiser at the turn of the century. In winter we had heavier and darker dresses. Mama would say, when we complained of just two dresses at a time, that it was better to have two well-made dresses than a closet full of "cheap, boughten stuff." Still, we envied our friends whose mothers did not sew and who had cheap, boughten stuff.

Mrs. McHugh lived near us. She sewed for a living, and I still remember how her rough hands rasped on silk. Mama took her sewing problems to her. What I did not realize was that sewing for a living did not earn much money, yet it was the only way that widowed Mrs. McHugh could support herself and her daughter. My father knew it was a poorly paid occupation, and that most women who held jobs received poor pay. This is why he was adamant that Elaine and I secure good educations and be able to earn a decent living before we married, because one never knew what the future held by way of divorce or widowhood. The neighbors thought this was a cynical attitude toward marriage, but Papa didn't care about their opinions on the subject.

When I was in the third or fourth grade, the children from the county orphanage attended our school, but when a measles epidemic broke out they stopped coming, and apparently went back to their own school rooms. In my brief acquaintance with them, I learned that at least two of the girls were not really orphans. They had no fathers, but had mothers whose employment did not pay enough to support them, or else took them away from home, leaving nobody to care for the children.

Our own mother never held an outside job. The only money she earned was as judge of elections. She was a Democrat, and apparently Democrats were in short supply in our community so she usually helped out at the polls, for which she earned the munificent sum of five dollars. Sixty years later I relearned what surely we must have been taught in grade school: that Oregon gave women the vote in 1912, and that Abigail Scott Duniway, the Oregon pioneer and suffrage leader, was a key figure in bringing it about. Actually woman suffrage lost by nineteen votes in Benton County in 1912 but other counties gave a majority.[12] Women had held the vote for only three years when we moved to Corvallis in 1915.

When I was young, I wondered if Mama wished she had a job outside the home. I think she sometimes wished she had her own money. Actually she was realistic enough to know there was plenty of work to do at home, and that women who held outside jobs received low pay. Papa would never have allowed her to work outside the home anyway. Today I ask myself about this patriarchy. Mama did sometimes refer to Papa as "the lord and master" but usually in a joking manner.

We had a family friend, a single woman who seemed middle-aged to me but was probably in her thirties, who clerked at Penney's. I think Mama envied her because she was not weighed down with children and housework. Mama rarely called unmarried women "old maids,"

1919. Elaine at three and Alison at five years old.

though everyone else did. She thoughtfully referred to them as "women of superior judgment." I used to feel sorry for this friend because she had no children. Our parents, bless their hearts, were always saying how glad they were to have us, and we children knew in our very bones that we were an important part of our parents' world.

Our mother was an interesting person to live with. She could whistle through a blade of grass held between her thumbs. She could make a whistle out of a piece of green willow. She could carve a stalk of corn into a tiny violin. She could play jacks with marbles. As a child in Snowflake, she didn't have "boughten" jacks or even a small ball to bounce, so adobe marbles had to serve as both. This meant she had to scoop up the adobe jacks while the adobe ball was in the air. With no bounce, she moved her hands swiftly.[13]

Our father was great on taking daily walks as a good form of exercise. We sometimes went with him, but what we really liked were the Sunday hikes in good weather. We hiked to the hills as a family, or down to the Willamette River with its clusters of rounded rocks along the shore. And every summer we went to Newport for two weeks. We

Top: Louise, Elaine, Alison, Newel H. Comish.
Above: Our family and new car, ca. 1930.

were enchanted by the ocean and the hard sand beaches, the soft sand dunes, and the dense brush which sometimes held huckleberries. Mama had learned a lot about plants, trees, and birds through reading books, and we learned from her during these outings.

No one else in our neighborhood went on family hikes or to Newport for two weeks. On the other hand, some children took music lessons but we did not. We were not really a musical family. Mama and

333 N. 13th, Corvallis

Elaine could sing quite well and even whistle, but the rest of us could not carry a tune in a basket. We never had a piano but the people next door did, and their only daughter, who was in her teens, played it. On pleasant evenings Elaine and I would dance barefoot in the grass outside the open window as she played. One of the wonderful things Mama did for Elaine and me was to make us ballet slippers for dancing on the lawn. Mama took an old pair of her own high topped black shoes and used the soft leather of the uppers to make soles for our slippers. She made the tops out of an old gray serge suit of Papa's. We laced our slippers with long black shoe strings. They were elegant, and we danced to the tune of "The Firefly," which the girl next door played over and over again.

Something else I remember about the girl next door was that, when her beau came to visit, she sat on his lap in the living room. Elaine and I used to peek through the window to watch them. Most people at the time did not have sofas. Chairs were what they had in the living room, and so instead of sitting close to each other on a sofa, a young man held his girl on his lap.[14] When Papa got tired at home in the daytime, he would lie down on the living room carpet and take a snooze. We did not have a davenport to snooze on until much later. In fact we acquired a davenport at about the same time we acquired a phonograph, which was a long flat cabinet, whereas the old-fashioned Victrola our neighbors had was tall and narrow. The real reason we got that phonograph was because I was failing music appreciation at school. Mama promptly bought records of the music that I was unable to recognize at school, and we played those records until I *knew* them.

I realized later that our furniture was sparse when we were young because Papa was saving for old age, and a large chunk of his salary went into house payments and into savings each month. When we became older, our folks did not want us to feel disgraced, and so they flossied up the living room with a new Wilton rug, the phonograph, a blue davenport, and two Windsor chairs. The pot-bellied stove gave way to a real fireplace, and the living room and dining room became one room, heated by the fireplace. We never had central heating in our Corvallis home. Elaine and I bought some jazz records, and we practiced the Charleston on the linoleum by the kitchen stove, with the phonograph sending its music in from the front room. Elaine even got a ukulele; her best piece was "Little Brown Jug How I Love Thee." We also talked Mama into cutting our hair short. And we went to a beauty shop and got permanents.

In 1927 we went to live for a year in Madison, Wisconsin, where Papa completed course work for his doctorate. We went on the train and slept in a Pullman berth. What an adventure! In Madison we lived in a third floor flat, experienced real snow and ice in winter, and in summer learned to swim in Lake Mendota. On Sundays, in good weather, we often walked as a family to Lake Wingra. I attended the high school attached to the University of Wisconsin, a tremendous experience because all the teachers were excellent, and whole new vistas opened to me. High school students had access to the university library, and I had a favorite spot under the circular staircase where I studied for hours. My father boasted that while he was getting A's his daughter was getting A+'s, and he assured me that, of course I could get a Ph.D. someday. There was nothing to hold me back. My mother agreed with him. And so at the age of thirteen, while living in Madison, I decided that some day I would.

When we came home again to Corvallis, we arrived in our first car, which Papa, accompanied by a fellow student, had purchased in Detroit. Papa learned to drive as he piloted it from factory to Madison. I think he had an accident on the way, broke the windshield and had it replaced, but he would never talk about it. Mama learned to drive the car in Madison. Because she had learned to handle a team of horses when very young, she saw no reason why she could not drive a car too. She took me with her when she practiced, driving slowly around blocks in a quiet residential area. When we returned to Corvallis, the woodshed had to make room for the car as well as the wood supply. And the next year I learned to drive because my father decided that fourteen was a good age, and so he taught me.

How Faculty Earn and Spend

Jessica Peixotto's 1922–23 study of faculty earning and spending at the University of California, Berkeley, might throw light on my parents' way of life in the 1920s because both Oregon Agricultural College and Berkeley were in Pacific coast states. Nine faculty wives encouraged Peixotto's study. They reviewed their own experience and talked with a number of "the most intelligent, capable and level headed" faculty wives. (Note Peixotto's careful adjectives.) Looking back, I am astounded at the action of these faculty wives because, in succeeding decades, wives were expected to be silent on salaries. Perhaps in the early 1920s at Berkeley, the New Woman was in evidence and overtones of the Progressive Era lingered. Dorothy Hart Bruce, faculty wife, concluded:

> Thus it appears that the professor's wife, if illness, or children or other dependents have any part in her life, cannot expect her husband to have leisure for research either during or between semesters, cannot expect freedom from debt, cannot expect her husband's income to increase in proportion to the increase in the size of their family and the needs of his growth and of her own, cannot expect sabbatical years, cannot expect any material expression in her home of her love of comfort and beauty, or any intellectual or artistic quality in her daily occupations; in fact can expect little but housework.[15]

Peixotto had already studied living standards of San Francisco workers. She now undertook to study ninety-six faculty families with assistance of graduate students and the nine faculty wives. Her study summarized the household work these ninety-six women did, and indicated how little domestic help most of them had. To help out financially, one-third of the wives of full professors were employed. Half the wives of associate professors were employed, as were around 40 percent of wives of men in lower faculty ranks. To earn extra money, male faculty taught for extension, taught summer school, and wrote textbooks.[16]

Peixotto concluded there was an academic standard of living with emphasis on acquiring and giving knowledge. The average academic man had a rational doctrine of spending, a theory that deprecated personal display, scorned quantity consumption, and, above all, competitive consumption. In this sense my father was an average academic man, not given to personal display, quantity consumption, or keeping up with the Joneses. My mother upheld his views.

My father regarded academic salaries as far too low, and although he praised President Kerr's ability to get the state legislature to fund new buildings at OAC, he regretted that Kerr did not raise faculty salaries. My mother, like two-thirds of full professors' wives in the California study, did not earn money but she stretched her husband's salary with careful spending, much sewing and canning, and by doing his typing. Peixotto wrote, "Only $60 a year as an average for professional expenses means that in most cases the faculty member, or his wife for him, has spent many hours at clerical drudgery."[17]

The term "role model" did not exist in those days, but I suppose that's what Peixotto became for me because my father would point out that she held a Ph.D. in economics and was a full professor. He always referred to her, and to all professional women, by the last name, just as he referred to men by the last name.

Peixotto graduated from the Girls' High School of San Francisco in 1880, but her father disapproved of women going to college, so she remained at home for over ten years, learning foreign languages, music, household management, and interior design. In 1891 she enrolled at the University of California to study political science and economics, and after a year's research at the Sorbonne, returned to UC where she received a Ph.D. in 1900.

One reason President Benjamin Wheeler hired Peixotto, in 1904, was to encourage increased enrollment of women at the university. Before long she was teaching and researching in social economics in collaboration with male colleagues. By 1912 they were joined by Lucy Stebbins, and later by Barbara Armstrong and Emily Huntington, all highly regarded.[18]

Because of Peixotto's expertise in household budget studies, the California State Civil Service Commission appointed her, in 1921, to investigate adequacy of state wages and salaries. She then obtained funding for the university to continue annual pricing of family budgets for three groups of workers—laborers, clerks, and executives. This was done through the Heller Committee for Research in Social Economics, which she headed.

The state government used these annually priced family budgets to set wages and salaries, and for purposes of arbitration. In keeping with the Progressive tradition, Peixotto and the other social economists at Berkeley studied causes, consequences, and potential solutions to social economic problems such as poverty, illness, crime, and unemployment. Old age, health, and unemployment insurance now exist in the United States partly due to efforts of the social economists at Berkeley.

I never met Peixotto, but my father might have, because he taught a six weeks' summer session at the University of California in 1924. That was an interesting summer. I was ten, Elaine was eight, and Newel was not yet a year old. We went by train to California, leaving our father to teach at Berkeley while the rest of us went on to Arizona to visit in Snowflake. I remember how hot it was in the middle of the night, when the train stopped at Needles to take on water for the engine. We woke up sweating in our berths. Although Mama often said with a smile that horses sweat, men perspire, and women glow, she admitted we were sweating that night.

In Snowflake, Elaine and I played with our cousins, tromped hay on the hay wagon, gathered eggs in the barn, and walked the path to the outhouse. After the Berkeley summer session ended, Papa came on to Snowflake for a quick visit, and then we all took an auto trip with relatives to the Grand Canyon before returning to Corvallis by train.

At the end of the 1920s, I was fifteen years old and knew that Peixotto had a Ph.D. in economics and was an exceptional professor at Berkeley, but I didn't know the details. And I had no inkling of my future as a faculty wife with my own Ph.D. in economics, and no inkling of how my own concern for social justice would play itself out.

2 The Great Depression and College Years

After the crash of October 1929, no one realized the country was in for a decade-long Depression, but we knew that times were hard. At Corvallis High School I was part of a movement to rent caps and gowns for graduation because we knew that many students could not afford suits and lovely dresses, and we knew many of the 147 students in our class could not afford to go on to college, even with room and board at home. We graduated in rented gray caps and gowns.

My senior year at Corvallis High School, I was news editor of the weekly school paper, *The High-O-Scope*. When it came time for Girls' League to publish its annual issue, I helped. I now wonder how far back in time these Girls' Leagues went, and whether they were related to the suffrage movement. Our Girls' League tried to get representation on the student council but failed miserably. In debate, Elizabeth Price and I won our district, went to state finals, and lost to two boys from eastern Oregon. There was no gender segregation in debate in Oregon high schools. Most teams had both boys and girls on them. High school students were always boys and girls, not men and women.

I attended Oregon State College (Agricultural had been dropped from the school's name) my freshman and sophomore years, walking the few blocks from our house at 333 North 13th. It rained often and I hated galoshes, so my memories are of wet leather-soled shoes, in which my feet were clammy and intensely uncomfortable. In college I repeated earlier activities, helping edit the daily *Oregon State Barometer* and participating in debate. There, women's and men's varsity debate teams were separate, and women's teams had different questions, with one of the women's questions usually related to the home.

Fortunately for me, my father could afford to send me to college. My only earnings came from grading papers for my history professor at forty cents an hour. I had a double major in education and economics, but my father insisted I also take a year of mathematics with the engineers. I was one of very few women in those classes and got good grades. In English composition, my essay about my grandfather, Alof Larson in Snowflake, appeared in *Manuscript*, the campus literary magazine.[1] Professor Frank Parr, in education, arranged for a piece I wrote about school assignments to be published in *School and Society*. He also recommended for publication a book review I wrote of H. E. Buchholz's *Fads and Fallacies in Education*. In my review, which appeared in the *Oregon Education Journal*, I noted that Buchholz advocated higher pay for men than for women teachers, so that men could support their families. I wrote that "women of the suffrage movement and the WCTU would express righteous indignation" at that suggestion. The final paragraphs of my review were continued over onto page thirty, which also included two unexpected pieces of information, in light of today's feminism. Across the top of the page was a picture of county school superintendents in session at the Oregon State Department of Education on July 11, 1932. Fifteen of the thirty-four people were women, and the president was a woman. Certainly a much better showing than in later decades.

The second piece of information read: "The fourth Friday in October of each year has been set aside by legislative enactment as a day on which the schools of Oregon shall give recognition to the life and work of Frances E. Willard." Willard, who lived from 1839 to 1898, worked toward prohibition, advocated for juvenile courts, social morality, and economic justice, and, in the words of the article, was also "a prophet of international peace through understanding and arbitration." The State of Illinois had placed her statue in Statuary Hall, Washington, D.C., "the only woman thus far honored in this way."[2] No wonder Willard's picture hung in the hall of my elementary school. Remnants of the Progressive tradition lingered.

After two years at Oregon State College, I transferred to Brigham Young University in Provo, Utah, where I completed my undergraduate work. I was eighteen years old and wanted to be outside the shadow of my professor father, an attitude which both he and my mother understood and encouraged. As I boarded the train, she said, "If you don't get homesick it will be a tribute to me as a mother." Frequent letters went back and forth.

BYU, a Mormon institution, did not charge out-of-state tuition, and we were already acquainted with two faculty women who had recently attended summer school in Corvallis and knew a Provo family who might offer me room and board. My father also knew Lowry Nelson, then teaching rural sociology.[3] I took a class from him but continued to major in education and economics. At BYU, I was elected president of the Associated Women Students and tried to get AWS represented on the student council, but failed. This was a repeat of what had happened at Corvallis High School with Girls' League. I gave up, but one faculty wife was very upset and urged me to fight further for representation. She remembered the long battle in our country for women's rights, but my generation had only token memory. I was on the women's varsity debate squad and on the staff of the *Y News*. As in high school, one annual issue of the student newspaper was put out by girls. (We were girls at BYU more often than we were women.) This issue was part of "Girls' Day," and appeared May 5, 1933, as *The Suffragette Issue of the Y News*. My senior year I co-edited the special issue, which we named *The Coed Cougar Issue of the Y News.*

During my senior year at BYU it became obvious that, upon graduation, there would be no high school teaching position for me. Jobs were extremely scarce but I went ahead and did my teacher training at Provo High School, teaching economics and coaching the girls' debate team. Unlike high school debate teams in Oregon, those in Utah were gender segregated.

I graduated valedictorian. Some of the women in our class had dropped out to get married, and many were engaged. A very religious Mormon family back in Oregon criticized me for not having found a husband at BYU—after all, it was an LDS matrimonial bureau. I had dated, but never seriously. Instead, I was bent on doing graduate work out in the world somewhere.

During my senior year, I had decided to do graduate work in consumption economics. With my father's long-distance help, I sent out several applications for graduate school and discovered that most colleges and universities did not offer work in consumption economics. Iowa State College did, and offered me a twenty-five dollar per month scholarship. My father would send me enough money each month to make ends meet. So off I went to Ames, in the fall of 1934, by train in the chair car. It took three days and two nights from Corvallis, going through Omaha. Whenever the train stopped for the engine to take on water, a group of young men scrambled off the top of the cars to stretch their legs. The railroads let them ride on top, free, because they were looking for employment.

Graduate Study at Iowa State College

Iowa State, like Oregon State, was a land grant college, strong in agriculture and in home economics. Elizabeth E. Hoyt and Margaret G. Reid became my major professors. They were in the Department of Economics and Sociology, headed by Theodore W. Schultz, who many years later would receive the Nobel Prize. When I went to Schultz's office to introduce myself, he said of course he knew me because he was a graduate student at Wisconsin in 1927–28 when our family was there. He recalled that when he came to our flat on Saturday afternoons to discuss economics with my father, we children were sent off with a dime each to go to the movies so the two men would have peace and quiet to talk.

Hoyt and Reid did not have offices with the men economists in Ag Annex, but were on the first floor at the back of Margaret Hall. I lived on the second floor. Built in 1894, Margaret Hall was a red brick building, French Renaissance style, with a tower at each corner and a gargoyle peering down from a roof edge. It stood near the library and near the home economics building.

When I arrived in Ames I put my money into a bank. "Don't keep it in your dresser drawer," my father cautioned."It isn't much, but keep it in a bank." Soon afterward the bank declared a moratorium and closed itself up. I had two dollars and thirty-seven cents in cash, and I had to eat. So I went to a grocery store over on Lincoln Way and asked for credit, which was given without hesitation. And that was how I got the milk and the bread which I kept in Margaret Hall, with the milk keeping cool on my window ledge between window pane and screen. After a while the bank re-opened, and I resumed eating my noon meal at the college cafeteria.

To earn my fellowship money, raised from twenty-five dollars to sixty dollars per month, I taught principles of economics to home economics undergraduates. All Iowa State students were expected to take a three-course sequence of introductory economics. The Division of Home Economics offered a separate listing of these courses for its own students, a convenience I later recognized as gender segregation. Was it discrimination too? I doubt that Hoyt and Reid would have seen it as discrimination because their courses were as rigorous as those offered elsewhere on campus. The first two courses used F. B. Garver and A. H. Hansen, *Principles of Economics,* the same text used across campus. The third course was consumption economics, the new field in which Hoyt and Reid were pioneers. Home economics students provided a much wider enrollment for consumption economics than would have been

Left: Alison Comish, 1934.
Right: Wynne Thorne, 1933.
Below: Margaret Hall, Iowa State College.

possible otherwise at Iowa State at that time. Indeed it was because of home economics that consumption economics became part of the curriculum at Iowa State, as explained by Elizabeth Hoyt:

> In the days when home economics meant to most people only cooking and sewing, Dean Anna E. Richardson of Iowa State College perceived that home economics must take account of the principles of economics as they relate to the use of goods and services, that home economics itself is, to a large degree, applied consumption. It was she and not the economists themselves who in the first instance made it possible for the study of consumption to have exceptional opportunities for its development at Iowa State College.[4]

Ironically, although home economics had initially sheltered consumption economics, on July 1, 1987, the Iowa State College of Home Economics lost its identity and became the College of Family and Consumer Sciences. The board of regents forced this decision saying "it was difficult to effectively market the college to prospective students and faculty under the old name."[5]

At Iowa State when I was a student in the 1930s, home economics freshmen had their own chemistry courses as well as introductory economics. Dr. Nellie Naylor, in charge of these courses, had written the text, *Introductory Chemistry with Household Applications.*

My friend, Bertha Fietz (Carter), a graduate student living in Margaret Hall, was aghast when she came to campus and learned she would be teaching freshman home economics chemistry because her own undergraduate work had been all "pure" chemistry—systematic, inorganic, analytical, organic, etc. But she found Dr. Naylor's approach—for example, the chapter on leavening agents in baking—made sense. Bertha appreciated the practical application of fundamental principles.

During my own time at Iowa State I did not encounter gender segregation in my graduate courses. I took courses with men in economic theory, history, and statistics and often was the only woman. I was fortunate to have Hoyt and Reid as my major professors. Elizabeth Hoyt was the first woman I ever met who graduated from Radcliffe, which meant she had taken Harvard classes. She knew Greek, Latin, philosophy, and anthropology, subjects of which I was ignorant. My own land grant college education had not offered these. And she had traveled around the world! She joined the faculty of Iowa State College in 1925.

Hoyt grew up in Maine and kept her community ties by spending her summers at Round Pond during her long life. When she was ten years old her mother died, and she kept house for her father and brother. As she got older, she earned money for education by selling buttons from door to door and working as a secretary. Hoyt was one of the first scholars to combine anthropology and economics. Her doctoral dissertation, *Primitive Trade*, was published in 1926, soon after she completed it at Harvard; forty years later it was reprinted as a classic. Her second book was *The Consumption of Wealth* (1928). I read my father's copy before I left for Ames. Her third book, *Consumption in Our Society* (1938), was published while I was at Ames, and her three other books followed.

Hoyt believed in standing up for one's own ideas, as indicated by her preface to *Primitive Trade:*

> The author expresses her gratitude to those members of the
> Faculty of Harvard University and Radcliffe College who gener-
> ously assisted her in the development of her thought, even when,
> in some instances, it ran counter to their own: to Professor A. M.
> Tozzer in anthropology, Professor R. B. Perry in philosophy, and
> Professor A. P. Usher in economic history. [6]

These were giants in their fields, yet she dared to disagree.

Often, when I stopped by her office, Hoyt would be sitting at her desk, leaning forward over her folded arms, thinking. She read broadly and sometimes brought to class slips of thin paper on which she had typed (using carbon papers so we could each have a copy) a statement from some author, which illustrated a point she was making. This was how I first learned about Lewis Mumford, Ralph Adams Cram, and Lafcadio Hearn.

Hoyt considered empirical studies important, but she was always looking beyond them to meaning and significance. Her theory of consumption used the idea of basic human interests: the sensory, social, empathetic, aesthetic, intellectual, and technological. In her final book, *Choice and the Destiny of Nations,* published in 1969, Hoyt described antagonisms capable of destroying humankind. She noted that knowledge of technology had increased more than other knowledge, and nowhere had the bits and pieces of human knowledge been brought together. She suggested that the concept of choice could bring together the diffuse contributions of the behavioral sciences, and she built her book on this concept.[7]

Hoyt was a great influence on me because she cared about values. Not all economists would countenance inquiry into values because they assumed ends as given, defining economics as "the science which studies human behaviour as a relationship between ends and scarce means which have alternative uses." This was Lionel Robbins' definition in an essay published as a thin little book, in London, in 1935, an essay which carried great weight among Iowa State economists.[8]

Puzzling aspects of the Depression had led to great concern about America's capacity to consume, the title of a study by the Brookings Institution, which emphasized purchasing power as a factor. Hoyt suggested I write a paper naming additional factors such as time and energy. She liked what I wrote and arranged for its publication in the *American Economic Review*.[9]

Margaret Reid was not only a colleague of Hoyt's but also her close friend. Reid had joined the faculty of Iowa State shortly before I arrived and had just published *Economics of Household Production*, her doctoral dissertation at the University of Chicago, written under the direction of Hazel Kyrk. In this book Reid recognized that no history of household production existed, so she depended mainly on economic history. For the twentieth century, she used sources such as *Middletown*, the United States Census, and studies of homemakers' use of time, done in the late 1920s by home economists under sponsorship of state Agricultural Experiment Stations and the Bureau of Home Economics of the United States Department of Agriculture.

Using the framework of economics, Reid considered factors affecting household tasks, and the cost and value of goods produced. She wrote of scientific management in the household and asked, does family production pay? In the United States, in 1930, approximately 14 percent of women classed as homemakers were gainfully employed. Reid wrote of barriers to women getting well-paying jobs and argued that families must weigh the costs of a woman going out to work. She urged that part-time jobs be developed for married women who needed gainful employment but whose household tasks kept them from becoming full time.

It was a great advantage to Reid to have the framework of economics because she could say that the family has particular values of its own, and that the economic approach combines scarce resources with alternative uses to meet the goals of the family. She did not presume to tell families what they ought to do. For example, she wrote: "Waste and economy can be judged only with reference to the ends which are desired. So long as families desire to live in independent homes and eat at a family table, the economy of boarding homes or a central community dining-room has no place in consideration of possible alternatives which might eliminate waste."

Apparently Reid was thinking of Charlotte Perkins Gilman whose book, *Women and Economics*, published in 1898, advocated common dining rooms. Gilman was the leading intellectual of first wave feminism in our country, but Reid rarely used the term "feminist." Yet Reid was addressing some of the same questions the early feminists had asked. However Reid said hers was a middle course, seeking to be objective without "muddying the waters" by tying arguments to particular kinds of extremes. She was concerned about the effects of household production on the status of women—the title of one of her chapters. The American Association of University Women (AAUW) had a Committee on the Economic and Legal Status of Women, which endured for several decades. "Status of women" was a respectable concept, whereas by 1930 the term "feminism" had acquired a negative connotation. To denote her middle position, Reid spoke of entering the lists with no point to prove. She urged examination of extreme positions. I have gone back over her references to find out if extremes were included, and they were. It's really a great reference list and contains important early feminist writers such as Gilman and Olive Schreiner.

At the conclusion of *Economics of Household Production*, Reid spoke of the reactionary and the revolutionary, saying that in both groups emotion rather than reason dominated. Yet Reid herself recognized that society regarded women's position as inferior. "Traditional husband-wife relationships have been based on the inferiority of women and superiority of men." "Increasing scientific knowledge does not support the idea that women are inferior. To continue such an idea is to add fuel to fires already kindled." She recognized discrimination and spoke of sex discrimination in toys and in types of activities for children, and discrimination against hiring married women. She was well aware of gainfully employed mothers' need for child care.[10] But Reid was not an activist. Only second-wave feminism, much later, would refuse to draw a sharp line between reason and feeling, and would insist on activism.

At that time there was feminist activity across the continent, though rarely so labeled. Veronica Strong-Boag, who researched and wrote about life on the Canadian prairies in the 1920s and 1930s, told of the frequency with which farm journals and prairie newspapers carried letters from women seeking information on child care and birth control, and asking what to do about abusive husbands. They wrote of heavy work loads, both on the farm and in the house. Strong-Boag argued that this was a persistent if often un-self-conscious feminism. These women wanted information on their legal right to egg and milk money, and on their rights to children and family property when husbands died or deserted them. Grass roots and elite women were bound together in seeing the need for help from husbands, household science, and government. They urged passage of married women's property acts, divorce reforms, and mothers' pensions. These attempts to redress inequities, Strong-Boag suggested, were feminism at its most pragmatic, but feminism "could make only small gains in face of recurring economic crisis on the farm and deep-running anti-feminism in the country at large."[11]

For Iowa in the 1930s, Reid tackled the matter of rural housing, publishing two bulletins on the subject. Among her findings was that only one in five farm homes had a bathroom, only one in four had electricity, and three-fourths of the families carried culinary water an average of ninety-four feet. These bulletins were sponsored by the Agricultural Experiment Station and the Iowa Extension Service, and by two federal agencies.[12]

With regard to the Iowa Extension Service in those depression years, Theodore W. Schultz once wrote me, "While at Iowa State I was favorably impressed by the Home Economics Extension program. It contributed more of value to women as they made choices in a changing economy than did the agricultural extension program for men."[13] He once told me that his wife, before she married him, was teaching high school with a contract that specified, "If you get married you are fired." After a time she did marry him and gave up teaching. I remember Schultz saying that his wife paid for the suit he wore to the wedding because, as a graduate student, he didn't have any money.

My master's thesis, directed by Reid, dealt with urban housing and was entitled, "Credit Facilities Extended by the United States Government for Home Ownership and Modernization." After I collected the material, it came time to write it up. Typing in my room in the early morning kept my roommate awake, so I retreated to the attic to be greeted each dawn by grackles on the window sill. They had iridescent black feathers and raucous voices. I typed steadily, hour after hour, draft after draft. Innocent dorm-dwellers thought the attic was haunted.

Actually it was a handy attic. Early on I had strung a clothes line there to dry the clothes that I washed by hand in the communal bathroom on our floor. Automatic washers and driers did not exist. The Maytag washer with a wringer, manufactured in Iowa, reigned supreme in many Iowa homes. Although Reid doubted that individual washing machines used weekly were economical, they were the people's choice. Of course our dorm had no Maytag. The water in Margaret

Hall was hard, and my white blouses and underwear yellowed. The real problem, though, was hair. The only source of soft water was the hand pump at the sink in the ramshackle kitchen on the first floor. I pumped water up from the cistern into a bucket. Since this water was rain and melted snow that ran off the roof, it was yellowish green and smelled musty. But it was soft. I took my bucket of water into a utility closet, which had live steam that could be coaxed out of a pipe. I put the pipe into the water, and when my water was heated, I carried it up flights of stairs to my own floor to wash my hair in the communal bathroom. Farm women were not the only women carrying buckets of water in Iowa in the 1930s!

On June 10, 1935, I received my master's degree and wrote home: "There were about 12 doctors' degrees and 30 masters', with 500 or more bachelors' . . . Two women received Ph.D.'s—and I sat near them and kept hoping that someday I could have one, too."[14] Even before I graduated with a master's, Hoyt and Reid agreed with me that I should go on for a doctorate. If I became a Ph.D. candidate at Iowa State, I would be the first woman in economics to do so.

It was customary for doctoral graduate students in economics to go elsewhere for a year to take more economic theory and gain a perspective different from that at Iowa State. Reid suggested I go to the University of Chicago. Hazel Kyrk, under whom she had studied, was still at Chicago. She would accept me as a graduate student and could arrange a small stipend and a waiver of tuition. Perhaps I would decide to remain at Chicago to finish a Ph.D.

Graduate Study at the University of Chicago

I spent the summer at home in Oregon and, in the fall, went to Chicago where I did, indeed, learn a great deal. In 1923 Hazel Kyrk's own doctoral dissertation at the University of Chicago had become a book entitled *A Theory of Consumption*. I carried my father's copy with me to Chicago, with his wavy underlining done with fountain pen. More recently Kyrk had written *Economic Problems of the Family*, the text in a course I took from her.[15]

Helen Wright taught me methods of social investigation, especially with regard to poverty. I took anthropology from A. R. Radcliffe-Brown, who wore a monocle. When he emphasized a point he opened his eye wide, the monocle fell out, and he caught it in his hand. Paul Douglas taught labor problems and chain smoked. When there was a winter storm, he went over to his first wife's house and shoveled her walks. Frank Knight and Jacob Viner taught economic theory. Students had a hard time keeping up with them. Charner Perry taught philosophy of value, and edited the journal *Ethics.*

I lived in Green Hall, the graduate women's dorm. Reid had lived there during her graduate work, just a few years before me. It was a dark gray Gothic stone structure, similar to neighboring campus buildings. Maids changed our beds and waited on table. I had never known real servants before. They were young women from Ireland, saving enough money to return home to marry. They were great favorites of Sophonisba Breckinridge, honorary head of Green Hall, who had lived there ever since coming to the University of Chicago at the turn of the century. Dinner in the evening in the dining room was a pleasant affair, eight to a table. Every three weeks we drew names and rotated tables, so everyone had a chance to sit at Miss Breckinridge's table. She was indeed a distinguished person. A biographer has written:

> Her students attest to her warmth, enthusiasm, and brilliance in the classroom. The combination of toughness and sensitivity she urged on students and colleagues was her own most distinguishing characteristic, manifested alike in her deceptively delicate ninety-pound frame, in her pale, thin face and sharply etched features surmounted by a mass of dark hair, and in her graceful but commanding treble voice tinged with the southern accent she never wholly lost.[16]

When I knew her, Breckinridge was seventy years old, had white hair, and was amazingly vital. She held a law degree, had been professor of social economy, and most recently dean of the School of Social Service Administration. In 1912, with Jane Addams, she was partly responsible for the Progressive Party's endorsement of bills regulating the wages and hours of women's employment. Miss Breckinridge, as we called her respectfully, had always taken up the defense of women in academia. She wrote in 1933, "Two great land grant colleges are denying the right of married women to continue in employment or the right of the academic woman to round out her experience by marriage." She went on to say that a dean of women (married) who was replaced by an unmarried one had appealed to the AAUW of her state, because there was no League of Women Voters or Woman's Party.[17] (I wonder what tools these women's organizations had in the 1930s to fight discrimination. They lacked Title IX and affirmative action, which we have today.)

Those of us who lived in Green Hall became acquainted with several remarkable people whom Miss Breckinridge brought to dinner. One was Marion Talbot. In 1881 Talbot and her mother had helped found the Association of Collegiate Alumni, which later became the American Association of University Women (AAUW). When the University of Chicago opened its doors in 1892, Talbot was on the first faculty as dean of women and assistant professor of sanitary science. In 1905 Talbot became head of the new Department of Household Administration and brought Breckinridge onto its faculty to teach economic and legal aspects of family life. Talbot had a long career at Chicago, during which she fought relentlessly for the right of women students to an equal education.[18]

The sisters Grace and Edith Abbott also frequently came to dinner at Green Hall. They were in their late fifties, but being so young myself, I regarded them as elderly women. They had been at Hull House with Addams, and in the early years of the century had worked with Breckinridge to combat unscrupulous cab drivers, lawyers, travel agents, and operators of fraudulent savings banks and employment agencies who preyed on the immigrants arriving in Chicago in great numbers. When I met them in 1935, Edith Abbott was dean of the School of Social Service Administration, and Grace Abbott had just become professor of public welfare, after serving in Washington D.C. in various capacities, heading the Children's Bureau and helping to write the Social Security Act. Earlier Grace Abbott had participated in the successful Illinois suffrage campaign of 1913, and went with Addams to the International Congress of Women at the Hague in 1915.[19]

An extraordinary visitor was Frances Perkins, secretary of labor to President Franklin D. Roosevelt. In my letter home, April 26, 1936, I told about getting ready for the dinner at which she would be present. "We are wearing our best clothes, waving our hair, shining our shoes, and everything." It was indeed a flossy dinner. We were served, for dessert, three kinds of ice cream on our plates, something unheard of during the Depression. I was fortunate to sit across from Perkins at dinner and shall never forget the story she told about Roosevelt. Perkins sat near him at an official dinner at which he was to speak. He leaned over and said, "Frances, before I rise to my feet to give this talk, remind me to buckle my braces. If I forget, I will fall on my face and it embarrasses Eleanor."

Perkins had worked hard for protective legislation for women in New York, a crusade which brought success after the tragic fire at the Triangle Shirt Waist Company in 1911. When Roosevelt became governor of New York he appointed Perkins to the state Department of Labor, and when he became president, made her United States secretary of labor. She had great influence on major legislation in favor of collective bargaining, retirement pensions, wage and hour laws, and unemployment benefits. The president often referred to her as Madame Perkins because she had kept her own name although married. Later on, her political enemies would say that keeping her own name was evidence that she was a communist. Susan Ware has described the New Deal network of twenty-eight women working in Washington D.C., who were concerned with social welfare issues and sought to place women in positions to influence policy. Among these were Perkins, Grace Abbott, and Eleanor Roosevelt.

In my letter home I wrote that Perkins was not a feminist. Perkins believed that if the Equal Rights Amendment passed, it would annul protective legislation for women. Breckinridge, Talbot, the Abbotts, and Eleanor Roosevelt agreed with her. It is a quirk of history that the Woman's Party, pushing for the amendment, took on the label of feminism, and the proponents of protective legislation refused it. Only today is the New Deal network considered to be feminist in a broader sense of the word. Ware has written that "this network of dynamic, intelligent, and committed women worked together as feminists for the advancement of their sex. Without them, the needs of women in government, politics, and relief would have been overlooked. These women worked together as social reformers for the preservation of democracy in a time of economic crisis [the Great Depression]."[20]

When I was at the University of Chicago campus, pacifism was a hotter issue than feminism. Japan was occupying Mongolia. Italy, under Mussolini, invaded Ethiopia, and Hitler was rearming Germany. The world teetered on the brink of another war, and most Americans wanted no part of it. Students planned a campus peace conference, and I was one of eight delegates from Green Hall chosen to attend. Miss Breckinridge's note to me, written February 26, 1936, reads: "I want to congratulate you on your election as a delegate from Green House to the Peace Conference to be held next week. The House will be very safe, we are sure, in the hands of the delegation selected. We know that you realize the very real tribute that was paid you and the responsibility that rests upon you as spokesman for one of the most dignified and responsible organizations in the Quadrangles."

We knew there would be delegates with communist leanings, and, sure enough, a resolution was put forth blaming wars on the American capitalistic system. The Young Women's Christian Association delegates

and most of the eight Green Hall delegates threatened to bolt the conference if such a resolution passed. This would deprive the conference of its
overall strength. The resolution failed. The *Chicago Tribune* was highly
critical of the conference. Publisher William Randolph Hearst was on a
hunt for communists, with a list that included President Robert Hutchins
of the university, as well as Susan M. Kingsbury, who chaired the AAUW
Committee on the Economic and Legal Status of Women.

After the peace conference, the students demanded a peace strike to
be held the third week of April. The university administration would
not permit a demonstration outdoors, or a parade, but promised the
field house. Prior to the peace strike, and hoping for a parade, 107 students, of whom I was one, filed through the library at four-thirty, on
our way to the president's office. President Hutchins was not there, but
we met with a dean and presented a petition with seven hundred
names. I wrote home about this and said I thought that, on the whole,
the University of Chicago students were against the peace strike or
were completely indifferent. Out of that meeting with the dean came
the decision that we could parade as long as we remained on university ground. The city police had orders not to protect peace strikers
anywhere. We could not have any outdoor ceremony after the parade.

At the field house there were many speeches from everyone.
Communists, socialists, laborites, one professor, and one reverend
spoke. Seventeen hundred were at the meeting, but only seven hundred were in the parade. We marched four abreast along campus
walks. There was one news reel camera filming us, and half a dozen
newspaper photographers and reporters. I wrote my folks that, if they
saw newsreels of the University of Chicago strike, I had on a gray coat
but so did scores of other people. I wrote that it was all very peaceful
because the fraternity boys who were against the strike had promised
not to throw rotten eggs, as they did the year before.

At Chicago my closest friend was Eleanor Parkhurst from
Chelmsford, Massachusetts, with degrees in English and sociology from
Wellesley. She came to Iowa State the same time I did, and was a graduate assistant to Elizabeth Hoyt. After a year at Ames, we both moved on
to the University of Chicago, where we lived on the same floor of Green
Hall. She enrolled in the university's School of Social Work and sometimes took me with her on assignments such as visiting court hearings.[21]

Another friend at Chicago was Fawn McKay who was working on
a master's degree in English. A native of Huntsville, Utah, she was
attending the University of Utah when I was at BYU. At Chicago, since

we were both LDS, we attended the Mormon branch meetings held in a small chapel across the Midway, and together we taught the women's class, using what we were learning in our university classes. It was exciting intellectually, and we felt appreciated. Fawn lived in Foster Hall, and we sometimes met on the basketball floor when Green played Foster. These were extremely slow basketball games because women were not allowed to run the full length of the floor. Neither of us was aware of what our future held. Before long she met and married Bernard Brodie, a political scientist. Fawn Brodie became a fine writer. Her first book, *No Man Knows My History* (1945), was critical of the Mormon prophet, Joseph Smith, and resulted in her excommunication by LDS Church authorities.[22]

As my Chicago year neared its close, Hazel Kyrk found an opening for me at Goucher College in Baltimore, which she wanted me to take in the fall, suggesting that after five years of teaching I should return to complete a doctorate at Chicago. I did not want to wait five years. The University of Chicago was much more strenuous than Iowa State, and I wanted to complete my degree quicker than that because I was thinking of marrying Wynne Thorne, who was then completing his own graduate work in soil science at Iowa State. (More later about how I first met Wynne.) Kyrk regretted that I did not want to teach at Goucher, but generously found me a three-week summer teaching job at Colorado State College beginning in August. At Fort Collins I taught consumer marketing to school teachers, many of them Texans escaping the Texas heat. All the students were older than I, a fact which some pointed out. I was twenty-two. I earned three hundred dollars and considered it magnificent pay.

Finishing the Degree and Beginning a Marriage

In the fall of 1936, I was back at Iowa State to take more economic theory, read lots of economic history for a minor, and prepare for my preliminary exams. This time I had a single room in Margaret Hall and typed undisturbed. My closest colleague was Virginia Britton from Akron, Ohio, also a student of Hoyt's and Reid's. Virginia undertook a small research project about employed women with children. She went to downtown Ames and asked the managers of various stores and two small manufacturing plants for the names of women with children who were in their employ. She visited these women and asked them to record how they spent their time for a week. No such study had been attempted before.

Virginia was one of many people whom I knew, on and off campus. I was particularly struck by the warm friendship among students, student wives, faculty and wives of faculty. Just as Breckinridge, Talbot, and the Abbotts had belonged to AAUW, so also did Hoyt, Reid, and wives of the male economists at Iowa State.

I recall one of Schultz's economics seminars in which a faculty wife spoke on household budgets, and I was impressed with the respect that the men accorded her. Women were so outnumbered among economics graduate students, that I sometimes felt myself a lesser individual, though I wouldn't admit it. I, too, had my turn speaking at the economics seminar. I wrote home on May 3, 1937:

> I worked on the seminar report, the relation of consumption to
> economics, and gave it on Thursday. It was given in the
> Modernistic room of the Memorial Union, where we have our
> seminars; a very ugly room. It went over all right, apparently,
> because I harangued the agricultural economics graduate assis-
> tants so much (to get even with remarks they have made on con-
> sumption) that they were roused to speech. And the faculty mem-
> bers, economics and sociology, asked lots of questions and
> laughed at the proper places. Once in awhile when I got stuck,
> Miss Reid would nod her head yes, to a question that I didn't
> think I could answer, and at different crucial moments, Miss Hoyt
> and Miss Reid each came in with a short discussion to set the peo-
> ple right and help me out a bit. My, but they are two wonderful
> women.

When I arrived at Iowa State the fall of 1934, I promptly became part of the LDS group. I was usually the only Mormon woman graduate student. Sometimes there might be two of us, but never more. The vast majority of men graduate students on campus were single, but some Mormon men were married and had children, a fact that worried the Iowa State administration because fellowships paid only fifty or sixty dollars a month. Mormons came together on Sundays and had lively Sunday school lessons, each of us taking a turn at teaching. Watching over and caring a great deal about us was the Cannon family. Professor Clawson Y. Cannon, head of dairy science, and his wife, Winnifred Morrell Cannon, were from Utah; they had three sons and a daughter. The Cannons invited us all to their place on holidays, and arranged other social gatherings. Our picnics were fun and I was delighted that a Mormon wife, Lorna Reeder, was the best softball player, even better than the men.

The first time I went to Sunday school, I met Wynne Thorne, an unmarried graduate student in soil science from Perry, near Brigham City, Utah. He graduated from Utah Agricultural College in 1933 and had been in Ames a year when I arrived on the scene. Graduate students across campus came together at "midweek dances" held in the Memorial Union. I went to these, sometimes with Wynne, sometimes with a graduate student from Corvallis. I was corresponding with another boyfriend from my Oregon State College days, who had gone on to Harvard, and I was also writing to a boyfriend from my BYU days. None could afford marriage, but they could afford to send me roses on Valentine's Day, much to my delight.

After my year at Chicago, Wynne convinced me he would make a better husband than "those other chumps," as he labeled his competition. By then he had completed his Ph.D. and was on the Iowa State soil science faculty. Wynne was one of those rare people who give one a deep sense of security. "He has cement inside of him," said one of my women friends. At the same time he was always fascinating to talk to. It was pleasant just to be in the same room with him, and he made it clear that he was in love with me. By spring 1937 we had decided we would get married in the summer. We hoped to have children but not till I completed my degree. When I told this to Elizabeth Hoyt, she said, "Oh, shoot!" commingling in her tone of voice her disappointment but also her blessing. She proceeded to get books on birth control out of the locked shelves of Iowa State College's library and loaned them to me. It was strange indeed that such books had to be locked up—all because of the Comstock law of 1873.[23] I find it appalling that contraceptive use by married couples was not legalized until a 1965 Supreme Court decision, and it was 1972 when it became legal for unmarried persons.

That summer I taught at Iowa State to have something to add to my vita and to earn money to pay my dental bill. Margaret Reid was writing *Consumers and the Market*, and I read and commented on her chapters as she turned them out.[24] It was a busy six weeks. And suddenly summer school was over. Some of the faculty predicted I would never complete my dissertation, but they did not know how stubborn I can be.

Wynne and I were married August 3, 1937, and he accepted a position at Texas Agricultural and Mechanical College (Texas A & M), a land grant college, not coeducational. We took up residence in College Station and watched the cadets—all students were required to take ROTC—drill in small groups on the road in front of the duplex in which we lived. I used the college library to gather material

Above: Eleanor Parkhurst,
Beulah Porter, Alison Comish.
Right: Alison and Wynne
Thorne at Texas A & M.

for my dissertation, my wedding-ringed left hand held up to ward off over-friendly students (always male) in the library stacks. My thesis was a library project on evaluations of consumption in modern thought.

Texas A & M was not a cordial world for professional women. There were only a handful on campus, mostly in extension. One was Jessie Whitacre, a graduate of Oregon Agricultural College who had been dean of home economics at Utah Agricultural College from 1918–23. At College Station she became our good friend, and we became aware of the strong network among home economists at land grant colleges.

In the spring of 1938, I left College Station for two months to return to Iowa State to work further on the dissertation. Reid was not there; she was on leave attending the London School of Economics. But Hoyt was there. Both of them were advising me on the dissertation. I lived again in Margaret Hall, this time on the third floor above the ancient swimming pool, small but still used.

On the evening of April 9 at around nine, I heard fire engines, and looking out my window, saw three engines down below me. No one rang a fire alarm. Most of the residents were out on dates because it was Saturday night. I hurried down the hall to see if there was smoke anywhere. There was. It was rolling out the elevator shaft. A young woman in a tub in the bathroom called to me, "What's happening?" and I said, "This place is on fire! Get out and get some clothes on!" She did. I dashed back to my room and gathered up a large stack of manila folders containing the materials for my dissertation. I discovered that my mind had frozen, and I had one great impelling urge to flee. I couldn't remember where the fire escapes were. The only reason I even went back to my room for those manila folders was because, when our family lived in Madison ten years before, and Papa was working on his doctorate, the man across the way from us had kept his own dissertation material in a briefcase by the front door and instructed his wife and children that if ever the flat caught fire, they must be sure to carry out the briefcase. "Save the thesis!" had been imprinted on my mind at age thirteen and now stood me in good stead.

But my stuff wasn't in a briefcase. It was a large stack in my arms, so large that two top folders fell, as the bathtub-person (now clothed) and I dashed down the stairs together. Smoke filled the stairs. I wanted to pick up my fallen folders, but my arms were so full I knew if I bent over I would drop everything. So I cried out to her, "Help me!" but she only said, "No, no, save yourself!" and dashed on down the stairs. So I left the two folders to perish and saved myself.

Once outside the building, we were prevented from returning by college men who had earlier searched the rooms for occupants. Shortly thereafter, my part of the third floor crashed down, filling the swimming pool. It was fortunate I had not returned, but I lost my typewriter, wristwatch, clothes, suitcases, quilts—all my things had perished. It was a great loss. There I stood in pajamas, robe, and slippers in the chill night air, teeth chattering from cold and fear. I telephoned the Cannons, and they took me in for the rest of the weekend. I wore their daughter Winnifred's clothes, which fit well except the shoes were too narrow.[25] On Monday I was given a room in the freshman dorm. The fire also destroyed the contents of Hoyt's and Reid's offices. Reid had a file of materials for a textbook she was planning to write on housing. It would have been the first college text on this subject, but she never wrote it.

To make a long story short, I made a very brief trip back to Ames, in December 1938, to defend my dissertation and to receive the Ph.D. at the winter commencement ceremony. I wore Dr. Cannon's academic robe, and I was the only woman to receive a Ph.D. at that commencement. Although my diploma says consumption economics, the history of the Economics Department says it was the first Ph.D. granted in general economics,[26] I think because until then doctoral degrees had all been awarded in agricultural economics.

President Charles E. Friley's commencement talk included a statement about trends of the time and the need for women to have intellectual pursuits as well as the importance of home life. Reid wrote that talk for him. And Margaret Reid placed the hood over my head and onto my shoulders. For me, for her, and for women it was an important moment.

I returned to Wynne and College Station. Six months later our two years at Texas A & M were over because Wynne had accepted a position at Utah State Agricultural College, his alma mater and also my father's. In September 1939 we went to live in Logan, and I began my forty years as a faculty wife there.

Looking back I realize I cared enough about equal rights for women that I tried to get Girls' League and Associated Women Students onto the student council. I didn't call myself a feminist; the term was in eclipse. The fact that I stubbornly pursued graduate work and was the first woman to earn a Ph.D. in economics at Iowa State showed that I believed women were entitled to advanced education, and I believed there were opportunities to secure it. I realize, however, that in those years of economic depression I was extremely fortunate in my opportunities. I also believed that a woman could have a Ph.D., marriage with children, and some kind of employment. Such an arrangement was nearly impossible for generations of women before me. As for social justice, my graduate year at the University of Chicago was an eye opener. It was a privilege to know women who were part of the Progressive movement and path-breakers in social work, and who substantially influenced New Deal legislation.

3 Producing Children and Books: The 1940s

Wynne and I left Texas A & M the end of the summer of 1939 to drive to Utah the long way round, via New York, where we saw the World's Fair and went on to Rutgers University, where Wynne attended the International Microbiological Congress. During this time Hitler invaded Poland and the tension at the meetings became almost unbearable. The German scientists clustered together. In the elevator I heard a Polish scientist say he could not go home and intended to go to Canada and join the Air Force.

We continued on our journey to Logan in Cache Valley where Wynne became associate professor of agronomy at Utah State Agricultural College, affectionately called the "A.C." because it was founded as the Agricultural College of Utah. This was the favorite song at basketball games:

> Show me the Scotsman who doesn't love a thistle.
> Show me the Irishman who doesn't love a rose.
> Show me the true hearted Aggie of Utah,
> Who doesn't love the spot (stamp, stamp)
> Where the sagebrush grows!

The stamp, stamp was everyone's foot pounding onto the floor in unison, which really shook the balcony of the field house, where most of the audience sat. We became ardent basketball fans.

We took an apartment four blocks from the college. The next June, on commencement day, our first child, Kip Stephen, was born, to be followed two years later by a daughter, Barrie. I did not seek a faculty position because of the policy that both husband and wife could not be on the faculty, but also because I knew that babies are a lot of work. But I was determined to pursue my own intellectual interests, including trying to get my dissertation published. I published only one article, which appeared in *Social Forces*. It was on evaluations of consumption in scale of living studies.

Tabernacle   Temple   Old   Whittier   5th Ward
                        Logan Hospital   School   Church

Throughout graduate school I had been interested in values, although Frank Knight, the famous professor of economics at the University of Chicago, reprimanded me and said that economists, as economists, do not deal with values. Some fifty years later feminist economists would point out that it is impossible for economic theory to be value neutral.[1] Knight said that philosophers, and citizens, dealt with values. I personally thought that mothers raising families cared about values. As soon as we reached Logan, I subscribed to *Ethics, The International Journal,* edited at the University of Chicago by Charner Perry under whom I had taken my one course in philosophy. The college library did not subscribe to *Ethics,* and the college offered no courses in philosophy, so I decided to teach myself.

My chief association with the college was through Faculty Women's League. We had been in Logan only a few days when Allie Peterson Burgoyne called on me and invited me to join League. Allie had known Wynne when he was a student at the college (1931–33) because she was assistant registrar and knew everybody. Many people remembered Wynne because he made himself conspicuous by organizing the independent students (Barbarians, or Barbs) and then snatching the campus elections from the fraternities and sororities (Greeks).

Allie Burgoyne and Blanche Condit Pittman had been among the very few faculty wives who held staff appointments. Blanche was clerk/secretary of the Agricultural Experiment Station, a position she had held for twenty years before she and Allie were summarily dismissed in 1936 because of federal and state anti-nepotism rulings. Neither of them had children. Had they had children, they likely would not have been on the staff to start with. What interested me was that, after losing their positions, these women turned to unpaid community

| | Industrial Arts | Old Main | Quad |

From 1943 to 1951 we lived between the "old" Logan Hospital and the Whittier School. All our children were born at the old hospital. Our address was 405 East 200 North.

From 1951 to 1966 we lived westward across town near the high school, in a square two-story brick house. Address: 226 West 100 South.

From 1966 on, our home was half a block west of the Whittier School, now the Whittier Community Center. Address: 365 East 300 North.

work of various sorts, remained loyal to the college, were especially active in the faculty wives' organization, and did not openly criticize anti-nepotism rulings. A year after their dismissal, they and others organized the Logan Branch of American Association of University Women (AAUW). Whether Allie and Blanche spoke together quietly about their exclusion from the college staff I do not know, because I did not join AAUW until my children were all in school. However, Luna Brite, wife of historian Duncan Brite, belonged to AAUW and often regretted that I, with a Ph.D., was kept off the faculty.[2]

It was Faculty Women's League that I joined at once, because this was one way to help along one's husband's career, because being with other women was pleasant, and because there was intellectual challenge and involvement in community good works.[3] League met every two weeks during the school year on Friday at three-thirty, when older children would be home from school, or good-natured husbands would come home early from work, to tend younger children. We dressed for League in heels, best dress, a hat, and gloves, usually white. I was a rebel and didn't wear white gloves each time. I also dispensed with the hat more often than any other member, but I certainly knew what was proper and how far I could push my idiosyncrasies.

For forty years my identity in the Faculty Women's League year-book was Thorne, Mrs. D. Wynne. At the end of the 1970s I became Thorne, Alison (Wynne). In contrast, my identity in the AAUW year-book has always been Dr. Alison Thorne.

The Second World War

On December 7, 1941 the Japanese bombed Pearl Harbor, and the next day the United States declared war. I was working in the kitchen and listening to President Roosevelt on the radio when, in the adjoining room, Kip, seventeen months old, tried to climb up a chest of drawers, having pulled out the lower drawers to make steps. Of course the whole thing toppled over on top of him, and I was pulling him out, undamaged, just as war was declared.

I took great interest in prices and shortages and began clipping out news items. Faculty Women's League invited me to do a program on this subject, and I did it wearing a maternity dress because I was expecting my second child. A chief cause of shortages was the need of the armed services for supplies. Bed sheets and toilet paper, for example, were hard to find. In the question and answer period following my talk, I was asked about toilet paper and gravely replied that it was being bought up by the military, but when they had enough, it would reappear on the market. And then, without thinking, I said, "If we just sit tight long enough, the toilet paper will come," a remark which brought gales of laughter and was soon relayed to husbands.

When price control and rationing became a reality, my neighbor Jo Turner, wife of the dean of forestry, and I, accompanied by my two small children, volunteered for the federal Office of Price Administration, visiting neighborhood grocery stores to check on prices. In Oregon, my mother, still very much a faculty wife, was a volunteer observer of aircraft, watching from a post in a large open area of that campus. She also found time to serve as president of the University of Oregon faculty wives' organization. No one paid attention to the fact that she was only a high school graduate.

The Agricultural College received funds to teach trainees of the air corps, navy, marines, and army engineers before they were sent over-sees. Some of this funding was for math classes, and two faculty wives who could teach math were given temporary positions at the college, positions which they lost when the war ended. Faculty men, besides their usual teaching, went to Ogden and Salt Lake City on weekends to help load military supplies.

I shall never forget a dark morning at five, when I heard trainees singing as they marched from the college, past our house, and on toward town and the railroad station. These young men had completed their course work and were being shipped to the South Pacific. Later we learned that most of them died there.

The war, I now think, was one reason why feminism was dormant in the 1940s and 1950s. Those of us with young children were deeply grateful to the men who made it possible for us to live safely and rear our young. The men of my generation bore the brunt of the war, and if I had been male instead of female, I might not be alive today. Why should I consider American women oppressed? Furthermore, in the war years women who wanted employment could find it, usually at good pay. From across the state, women came into war-related industries, especially the air force base, ammunition plant, and ordinance depot. A few day care centers for their children were created, but Utah had fewer than other states, and when the war ended they quickly vanished.

At first Wynne was exempted from the war because he taught agriculture, but later he became subject to the draft and was assigned a number which was placed in the national fish bowl, or draft lottery. His number happened not to be drawn, so he did not serve.

Writing Books

In the meantime Wynne and I thought we would like to have more children but ran into bad luck. I had an ectopic pregnancy and other difficulties that resulted in surgery. It looked as though two would have to do. It was then that I decided to write a book about homemakers' values and gave myself five years to do it. Astonishingly, my aches, pains, and mental depression vanished when I set about this intellectual task, though it was a challenge to find time.

With two young children, I was very busy, but like my mother, I sent the sheets and towels to the laundry to come back ironed, and our cotton underwear, pajamas, and Wynne's shirts came back wet wash. Like my mother I did the diapers by hand with a handwringer attached to the laundry tub in the basement. By now we were living in a tall, old fashioned, two story white frame house just off the Boulevard, a street which curved along the edge of the hill between the college and downtown. All our bedrooms and the only bathroom were upstairs, but the kitchen was large and pleasant, especially when the west sun streamed through the windows. I kept the potty chair hidden under a large cardboard box, next to the refrigerator.

I kept my book writing materials in a cardboard file drawer that sat on the dining room buffet, parallel to and against the mirror. I stashed manila folders of reading notes in it. I depended heavily on the college library and perpetually checked out books, especially some old house-keeping ones placed there in earlier days. It did not occur to me to read suffragist and feminist literature, but I did come across Inez Irwin's *Angels and Amazons* and found it powerful stuff.[4] I was unaware that the library contained three volumes on the life and work of Susan B. Anthony.[5] Occasionally I went to Salt Lake City to use the library at the University of Utah.

Two hours comprised the longest continuous period I could snatch for study and writing. And then suddenly, in 1947, Dean Ethelyn O. Greaves invited me to teach the course on consumer buying problems because the regular teacher was going on leave. This was an opening wedge against the anti-nepotism ruling and I accepted but, after teaching two quarters, discovered that I was successfully pregnant and gave up the class. Routine teaching and grading papers were not as interesting as pursuing ideas for my manuscript.

Wynne had become a full professor and head of the Agronomy Department. He also served for one year as acting dean of the School of Graduate Studies and, in this capacity, began a seminar on science and values for interested graduate students and faculty. There were still no classes taught in philosophy at the college, apparently because philosophy was not assigned to the land grant college, and because the administration feared philosophy would undermine the faith of Mormon students. I attended Wynne's graduate seminar on science and values and enjoyed it immensely.

Our third child, Sandra, arrived on February 18, 1948, and soon came down with colic which lasted six weeks. There seemed to be no real cure for colic. Is there one today? Wynne was at the college from eight to five every weekday. He spent his early mornings, early evenings, and weekends writing a textbook on irrigated agriculture. I was exhausted after each day of a crying baby, so Wynne, to comfort her in the evenings, held her over his shoulder with his left hand and wrote with his right. A secretary at the college did his typing, so I never typed his manuscripts as my mother had done for my father.

Several months later, when the manuscript was finished, Wynne asked me to read it and smooth out and simplify the language. "If you can understand it," he said magnanimously, "then the freshmen should be able to understand it." Not exactly a compliment to my brainpower but I am a competent editor and improved this work, which became *Irrigated Soils: Their Fertility and Management,* published by Blakiston in 1949, with Howard B. Peterson as co-author.

Our house was a mess during the weeks of final editing. I kept Sandra's formula made up, her diapers washed, and the household fed. On the whole, for me, it was complete intellectual absorption, with a lick and a promise to housekeeping. It was sheer delight to have a sustained intellectual task. I had my own book manuscript, of course, but too readily dropped it when other tasks became overwhelming. With Wynne's book we had a real deadline to meet, and a real publisher to spur us on.

Sandra was seven months old when I became pregnant with our fourth child, which was fine because I was then thirty-four years old and thought we should finish up our family in a hurry. I completed the final typing of my own manuscript just before Avril was born June 20, 1949. As I lay in the delivery room with this fourth child about to come forth, the birth process was reflected in young Dr. Gordon Harmston's spectacles. This was long before today's practice of giving women a mirror to see the birth of their children. Wynne was not present because fathers were banned from delivery rooms although, in that same hospital nine years before, he had been present at the birth of our first child.

The nurse and Dr. Harmston and I were busy bringing this baby into the world. "It has red hair," said Dr. Harmston, who could see the top of the head. "But it's facing the wrong direction and it will be a hard birth." I thought about this for a little while, and suddenly there came a really whopping big labor pain, and Harmston exclaimed, "It has turned itself around 180 degrees! I've never seen a baby's head pivot like that before!" Shortly thereafter, Avril was born.

I believe one's body has a great deal of wisdom of its own. In those days, and it was 1949, we as women knew remarkably little about how our bodies functioned. *Our Bodies, Ourselves,* a collective work of second wave feminism, would not be written for another twenty-three years.[6] My mother always said, "We don't have any trouble giving birth in our family." I trusted her judgment and figured my body would manage somehow to bring forth children. Also important was her attitude that a new baby was the most joyous thing that could happen to one, and waiting for it was a matter of happy anticipation. I literally felt that way.

So now I had a new baby, and I also had a book manuscript which I sent to several publishers, all of whom sent back rejection slips. I thought it was a good book. I had tackled something that nobody else had tried, and I considered it a refreshing piece of writing. One publisher's assistant suggested I break it up into sections and try women's magazines. But I didn't have time to do that. I typed the final copy on translucent sheets of paper that could be copied in the School of Engineering by an offset process. This was before the days of Xerox. The double spaced typed manuscript was 162 pages long, and the cost of each copy was eight dollars. I had eight copies made.

I named the manuscript, *Let the Dishes Wait: A Philosophy for Homemakers.* Wynne had provided the title by saying, "Why not call it 'Let the Dishes Wait,' since that's what the dishes have done most of the time you've been writing your book." It was with laughter that he suggested the title, and with laughter that I accepted it.

The Shadow Manuscript

My would-be book is now fifty years old, its paper yellowed. I think of it as a "shadow manuscript" because, being unpublished, it lay in shadow, and because it dealt with domesticity, a shadowy realm involving women's household work, unpaid and considered less important than paid employment. Occasionally a "shadow price" has been placed on this kind of work.

My book reflected the life of white, middle class wife-mothers of Cache Valley in the 1940s. Very few of us had employment. None of us had hired help. It seemed to me that we all belonged to clubs. There were various kinds including civic, literary, study, bridge, garden, and gourmet cooking. These usually met in homes. For some women there was AAUW, which met monthly on the campus on Saturday afternoons. For a great many there were weekly meetings of the LDS Relief Society, held in the ward church houses.

Natural gas was not yet piped into our valley so most of us had coal-fired furnaces that, after a long winter, left a thin layer of soot on walls and curtains. That's why spring cleaning was so vital.

Mass consumption was taking over and women's magazines were in a comfortable relationship with advertising. I was trying to get women to think for themselves. Some pieces of advice I thought better than others. Nursery school leaders I would listen to. The psychiatrists were speaking up but I was dubious of some of them.

Here I have paraphrased excerpts from the shadow manuscript and added contemporary comment, sometimes because of historical changes and sometimes because of my own changed thinking. The names of chapters are capitalized.

What Matters Most

I wrote that we lived in a constant psychological hailstorm. We were continually pelted with cries to buy new clothes, new cars, new refrigerators, new novels, and new furniture. We were told to make an outdoor fireplace, to send our children to camp, and to aid foreign relief. We were urged to do hundreds of different things. Advertisers, neighbors, our families, and the schools sought to tell us what to buy, what to do, and what to be.

Some people had a clear-cut set of ideas of what they wanted out of life, a clear-cut set of values. They walked intelligently amidst the fierce barrage of advertising, and the subtle barrage of neighbors and culture, and the more honest barrage of schools. But other people had a fuzzy picture in their minds of what they sought in life. They fumbled, tried this and that, and fell easy prey to loud advertisers.

I wrote that this urge to conform was being exploited by advertisers, and in various places throughout my manuscript, I criticized advertising. A woman on the staff of the radio station in Cedar City, Utah, asked me if she could read *Let the Dishes Wait* over the radio, and I consented. When she had finished her programs she returned the manuscript with thanks, saying that people liked it, but at the insistence of the radio manager she was forced to eliminate all criticism of advertising.

I now know that advertisers and manufacturers had a great influence over what appeared in print in the 1940s and 1950s. Frances Fitzgerald in a study of public school texts found that, in 1939, the Harold Rugg books on American civilization were attacked by the Advertising Federation of America, the National Association of Manufacturers, the American Legion, and a columnist of the Hearst Press. By 1944 the series had disappeared, and other liberal texts and publications were also being attacked. By 1950 school texts reflected policies of the National Association of Manufacturers, and anyone who wrote boldly against advertisers was suspect.[7]

My own suggestion in dealing with the psychological hailstorm was this:

1. We should ask ourselves where we got our values.
2. We should know something of how others live, but not necessarily be bound by others' ways.
3. We must use wisdom in compromising among values.

I quoted from the home management text by Ella Cushman of Cornell, telling about a Mrs. Avery, who when married, had been given Wedgwood china, beautiful table linen, and fine silver and glass. But she liked to go on field trips with her husband and his classes, and when they returned they liked to invite students to stay for supper. Mrs. Avery made some simple, attractive luncheon sets from red and white plaid that required no ironing, and bought pottery seconds in plain ivory. She stocked foods for quick, appetizing meals, and laid away the fine linen and Wedgwood.

In 1949 I liked the practical Mrs. Avery and commended her good sense in putting away those things that took so much time and energy to care for. Today I can make another point: Mrs. Avery became a visible faculty wife. Cushman noted that this couple had a mutual interest in plant science. We now know that Cornell had faculty wives who were trained in botany and unable to get positions on the faculty themselves.[8] I wonder if Mrs. Avery was one of these.

The Imperfect Housekeeper

One purpose of my book was to urge home keeping women of the 1940s to give up the pervasive ideal of perfect housekeeping. "There are three kinds of dusting," said a homemaker. "One where you dust every single thing and every crack and corner; one where you dust only what shows most, as the top of the piano and table-tops; and a third kind where you just draw the shades."[9]

This unorthodox quote was in a college textbook on home management published in 1932. It went on to say that it is just as important to know when to draw the shades as to know how to dust correctly. Unfortunately, books on home management spent more time telling us how to dust and clean correctly, than in telling us when we were justified in pulling the shades, or in just leaving the shades up and refusing to apologize for the mess the house was in. Indeed, a more recent generation would tell us to write "Welcome" in the dust.

The ideal of perfect housekeeping occurred after the Civil War. Bertha Damon in her book, *Grandma Called It Carnal*, described the worship of good housekeeping in a small Connecticut town of this period, when women had just begun to "show off" by employing many separate rooms.

> 'Perfect housekeeping' became a fetish, a cruel god that demanded and received human sacrifices. Whatever gifts of mind or body a North Stonefield woman had, if she were not a 'perfect housekeeper' she had no claim to consideration. That was that. Anybody who was anybody kept her house in a state of hard, intolerable neatness. There is a neatness that is warm and lovely; it is one of the fine arts. Its origin is love for possessions that are intimate, that serve. There is a neatness that is cold; it comes out of bitter energy, lack of worthy occupation, and sometimes, not always, the desire to lay down laws for one's family, to make them miserable, and to be a martyr oneself. The love-neatness knows its place, knows it is but a means to an end, the end being a fine happiness in family life. But the hate-neatness is an end in itself. In almost every North Stonefield house some rooms were shut up and never used; some rooms had the sun entirely excluded by shades; some of even the most inhabited rooms had newspapers laid cheerlessly along the trails frequented by the menfolks.
>
> There seemed to be no limit to the pains which women were willing to take in order to conform to that severe standard of 'perfect housekeeping.' 'She keeps her kitchen floor so clean yer could eat yer bread 'n' milk off of it': emulation of that appetizing achievement led to endless damp drudgery on hands and knees.[10]

An early housekeeping book, written by Mrs. Christine Herrick in 1888, set up in all seriousness unusually high standards for clean woodwork. She wrote that the doors need daily attention even in homes where there are no children, while in the chambers from which little ones run back and forth constantly the task must sometimes be repeated every few hours.[11] Imagine wiping the woodwork of doors every few hours!

George Norris, United States Senator from Nebraska, wrote in his autobiography how as a boy back in those days, he once proposed a debate in school on the topic: "Resolved: there is more pleasure in living with a neat, cross woman than with a good-natured slouchy woman." Since no one wished to defend the slouchy woman, Norris did and won the debate.[12] Such a defense was rare.

In my experience of the 1940s, fear of being known as a sloppy housekeeper made many women clean the corners of basement and attic, even though visitors never penetrated there. But we did expect people with new houses to throw open their closets with a flourish to show off their spaciousness. Those of us who resided in old houses felt lucky that our friends were not interested in our closets.

I saw women, sensible in other ways, rush around to get the spring cleaning done in half the usual time because club was meeting there. It was a rare woman who said, "I'll be glad to have club any time. I don't go to a lot of fuss about cleaning. You'll just have to take the house as you find it." And certainly the guests did not peer into corners, rub a finger on the chair rungs, and study the wallpaper at close range.

Were there any worthwhile reasons for good housekeeping? Yes, I wrote. Perhaps we kept our houses clean to further physical and mental health, or because we achieved aesthetic and craft satisfaction out of it.

I noted that, as homemakers, we did dozens of tasks every day, most of them in a hurried manner so we could get through everything. Each of us yearned for a chance to do one thing thoroughly for a change, to make just a bit of perfection. How many women had said, wistfully, "I wish I could have all my house looking the way I want it, just once!" I wrote that it was unfortunate to wish to make the whole house perfect. The danger of the too perfect housekeeper was that she visited her ideals of cleanliness on her family with constant admonitions of "Wipe your feet! See the marks you left on the towel! Don't cut out paper dolls now; they make too much mess!"

I wrote that young children cannot play without making disorder. They regard furniture as potential trains, houses, and tents. They make a boat upon the stairs, patterned after Robert Louis Stevenson's poem.[13] They turn chairs upside down on the stairs to make the boat, and then ask for a pail of water and a piece of cake so their boat will be like the one in the poem. At our house we usually lacked the cake, so the children resorted to slices of bread. Result: crumbs all over the stairs and a pail of water that kept tipping over.

Nursery school leaders were spreading their ideas that children needed messy play. They needed not only a sand pile but sand with water in it. They needed not only paints but finger paints that were actually smeared onto paper with fingers, thumbs, and even elbows.

I wrote that, above all, a sense of humor was needed to bridge the gap between the perfect housekeeping ideal and the inevitable clutter of living. Humor was concerned with the immediate incongruities of life, those which do not affect us essentially. But if a woman's house-keeping affected her deeply, if it was an important ideal to her, then she could not laugh when she got caught in a messy house.

THEY THAT WASH ON MONDAY

Washing and ironing in the 1800s took a great toll on women's time and energy. I began this chapter with a quotation from Marion Harland, written at the turn of the century. Marion Harland was the pen name of Virginia Payson Terhune, the wife of a minister and a prolific author of household advice books and newspaper columns before and after the turn of the century. She was so fond of her early description of washing by hand that she repeated it in a book written after washing machines came into use. It is such a long sentence that I laid it out as found poetry.

It is—
and it has been from time immemorial

and it will be
until the end
of this rolling old globe of ours—

the law of thrifty housewives
that eyes,
anointed by the blessed sleep of Sunday night,

shall be unsealed by cock-crow
to smart and water in the smoke of boiling suds;
that hands,
lately folded in prayer and crossed
in sacred decency through the hallowed hours,

shall rub and redden and roughen
over the bleached ridges
of wooden washboards,
or the luckless laborer

lose temper and cuticle
against the treacherous grooves of metal 'patents';

that what with lifting boilers and tubs
and wringing and starching and hanging out
and folding down,

the priestess of that unblessed day in the calendar
shall be, by Monday night,
separated from Sunday quiet and Sunday thoughts

by an abyss of unsavory odors and sweltering heats;
by such backaches,
and headaches,
and armaches,

that the recollection of the holy season
is a dream of doubtful distinctness.[14]

Although washing was not that difficult for middle class housewives in the 1940s, many of my friends were still getting up at five on Monday morning to get the wash out early. I didn't rise that early but I had a washboard and used it for the diapers.

I described the efficiency movement, which began with engineers streamlining movements in factories and then spread to households. Lillian Gilbreth was an enthusiastic advocate. She invented a pin and string method of measuring the distance a homemaker traveled in doing work in her kitchen, and she emphasized the one best way in the kitchen, in ironing men's shirts, and in making beds.

In response I wrote that some women were not interested in making beds in record time and were content to amble back and forth from one side of the bed to the other, while throwing on sheets and blankets and tucking them in. Perhaps their minds were occupied with something else. Personally, I was of this school.

I said it remained the province of each homemaker to decide whether beds should be taken apart and made anew once a week or once a day. Most of us felt once a week was sufficient, especially if there were other uses we and our families wanted to make of our time. This was where our sense of values came in. It was also our sense of values that made us rule that beds were not to be sat upon in the daytime for fear of ruining the bedspread, or else made us buy ordinary, darker colored spreads so we could be nonchalant when people sat on them.

Advice to homemakers on how to do household tasks prevailed in abundance. Not all of this advice was expert advice. When World War II broke out, the women's pages in newspapers bristled with suggestions on how to be thrifty.

"Never throw away your orange peels," urged one writer. "This is wasteful. You should save them and make marmalade."

"And where, dear madam," thought I, "are we to get the sugar for marmalade, now that sugar is rationed?"

Many women felt it was easier to get through their work when laid out by certain days: one day to wash, the next to iron, and somewhere along Friday or Saturday, a thorough house cleaning. But I had a neighbor who, on occasion, did her washing in the evening, hanging it out as late as midnight. She liked to do the weekly house cleaning in the evening too, finishing up by going into the garden by moonlight to gather flowers for the living room.

Traditional housewives considered her to be a poor manager. In my eyes she was a good manager. It all depended on one's goals. To her, housework was a very minor aspect of living. She was active in community affairs and her home was wide open at all hours to friends and especially to children. She did not let housework interfere with her enjoyment of the daytime hours, and she was eternally grateful to an early friend of hers who taught her "how to do housework at night." This neighbor was Jo Turner, with whom my two offspring and I walked on certain days to check grocery prices for the Office of Price Administration during World War II.

My manuscript then turned to an early home economist, Caroline Hunt, who in 1908 had written:

> It is indeed good to be alive on the west shore of Lake Michigan of a bright winter's morning, and yet, although I have spent hours walking on the shore on Saturday mornings, I have never seen a person besides those who were with me. Where are the mothers? Why don't they bring their children down there? Don't they know the fun of tramping up the shore and building fires and having little camp lunches, and of watching the winter landscape?[15]

I wrote, "Where were the mothers indeed? They were home, of course, preparing for Sunday by vigorously cleaning house, or vigorously baking, or vigorously buying supplies in the stores. But there is no law except custom that says the face and feel of Saturday must be one of cleaning, baking, and shopping."

MAKING ENDS MEET

I wrote that we all need money to live. There was scarcely a family to be found that thought it had enough to live on, whether it had two thousand or fifteen thousand dollars a year. The typical American family had an annual income of three thousand dollars in 1947.

I wrote that as we looked over our list of essentials, we knew we wanted food, medical care, sanitation for physical health, clothing, housing, insurance, and savings. I hoped families would have a feeling of surplus with their income, a sense of being free to choose. This meant thoughtful discarding of things that gave shallow satisfaction.

There were desires to express our own individual talents, desires for things which we enjoyed for themselves because they enriched our lives. For example, our neighbors the Browns liked music. They decided to sell their car and use that money for a really good record player and some records. The money they had spent on gas and oil and straightening fenders now went for music. Mrs. Brown played records as she did her housework. She was not bothered with neuroses because her free half-a-mind was on the music. Their children were growing up with remarkable music appreciation. Today I admit that, after a time, the Browns had to get a car again.

Instead of buying a new spring dress one year, I bought Thomas Craven's book of art reproductions to teach myself and ended up teaching my offspring as well. We postponed re-upholstering some furniture and bought a tent and sleeping bags instead so we could go camping. Today I admit that I finally had to buy a new dress, and we did re-upholster.

In a subsection titled "Where Is the Money Coming From" I suggested alternatives such as the father working overtime or the mother possibly getting a job. There were ways women could earn at home. Children, too, sometimes earned. It was a sketchy treatment. While I recognized the double burden of earning mothers, I failed to mention that women's wages were much lower than men's.

In a subsection titled "Make Instead of Buy," many of the examples showed the influence of the agricultural era and the Great Depression. In the 1940s there were extension service bulletins that gave instructions on how to do these things.

Homemakers could make money go further by sewing for the family. Outgrown clothes could be cut down for the younger children. Coats and dresses could be made, although making underwear did not pay out. We could cut worn sheets down the middle and sew them up with the outer edges together. We could turn shirt collars and mend more. We could do our own clothes cleaning and pressing.

We might bottle and can food and make our own jam and pickles, but we did not save money that way unless we had a garden or other access to low-cost food. Even with our own gardens, canning peas and greens rarely paid out.

We could cook cereal every morning and not use dry cereals, which cost more per dish. We could make our own bread, cake, and pie, never buying the commercial product or the ready mixes. We could reduce waste by care in cooking, urging the family to slick up their plates, and learning to use leftovers.

We could cut hair at home, do our own furniture re-finishing and upholstering. We could make our own soap, furniture polish, and floor wax. In smaller towns, families could keep a cow, rabbits, and chickens.

In all these ways we could save money. However, few household tasks had been systematically studied to show how much money was saved. Above all, we had to remember that while making over clothes and baking bread did not cost much money, they did cost the mother's time and energy. Was that her idea of a joyful life? Perhaps it was a pleasure for women who liked handicrafts but, for those women with a dislike for sewing and cooking, the resentments more than outweighed the money saved.

I wrote that one of my peculiar joys in life was to throw away socks when the hole in the heel was as large as a fifty cent piece. Sometimes I was inclined to do it when the hole was only the size of a quarter. Yet my friends methodically darned such sad specimens. This was in the days before nylon reinforcement of toes and heels. Nylon would prove to be a godsend.

Also, I noted that we needed a good sense of values to give us the courage to abandon purely conventional ways of living, and to develop our personal capacities to appreciate. The wise homemaker knew how to buy sheets, but more important, she knew her family's latent talents, whether for sports, music, flowers, or science, and she encouraged their development.

Come to Dinner

This chapter was no great shakes, unless you were interested in what one faculty wife, namely me, went through in preparing to have departmental couples in for dinner. Underneath it was a confession that my physical energy did not stretch and we could not afford hired help. I decided informality worked best, and wistfully hoped for good conversation because I really didn't like the usual bridge playing. I tackled the matter of children's birthday parties, and ended with a few good-hearted remarks on the importance of hospitality.

Time Off

The overworked mothers of the nineteenth century hardly knew the meaning of the word "leisure." Their days were so full that it was common to say: "Man works from sun to sun but women's work is never done." In Mrs. Herrick's housekeeping book, written in 1888, there is one lone reference to relaxation. At the very end of the book she said:

> Even the busiest woman, by a little plotting, can snatch five or ten
> minutes during the day in which to glance at the daily paper, and
> learn enough of the progress of events to be able to converse know-
> ingly with her husband upon current topics. If she learns only suffi-
> cient to render it possible for her to make intelligent inquiries, and
> stimulate her husband into giving her a fuller version of the news she
> has only caught an inkling of, so much the better. The average man is
> never more happy than when in the position of enlightening some
> one who receives gladly the words of wisdom that fall from his lips.
>
> When the tea-table is cleared, and the husband and wife settle
> down for the evening, the pleasantest part of the day should be just
> begun . . . Most men like the pretty domestic picture a woman
> makes when she is at work making or repairing little garments, or
> indulging in a rare bit of fancy-work.[16]

Today my comment would be that housekeeping books at the turn of the century reflected woman's sphere. I discern manipulation whereby the wife enlarged her own learning in order to please her husband. It seems unjust that Herrick parcels out learning to men and keeps women in their proper sphere.

In the 1940s women with children were still putting long hours into household tasks, amounting to fifty-six hours a week, which averaged eight hours every day according to time studies. There didn't seem to be much leisure because we got it in scraps, perhaps half an hour in the morning, an hour in the afternoon, and a couple of hours after the dishes were done at night.

Studies showed the two biggest leisure time activities were reading and informal social life, such as talking to the family, friends, or neighbors. I suggested other sorts of activities such as just sitting, a chance to catch the mood of a day, to contemplate the ways of a child at play, to meditate on one's whole way of living. Today television dominates, but it did not spread across the country until the 1950s.

In the late 1940s occasional articles warned women they should use their spare time to keep up with whatever occupation they had before marriage because they might become suddenly widowed or divorced, and, besides, what would they do when their children were grown and gone?

The most thought provoking article on this matter was Ann Leighton's "The American Matron and the Lilies," which appeared in

Harper's.[17] She said that keeping up with former interests was like "holding a small dry bundle aloft while tides rise around." I said that the tired mother should not be saddled with a guilty conscience because she used her leisure time in just sitting, or in going out to club. For those mothers who did want to keep up with former interests, life would be complicated, but they should certainly keep trying.

However it was very important to recognize that most mothers who worked for pay did so because they had to. Their paycheck was badly needed to support their families, and they should not be criticized for taking employment.

Yet a new kind of advice had begun to appear, this time from psychiatrists. One of them, Marynia Farnham, said it was harmful for a mother to pursue a career because being a mother meant being protective and passive, while a career called for aggressive and self-assertive traits. She predicted that women would become psychologically ill trying to harmonize motherhood and a career.[18]

In 1949 I sensed there was something wrong with Marynia Farnham and wrote that we should not believe anyone blindly. I went on to quote Elsa Denison Voorhees, a psychologist, whom I considered more sensible:

> Life itself . . . will probably remain, for most women, unorganized, bewildering, and inexplicable; but that is no reason why the thinking of any woman about herself and her own process of living cannot be clear and purposeful . . . How can she arrange her life as a whole in order that she may—with luck—get the greatest possible satisfaction from it throughout its probable length, with a sense of well-being for as much of the time as possible, and with *an unwavering certainty of her right to grow and to live intelligently.*[19]

The italics are mine, today, because this was a feminist statement.

MIRROR, MIRROR, TELL ME TRUE

It was considered a feminine privilege to care about clothes and appearance. Women were indulgently believed born with a looking glass in the hand. But I wrote that actually there were as many attitudes toward personal appearance as there were people. After some discussion of these attitudes, I tackled the motives of clothing textbooks for high school girls, and criticized women's magazines.

Bear in mind that the women's magazines of the 1940s were dignified and in many ways helpful to women in their daily lives, in spite of their comfortable relationship with advertising. In the 1940s I regretted the enormous emphasis of women's magazines on glamor.

My friends and I weren't thinking of beauty as we went about our housework. I wrote that we didn't pretend to be glamor girls. Most of us wore cotton dresses, or worn out afternoon dresses, and they weren't always crisply fresh. Nobody could afford the money or the time to have a clean house dress every day. Nor did we prance around at our housework wearing high heels, even though advertisers thought so. We tried to wear sensible shoes, or else we were getting the last ounce of wear out of some shoes lying around. We wore bobby socks or old stockings with runs in them, getting the last ounce of wear. Mothers finished wearing out the hose that their school and business daughters had discarded.

On days when I cleaned the basement or planted the garden, I did not have time to give thought to my appearance. If I got my hair combed and face hastily damped and wiped, I was doing well. I enjoyed wearing slacks or levis for really big household jobs, and so did many of my friends, even though the glamor magazines and charm books assured us that we were incorrectly built to look good in pants.

HOME IS WHERE MOTHER IS

I wrote that the fuss made in this country over Mother's Day would lead one to believe that the American people worshiped mothers. Much of this behavior, however, was only sentimentality, which made real mothers squirm uncomfortably when songs were sung that quavered with tears, and readings were read that dripped with feeling, and greetings were sent heavy with roses and adjectives.

There was a man who happened to see an old grandmother rocking on her porch and knitting. He thought, "Oh, what a gentle grandmother! How she toils for others! How she deserves our kindest consideration!" And he built in his mind his picture of her. His tears started as he gazed on her gnarled, work worn hands.

A little boy, not old enough to be sentimental but old enough to seek conversation, sat swinging his feet off the edge of the porch. Presently he asked, "Grandma, why do you knit?" Grandma returned his look and answered, "Oh, just for the hell of it."

In great contrast to sentimentality over mothers are the brickbats which a psychiatrist named Strecker hurled at moms. In his book, *Their Mother's Sons*, Strecker said a very great many mothers of this country ruined their children by binding them so close, psychologically, that the children failed to grow into mature adults able to stand on their own feet. One-fifth of the men eligible for draft in World War II were so neurotic or mentally unbalanced as to be failures. "Mom" was to blame. Strecker got right heated in his accusations of mom. It didn't matter whether Mom waited on her offspring hand and foot, or whether she was a beautiful addle-pate, or be-spectacled intellectual leaving said offspring to fend for themselves.[20]

Brickbats had been hurled at mothers before. I wrote that the wise mother walks down the middle of the road, not along the edge where the bouquets were thrown, or the other edge where brickbats were hurled. I struggled with what should be the characteristics of a good wife and mother, with statements about cheerfulness, sense of humor, and serenity.

I wrote that she helped her family to develop their personalities. (To develop personality was a common phrase in the 1940s.) At the same time she did not neglect her own personal growth. There were ideals in the home. She and her husband had a good set of values, which they pretty well agreed on, and their children absorbed these, though the parents didn't expect their offspring to grow up exactly like them.

I said it was almost impossible to put into words the home-like feeling which good mothers created. Not only the children, but their father admitted that when they come home after school and work to find mother gone, the whole place seemed awfully empty. It wasn't warm, no matter what the thermostat registered.

I admitted everything was not perfect, although some women apparently thought so, according to Ann Leighton, in her article "The American Matron and the Lilies":

> The standards she sets herself she could ask of no one else . . . The perfect wife. The perfect mother. Her husband's great love and attractive to other men. A healthy family of at least three and the figure of a teen-age girl. A permanent position in her community through which she streaks like a comet. A mind posted beyond domestic drudgery on a world she has scarcely time to observe. All she asks is the most from life, from love, from friendship, city, country, the world of art and music and literature . . . She works like a slave to live like a queen . . .
>
>   She believes that it is better to do nothing than to do anything badly; so she tries to do everything well. If she cooks, it must be good cooking, French, exciting, and for the children, the work of an expert dietitian. If she cleans, her house will look sleek and loved,

better than one cleaned by strangers for pay. Her children have care beyond any a nurse can give. Her garden, her animals, her canning, and even her flower arrangements look ready for expert appraisal.[21]

I wrote that this was all too strenuous to make a good homemaker. The wise wife and mother was more leisurely. A perfect matron like the one above would leave her family a nervous wreck.

In this chapter I also said that the process of managing people was not the same as just living with them and enjoying them. Managing involved bossing, only in a nice way of course. To enjoy people one talked on the same level with them, and treated them as something important in and of themselves.

I wondered how much of my own talk with our offspring was management—instructions and urgings and commands. I found myself saying in the mornings: "Hurry and get dressed. Get your work done. Eat your breakfast before the mush gets cold. (I knew the modern word was "cereal," but it was still mush at our house.) Your face isn't clean; go wash again. Did you brush your teeth? Get me another spoon so I can feed the baby. Go down and bring up a bottle of tomato juice. Take care of the baby while I run upstairs. Don't leave chewing gum there! Turn the radio lower. Remember to wear your boots. Shut the door tight."

Some days after school when they came home brimful of the latest happenings and anxious to tell them, then we really conversed. As we played Flinch or Authors we paused to talk. Sunday walks were a good talking time, but here again the radio competed, and maybe they did not want to go walking. At dinner at noon, and supper at night, there was time to talk, though never at breakfast at our house. When I sat down to dinner and supper, I pretended I was not a cook and cleaner of the house, but just one person talking to other persons. I refused to think about who was doing the dishes after the meal was over, and what else I should add to my shopping list.

JUST A HOUSEWIFE

"And what is your occupation?"

"Oh, I'm just a housewife."

How many women gave this answer!—whether in applying for a library card or a driver's license or in appraising themselves.

I wrote that when my first two children were babies, and I was tied hand and foot to feeding schedules and diaper washing, an older career woman sniffed when she heard I had apparently buried my

Ph.D. and had gone domestic. Her sniff set me to wondering what's wrong with going domestic. Why did this woman, as well as so many of my own homemaking friends, speak of this occupation as being just a housewife? Perhaps, thought I, if we dug up all the possible reasons for this attitude and studied them carefully, we might improve our morale. At least hauling the problem into the light would straighten out my own emotions about my occupation. I worked my way through answers to arguments that housewifery was menial, monotonous, and isolated; that one must be a jack-of-all trades to do it and it was unpaid.

Marion Harland, writing housekeeping books at the turn of the century, prefaced many chapters with bits of interesting information designed to lift the morale of housewives. For example, in the chapter on bread making to be found in her book, *The Housekeeper's Week*, she introduced her bread recipes with two incidents:

> Jane Carlyle with good blood in her veins, and common sense in her pretty head was a worthy companion in intellect to her husband the great Carlyle. Although well born and delicately reared she had to cook for her dyspeptic husband, especially mixing, raising, and baking the bread which with oatmeal porridge made up the staple of his diet. At first she railed at it as degradation, but one dreary night while waiting for the dough to rise she had a revelation. 'After all, in the sight of the higher Powers, what is the mighty difference between a statue of Perseus and a loaf of bread, so that each be the thing that one's hand has found to do?'

The other incident dealt with Emily Bronte, who in the corner of her kitchen on baking day would knead the dough, her eyes fixed in the intervals of the task upon the German book propped against the wall "out of reach of flour-dust or spatter of yeast." Her father was also dyspeptic. Her neighbors knew her as "the Parson's daughter who made the best bread in Haworth." Marion Harland wrote, "I have talked with them and heard their commendation of her housewifery, particularly of her beautiful darning and her 'main good luck in baking . . .'"[22]

In 1949 I wrote that thriving schools of home economics sought to breathe an aura of respect around the business of being a housewife, even though in the beginning home economics carried a negative connotation. Isabel Bevier, an early founder, wrote that home economics was associated in the West with agricultural colleges, whose standards of scholarship in earlier days were not as high as those of the classical schools, and in the East home economics was associated with schools of cookery and sewing.[23] I never dreamed that, by 1985, home economics as a field would disappear, belittled I now believe by the fact that it was a women's field. Human ecology, and family and consumer sciences have replaced it.

During the Second World War Elizabeth Hawes published her book, *Why Women Cry,* in which she wrote "I have never met a contented housewife. But as there are such a vociferous bunch of people constantly preaching that women's place is in the home—and as these are so many of them prominent and upstanding members of the community, I must force myself to assume that somewhere there is a female who is perfectly contented with the lot of housewife."[24]

Hawes argued that some women are better off having something to do away from home, and she organized child care centers and cafeterias for employed women during the war. This was reminiscent of Charlotte Perkins Gilman's book *Women and Economics* (1898) which urged professional cleaners to go through the houses, nursery schools to care for young children, and the creation of a common eating center. After all, Gilman wrote, if the only bond that holds a family together is the tablecloth, it is not much of a bond.[25] Gilman was the leading intellectual of the first feminist movement at the turn of the century.

I wrote that there must be opportunity for those women who needed outside employment to supplement earnings or to fulfill their talents. Good nursery schools and a better system of child care were badly needed. Homemakers must not feel completely tied. They needed a feeling of choice, a feeling that they chose homemaking because they honestly preferred it, but if they wished to branch out into a specialty they should have that choice.

It is obvious that my shadow manuscript dealt primarily with non-employed, white, middle class homemakers, whose husbands could support them, and who therefore could have a feeling of choice. I failed to consider families in real economic distress, especially families headed by women.

ARE YOU HAPPY?

Happiness was an American ideal. It was generally believed that everyone had a right to happiness, and we thought it could be handed to us on a platter. Most movies, novels, and stories had happy endings. Advertising assured us we would be happy if we bought its perfume, sterling silver, kitchen cleanser, and hand lotion. I wrote that this placid state of eternal happiness was impossible. We would get mighty bored in a continual placid, happy state.

I said that human beings needed action. The human spirit deteriorated if it didn't bump against obstacles to overcome. I described how when my husband left on a trip, I would pop around and get the work done, and outline my days. We ate regularly. Nobody got sick. Shopping was uneventful. And I got three books read, but there was no zest.

Suddenly the head of the house was home. He trailed in with luggage, a bushel of ripe peaches, and unexpected relatives to stay the weekend. Life was a pandemonium. We concocted supper for everybody and washed two dozen fruit jars for the peaches, which must be bottled tomorrow. The offspring were deliriously happy. I was having a good time, too, talking to the relatives and figuring out how to stretch three slices of halibut to feed eight people. A stormy life has more chances for happiness than a quiet life with never a ripple. Happiness seems to be a byproduct of activity.

Then I discussed the moods of women, including before menstruation, and morning sickness in pregnancy. It was a common sense approach since I didn't have any real expertise in these matters, just my own experience and that of friends and relatives. I quoted others saying that women are more neurotic then men. I wondered if this was an inborn tendency or something acquired as we grew up. I did not think to ask who had the right to judge women as more neurotic than men. This whole problem would be faced head on by second wave feminism, years later.

I wrestled with matters of drudgery. I wrote about fatigue, with graphs showing the rise and decline of energy during the day. I didn't know, then, about individual biological rhythms and that there are night persons who do not start the day with a burst of energy. The very title of this chapter gives one pause today when the stresses of life are paramount. The idea of happiness would dominate the 1950s, and of course it has long remained a motivation used in advertising.

Educating Our Daughters

I summarized, historically, the opening of men's higher education to women, the struggle of home economics for academic respect, and then, in the 1940s, how certain psychiatrists and other writers urged that women be educated only in fields "related to motherliness." I observed that they sounded like the Wisconsin Supreme Court decision of 1875. It refused to admit Lavinia Goodell to the bar because the law of nature destines and qualifies the female sex for the bearing and nurture of the children of our race and for the custody of the homes, which are surely not qualifications for forensic strife.[26]

Of course women needed a broad education, and I wrote that both men and women must be able to earn a living and both needed personal-social abilities, but women needed more of the personal-social abilities. Today I am not so sure women should be assigned more.

Soon after I completed my manuscript, Lynne White, Jr., president of Mills College, published his book, *Educating Our Daughters* (1950), emphasizing sex differences in biological makeup and social roles. He wrote that women's curricula would enable women "to foster the intellectual and emotional life of her family and community" and infuse the home with beauty, culture, and gourmet cooking. He created a furor when he put these ideas before the national convention of AAUW in 1947.

In contrast, Harold Taylor, president of Sarah Lawrence College, insisted such an education would promote rigid, subservient behavior, fashioning women in terms of men's needs instead of their own fulfillment. Courses in family living, child rearing, and responsible citizenship were as important for men as women. A distinct female curriculum would reduce common ground for intellectual companionship, and handicap those women seeking advanced study in the professions. Mildred McAfee Horton, president of Wellesley College, who had directed women of the United States Navy during the recent war, was alarmed that women who expected to marry refused to compete for high status job because they regarded such positions as unfeminine.[27]

It was a great disappointment to me that I could not get my manuscript published. It didn't occur to me that one reason was because men controlled the publishing world, but it occurred to Dale Spender who published a book in 1982 entitled, *Women of Ideas and What Men Have Done to Them: From Aphra Behn to Adrienne Rich*. In her section on the 1950s, Spender mentions my unpublished manuscript as a casualty.[28]

4 Search for Values

In 1951 the tall, two-story white frame house we were renting suddenly became too small when we realized our fifth child was on the way. After some negotiation, we bought a large two-story brick house across town. In a way I was sorry to leave the rented house at 405 East Second North. We had lived there for seven years, including the war years, and I would miss the magnificent view of mountains to the east, south, and west. There we had taken our first steps in astronomy.

In 1948, while living in the white frame house, I had dragged Kip, age eight, to a lecture by William Peterson of the college faculty. He spoke on astronomy. Kip was so interested that I asked him if he would like to try astronomy as a hobby. We began by trying to portray the planets in a manageable size on a long stretch of shelf paper pinned across a wall of the kitchen. We did draw the correct order and the relative sizes, with Mercury very small, Jupiter very large, etc. and we made the sun a slight curve on the left edge of the paper. Then I realized we couldn't get the relative distances onto the paper. The distances were just too great. I had converted distances to feet. We went out on the corner of the sidewalk and said, "This is the sun on our corner, and it is four and a half feet in diameter." Then we stepped a brief way, and marked Mercury on the sidewalk with a piece of chalk. A bit further and we put on Venus. A bit further and we had Earth. We had one planet out by the hedge, but Pluto had us stymied. We calculated that it was located at Tenth North street, which was the edge of town. Pluto, the size of a finger tip, was orbiting the whole town of Logan, held in place by our four and a half foot sun sitting on the sidewalk corner!

I also bought a star map and puzzled over it for a long time because, looking down as it lay in my lap, I found the directions were all wrong. After a time it occurred to me that I could lie on my back on the bed, hold it over my head, and, by looking up at it, find the directions were correct. On pleasant nights the youngsters and I would go over to the nearby Whittier school grounds, lie on our backs, use a flashlight to look at the star map, then shut off the light and locate

Cassiopia and other constellations. We had a wonderful view because this was years before saturated lighting of the night.

Although my shadow manuscript, *Let the Dishes Wait*, had found no publisher, people heard about it and wanted me to speak to PTA meetings, women's clubs, and even Rotary Club. Wynne was a Rotarian. I gave the talk all over northern Utah, sometimes calling it "Wisdom in Homemaking," but people preferred the title, "Leave the Dishes in the Sink," the local phrase then and today for not doing dishes promptly. Around here nobody said, "Let the dishes wait." For years and years I gave talks under this title, changing the substance to encompass what I was learning from experience and from reading.

Ultimately I wrote up this material.[1] The new manuscript had a section on "the quick pick-up," based on events in our big, square, brick house in the early 1950s. We were living near the high school, and the Woodruff elementary school ran along our backyard fence. I could look down into the fourth grade room from our upstairs sleeping porch. When we first moved there, Kip and Barrie were students at the Woodruff and came home for dinner at noon because school hot lunch was optional.

Lance was born July 3, 1951. He was a remarkable baby, even tempered and rarely sick. We had become a household of seven. It's hard to keep a neat house with four youngsters and a baby, and so this is what I wrote:

The Quick Pick-up

Now I am fully aware that in well regulated households there is a quick pick-up and straightening before one retires. Christine Herrick, in 1888, commended this practice in order to outwit early morning visitors. Home management books commend this practice today. Fortunately, or unfortunately, depending on point of view, I was never taught this habit and, as we were all pretty tired by night, we simply dropped our books, games, and other occupations and fell into bed after cursory tooth brushing. So next morning, of course, the front room was a shambles.

A husband, two school age children, two very young children, and a baby were my score at the time of which I speak. Breakfasted, husband and schoolers took off, sort of shutting their eyes as they rushed through the shambles and out the front door. The living room and adjoining dining room belonged to small ones during the morning, to make tents and boats with furniture and blankets, to cut out from catalogs, build with blocks, and generally make a mess. Mother, meaning me, bathed the baby, made formula, washed diapers, and started noon dinner, the hearty meal of the day to which husband and schoolers would presently return. Naturally I would be a little weary by eleven-thirty, but, with the potatoes on to boil, I said to the two little girls, "Now for the quick pick-up."

I marched into the living and dining rooms with the laundry basket and heaved into it the larger toys and other out-of-place items. I marched to the back porch and deposited the basket. Then returning to the living room, I scooped up all small items like marbles, crayons, stray bobby pins, and green houses and red hotels from Monopoly. These I dropped into my apron pocket and then marched into the kitchen and dumped them into the trash drawer.

If anything that is small is ever lost in our house, you can always find it in the trash drawer. It may take awhile to find it, but you know it is there. Today's generation of young mothers also believe the trash drawer is a good idea, but terminology changes and they call it the junk drawer. The generation before mine also had such a drawer. I recall a great-grandmother telling me she had kept her drawer lined with linoleum because of the nails and rough things that it sometimes contained. One family calls it the "guzzinta" drawer because everything guzzinta it.

Now, on with the quick pick-up. I quickly made square heaps of magazines and newspapers and books. Some other day they could be sorted out. We put all furniture back into place and heaved the blankets around the corner onto the stairway landing. The youngsters steered the vacuum through the paper scraps. It is illegal, in a quick pick-up, to do anything about corners. I closed all drawers and cupboard doors, and then looking out the window, saw approaching my spouse and two schoolers. If dinner wasn't quite ready, I quickly set the table. All mothers know that, even though you have a meal practically ready to dish up, if the table is bare of dishes the family moans, "When do we eat?" But a set table will hold off a hungry family for twenty minutes.

Enter husband and schoolers. "Gee, the place looks clean," they might say in unison, because they remembered the shambles of the morning and of the evening before.

Once upon a time I started to write a theory of drawers, but my husband said only one statement could be made about the Thorne drawers, namely, that they were all trash drawers. "No," I argued vigorously. "They are not all trash drawers. You never find underwear in the bread drawer, or bread in the underwear drawer. Therefore I do have a system."

The reason we did happen to have an underwear drawer in the kitchen was because all our bedrooms were upstairs, and the young children sometimes had accidents that required a change of panties, and I certainly was not going to trot upstairs every time underpants were needed. There was, however, a decent distance between the bread drawer and the underwear drawer.

In giving these talks, I used to admit boldly that I rarely dust the window sills at our house. After all, we do have glass curtains and the window sills do not show. It was surprising how often someone would come up to me after my talk and say in a very, very low voice, "I never dust the window sills either, but I never dared say so in public." It turns out that there is a large sisterhood of non-dusters-of-the-window-sillers.

In giving these talks on my kind of housekeeping, I refused to say outright that I was a sloppy housekeeper. Nor would I admit that my standards were lower than those of other women. Sometimes I would say that we had a double standard at our house because, on Saturday, the children and I could whip in and clean up the place if the spirit moved us. The only trouble was that the spirit didn't move us very often. But if we did do a good cleaning, the children knew enough to step lightly for awhile, although before long we were back to our old ways.

For ten years I beat around the bush, refusing to label myself a sloppy housekeeper but unable to find suitable terminology. Then Irma Gross and Elizabeth Crandall published a textbook on home management, in which they devoted several pages to conventional and flexible standards. Conventional standards are what you think most people have. They are quite high quality standards. Flexible standards show that you have thought about your standards and decided to change them deliberately to fit your own situation. Gross and Crandall observed that sometimes a student would say, "Well, anyone can let down." But flexible standards are not letting down; they are deliberate change, a purposeful withdrawing from strict allegiance to the conventional.

One of their students, who married after graduation and had four children under six, was helping her husband with the clerical part of his graduate work. She wrote back to her teachers thanking them for the idea of flexible standards. She told how few things she ironed. "As for cleaning—remember I'm nearsighted. I mop the kitchen floor only when my feet start sticking to it!"[2]

All my children are nearsighted. One day as we sat at the kitchen table, I asked them to take off their glasses and tell me how the kitchen looked. "Mother, it looks fine!" they said with enthusiasm. "You can't see

226 W. First South. Logan High School was to the east. Woodruff School was behind us. First Ward Church was directly across the street.

You let us roller skate in the living room.

the dirty places and the chipped paint on the walls. The floor looks clean too!" So then it occurred to me, why couldn't one give a party and invite only nearsighted people and ask them to leave their glasses home . . .

When we acquired the large, square, old brick house in which we reared our family, the carpeting in the adjoining living and dining rooms was already ancient. It was down to the threads, and, every time we had company to dinner, I would shave the carpet before they arrived by taking the scissors and clipping the upstanding strings along the seams.

It was lovely carpeting for teaching children to skate. Very young children could keep their balance and go round and round the dining table on carpet until they graduated to kitchen linoleum or outside to the sidewalk. The carpeting was good for hopscotch because it had a slightly visible pattern that was about right in way of squares. We did not hesitate to play marbles on it either. So much had I extolled this ancient carpeting that one mother, who possessed young children and brand new carpeting with a heavy pile, suddenly felt that her youngsters were being deprived, so she acquired some ancient carpeting and installed it in a basement playroom.

People sometimes ask me how I have the gall to go about giving talks on my imperfect housekeeping, and I blithely reply that it is because I come of a long line of poor housekeepers. Consider my grandmother. She raised nine children in four rooms in Snowflake, Arizona, a tiny town at five thousand feet elevation. It really does have snow sometimes in the winter, but was not named for the weather but for Brother Snow and Brother Flake, who were the founding fathers.

Now if you have nine children in four rooms, there's only space for beds, and one can only hope to keep a trail open. Grandma cooked for her family and washed their clothes on the scrubbing board without benefit of a washer. Grandma didn't bother much with gardening and flowers. If she had a spare moment she was sitting, reading, in a rocker. She read prodigiously. When a teachers' institute was held, she would attend just to see what the teachers were learning those days.

Very early in her married life, Grandma had taken it upon herself to keep a journal of the important town events, the births, deaths, marriages, celebrations, and other happenings. She kept it till the day she died, and it ran into several laboriously hand-written volumes. One time the governor of Arizona came to Snowflake to give a patriotic talk, and knowing Grandma was keeping this journal, he asked her for historical information for his talk. She then recorded in her journal, "I wrote the speech for the Governor of Arizona, and he gave it pretty good."

My Life as a Faculty Wife

Shortly after we arrived in Logan in 1939, Robert L. Evans, then head of the Agronomy Department, suggested forming the Agronomy Wives. Professor Evans made the original suggestion, but from then on we women took over. We met once a month, but not in May and not through the summer because of gardening, canning, family outings, etc.

Evans felt that if the wives came to know each other well, this would have a pacifying influence on the competition evident among some of the faculty, for example competition over who did research on barley and who did it on wheat. I don't know if we had a pacifying effect, but we women got along splendidly and had good times at our meetings. We had intellectually stimulating programs, which we presented ourselves, and twice a year gave a party to which our husbands were invited.

At one of these parties the women did skits, each portraying her own husband, much to the consternation and yet delight of the men. Mabel Tingey came on stage wearing layers and layers of Del's clothing, looking as he did when he went duck hunting. As she carried on a running chatter, using Del's earthy vocabulary, she pulled off one jacket, then a second, then one sweater and then a second, and then two pairs of trousers, and stood revealed in red long-handled underwear. A striptease long to be remembered! It was Mabel, a gifted artist, who always made the Agronomy Wives' yearbooks. She was also our historian, creating scrapbooks filled with news clippings of Agronomy Department families.

Turnabout is fair play, so at a later party the men gave their version of their wives' behavior. This was in the winter of 1951–52, when Wynne had become department head following Evans's retirement. Wynne introduced the men's skit and then presented Mrs. Thorne's behavior. His script, which he composed and typed himself, has a footnote to the first page that says "In each scene, the lady is on stage and pretends conversation with her kids who are off stage." This is his script:

> Ladies and gentlemen of our TV audience. We all look forward to one of the greatest treats of all time. In a few short months we will bring into your home the coronation of Queen Elizabeth. You will then be taken into her palaces and with her to select social functions.
>
> In order to prepare you for all of this royal splendor, these overwhelming affairs of state, and the social graces of the royal court, we are selecting a few distinctive groups of our American citizens.

By following this aristocracy of America into their homes and their professional and cultural organizations, we can better compare the best of America with the royal trappings of Europe.

For the first introduction to the royalty of America we are taking our cameras West to the heart of our inland empire. Here we find Logan, Utah, the great educational, cultural, social and scientific center of all the Americas. And without doubt the most elect of all groups in this great area are the Agronomy Wives of Utah State Agricultural College. The pageantry, sparkling repartee, social graces and learned discussions that occur at these eagerly awaited monthly assemblies are noted far and wide.

The spacious and elaborate homes of these notables form a fitting background for the enchanted hours of these meetings. In order that you can more fully appreciate these gala affairs let us visit a few of the homes to see the many preparations required to make these meetings the talk of two continents and the envy of the world.

It is altogether proper that we should go first to the home of the chairman of the great department. Here, one hour before the noted guests are due to arrive we glance into the living room and find Mrs. Thorne making her preparations. (She is sitting, typing, with floor and house littered.)

The daughter Barrie inquires: Mommy, aren't Agronomy Wives coming tonight?

Mrs. Thorne: Hush. I'm preparing a speech.

Barrie: Yes, but if you don't clean up a little there won't be any place to sit.

Mrs. T.: Now Barrie, I am not going around the state telling people not to be a slave to their home and then come here and spend all my time cleaning up.

Barrie: But Mommy, don't you think we ought to clean up just a little?

Mrs. T.: Oh, all right. Kip, come here and carry that sack of potatoes off from the easy chair and put it on the back porch.

Kip: Now Mother, you said the easy chair was a handy place to keep potatoes.

Mrs. T.: Take them away and kick your shoes and old clothes behind the davenport where you can find them in the morning. Sandra, push those paper dolls under the corner of the rug. Avril, turn the cushions of the sofa over, so the trash on top will fall under. Barrie, take the dishes off the table and put them in the sink. Maybe the neighbors will come in tomorrow and offer to do them. There. That is just like I said we should do in my book. Nothing like following your own advice. And thank goodness they can't see what the rest of the house is like or the Agronomy Wives would think I am a sloppy housekeeper instead of a casual one.

Women and Higher Education

One of the continuing threads of my life has been a concern over women and higher education. In 1950, I had a chance to express my views as part of a symposium on this subject, sponsored jointly by women faculty members, the Associated Women Students, and the Logan Branch of AAUW. The symposium was part of inaugural week for a new president, Louis Linden Madsen. Dean of Women Ione Spencer Daniel proposed the idea, and, although she had some trouble convincing the administration of the importance of such a subject, the symposium did take place.[3] Scarcely any men attended but a great many women did, and some months later we repeated it at a meeting of the Provo chapter of the AAUW. Just as Marion Talbot, Sophonisba Breckinridge, and other early women had fought for opportunity for women in higher education with support of the AAUW, we in Utah were doing the same thing.

I was the first speaker and was introduced as having a Ph.D. and four children ranging from ten years to sixteen months in age. I said that foods and clothing courses had not been as important to me in rearing children as had a broad education, which gives a framework on which to pin ideas. Children benefit from intellectual stimulation, and I gave several homey examples.

Another speaker was Juanita Leavitt Pulsipher Brooks, already known as a writer of western history. Before she was old enough to vote, she had married, had a child, and was widowed. After some years of teaching, she married Will Brooks, a widower with four sons. Juanita and Will then had four children together, bringing their total to nine. Juanita was teaching English at Dixie Junior College in St. George, Utah. Before marrying Will, she had earned a masters' degree at Columbia University.

When Juanita Brooks rose to her feet, she began by saying that after hearing Alison Thorne she had thrown away her planned speech and would tell how higher education had helped her raise a family. She then said she had learned from Matthew Arnold the sustaining phrase "to be educated is to see life clearly and to see it whole." As I recall, she went on to say:

> I inherited these four boys from Will Brooks, and one of them kept playing hooky and running away from high school, going off into the desert and mountains with companions. When a boy who is supposed to be in school appears covered with dirt and carrying a pair of burrowing owls, seeing life whole helps one to decide how great the offense is. At first we thought it was because he needed glasses, so we got him glasses, but he still played hooky. So I said to him that, since he was off in the desert and mountains, why didn't he make a collection of the owls' nests and other things he found, and I would show him how to make a natural history collection, as I had learned to do when I was a student at the BYU. In order to make such a collection, he left his friends, who were not interested in such things, and went off alone. He made such a good collection that he was able to sell it for two thousand dollars. So then he finished high school and paid his own way through college.

Another speaker, Vera Weiler Bennion, was older than the rest of us. Vera and her husband had graduated from the Agricultural College, in 1913, in a class of one hundred. They were the only graduates who went out to make a living on the land, homesteading in Daggett County. Although she could not manage her wood stove as well as the woman on the next ranch, Vera found she could serve on the school board better. She raised the first turkeys in that county and learned from an extension service course how to landscape. She said, "As a result, with plenty of water, land, and manure, believe me I landscaped the whole outfit!" With her four children grown, she was doing community work, including membership in the Utah Women's Legislative Council, of which she had been president. She also knew a great deal about politics, having helped her husband, Heber Bennion, get elected secretary of state. She concluded by saying a college education should train women to be leaders in government in the fields of public health, in safety education, and in movements for peace. The women in the United States who have raised their families and are no longer burdened with housework are a great undeveloped resource.

Another speaker, Dr. Ida Stewart Brown, assistant dean of students at the University of Utah, was a young woman without children whose husband died in the Second World War. She was apologetic for not having a family and praised the wife-mother role. "But," she said, "there is danger in a college education if it takes away the femininity, which makes a woman distinctive from a man." While the other three of us were mothers and community workers who spoke from our personal experience, Brown was speaking from her training in psychology that, increasingly in the 1950s would emphasize marriage and domesticity, urging women not to be overly intellectual.

The Climate of the 1950s

This decade would prove to be different from others of the century. For one thing there was the baby boom. In the aftermath of the war, people wanted families, and young people married earlier than any generation in the century and spaced their children closer than did their mothers. One study of college alumnae found that in 1950–55 only 2 percent of college women expected to be employed all their lives, including the child bearing years. In the 1920s it had been 14 percent. By the 1960s it would be 45 percent.[4]

In the 1950s women's clothing emphasized femininity. As historian Lois Banner has written, fashions came to resemble those of the Victorian period, with skirts falling to mid-calf and becoming full, held out by starched crinoline petticoats. Waists were bound in by girdles, and for evening there were boned corsets called "merry widows." Breasts were supported to appear as large as possible, usually with the use of padding. Shoes came to sharp points, and the popular heel height was three inches.[5]

I wore a girdle when I went out, and a padded bra. My dress shoes had pointed toes, but heels of less than three inches. It was dowdy to wear rubber soled Girl Scout shoes to social events, but I certainly wore them at home and for walking to town. Schoolgirls, including my daughters, wore full skirts with stiff petticoats. A teacher remarked that, when the girls of her class sat down, it sounded like a great crumpling of newspapers. Then, after a time, skirt lengths began to rise at a slow and steady pace. I was lucky. I never had to let down hems. What a daughter wore one year was still the right length for her the next year despite her growth.

As for hair styles, the college edition of Webster's *New World Dictionary* (1953) showed female pictures with 1950s coiffure, and with a strong distinction between male and female appearance. We used such a dictionary for years. Yet not until second wave feminism arrived did I take a really good look at those pictures, particularly the one on page 1,695, which had two pictures to illustrate "yoke." The top one was of two oxen with a yoke across their necks. Below was a young woman, with upswept hair and ribbon. Her dress had a yoke across the shoulders, her head was slightly inclined, and her eyes were modestly downcast. She looked more docile than the oxen. When a revised edition of this dictionary ultimately was published, the oxen were still there but the girl had disappeared. Indeed, most illustrations were of things, not of people, but pictures of males were still more frequent than those of females.

Reading Philosophy and Discussing It

All these years I was studying philosophy on my own because I needed an ongoing intellectual project, and because I really believed that somewhere in philosophical thought lay nuggets of wisdom helpful in living one's life. Ever since that philosophy course, in 1935, under Charner Perry at the University of Chicago, I had been curious about whether philosophy could give insight into the everyday problems of wives and mothers. It seemed to me that philosophy ought to be as helpful in women's lives as in men's. But I couldn't find anyone who had succeeded in making such a connection. I took generic "Man" for granted, and when reading about philosophy for Man assumed it to be philosophy for human beings. When I read "the person, he," I generously acknowledged that it included "the person, she."

Wynne became interested in philosophy too, and we had two regular occasions for discussing these ideas with other people. One was the adult Sunday school class of the LDS Fifth Ward, a large class that Wynne and I taught together through the 1940s. We would take the official title of a lesson, put under it the philosophical and other ideas that occurred to us, and encourage lots of discussion.

Apparently we were not the only ones doing this sort of thing. In 1942 Juanita Brooks wrote a letter, in which she said, "I retain my fellowship in the church because I like it and I need it and I want my children to have its benefits, but I refuse to surrender my intellectual independence to it. I'm amazed with the things I can get away with, with the fact that they have me teach a Sunday School class—students in their early twenties—and we do not follow the lesson outline. Neither do we always present the orthodox point of view. . . ."[6]

In December 1942 I was reading William James's, *Varieties of Religious Experience* and using it in Sunday school class.[7] I typed my notes on our portable typewriter, with Barrie, the baby, on my lap held in a framework of body and desk. She was a quiet child and did not topple. Once I happened to mention to historian Leonard Arrington (who was on the college economics faculty and taught Sunday school in the Tenth Ward) that I was using William James in the Sunday school class I taught. "How do you dare?" he asked. But I continued to do so. Not until years later did I learn that our Fifth Ward Sunday school superintendent protected Wynne and me from attempts of higher church authorities to oust us from teaching.

Moving to the big square house in 1951 made us members of the LDS First Ward, with the chapel just across the street. Wynne gave up teaching Sunday school because of the burden of his work at the college, but I continued, sometimes teaching the adult class, and sometimes the young people of high school age. I also did a monthly lesson for the Relief Society.

The second opportunity that Wynne and I had for discussing philosophy with other people was "Thoughtless Thinkers," an informal group that lasted over forty years. On Sunday evenings once a month, we met in one another's homes (without refreshments, thank goodness) to discuss ideas, beginning with religion but usually moving on to philosophy, ethics, science, art, education, or public affairs.[8] Our meetings were open to anyone who was interested. Some were faculty couples, and some were not connected to the college. There were several widows and one woman who attended consistently and who left her husband home. Occasionally we had an outside speaker. This was how I first met Sterling McMurrin, who was teaching philosophy at the University of Utah.[9] I asked him for a list of helpful books on religion and philosophy, and Wynne and I bought and read them.

In those early years we read the philosophy of personalism because it gave individuals considerable control over their own lives. We believed that no one person, book, or organization could be used as an authority to stop or place a barrier on discussion. In this spirit we read Ralph Tyler Flewelling's *The Things That Matter Most.* For many years I subscribed to *The Personalist,* which Flewelling edited at the University of Southern California. We also worked our way through Nicolas Berdyaev's *Slavery and Freedom,* which explored strengths and pitfalls of self-realization. Berdyaev wrote, "Personality is like nothing else in the world. There is nothing with which it can be compared . . . When a person enters the world, a unique and unrepeatable personality, then the world process is broken into and compelled to change its course in spite of the fact that outwardly there is no sign of this."[10]

Over the years Thoughtless Thinkers was an intellectual adventure. Wynne described our discussions in his tribute to Clara Nebeker Hulme when he spoke at her funeral in 1966. Mrs. Hulme, the oldest person in our discussion group, had been a widow for many years. She was filled with the excitement of ideas and read continuously and widely. She was public spirited, having been the moving force behind the building of the first LDS recreational girls' home in Logan Canyon, the first PTA in the valley, and the first kindergarten. During the war when my neighbor Jo Turner and I were checking grocery prices for the Office of Price Administration, Clara Hulme was director of the program for our entire county.

Mrs. Hulme, as we always called her, was also a "vigilant supporter" of the college, and did not hesitate to speak to administrators if she felt they had taken a wrong path. With several other older women, she often sat on the front row at public lectures given at the college. A few years before her death, she told me that she did not want to be extolled at her funeral as a perfect housekeeper, as was customary at women's funerals. Instead, she wished to be remembered as a humanitarian. Wynne, in his talk at her services, never mentioned housekeeping. He said that she, along with others in our discussion group, had been reading Paul Tillich, Teilhard de Chardin, and Edmund Sinott. In his book, *The Biology of the Spirit*, Sinott argued from a scientific background that there is some undiscovered process in nature that tends to pull matter together into living systems, and this is the basis of goal-seeking, both mental and spiritual.[11]

Turmoil and Then a Sabbatical

The first years of the 1950s were difficult ones at Utah State Agricultural College. Louis Madsen remained president only briefly because the governor of Utah was manipulating the board of trustees, and the board was preparing to get rid of faculty who displeased them. Wynne chaired the Professional Relations Committee of the Faculty Association and led the battle for faculty rights. He was fearless, though well aware he stood in danger of losing his own job. He reasoned he could find work elsewhere, and some of the faculty could not.

Dean of Women Ione Daniel lost her position because the board considered her too outspoken politically, and it passed a ruling that if one member of a married couple was in administration, both could not be employed by the college. Ione's husband, Theodore Daniel, had solid standing on the forestry faculty, and because she was an administrator she gave up her position exactly as the board anticipated. This anti-nepotism ruling continued into the 1960s and would keep me off the faculty because Wynne was in administration. Ione became visiting teacher for the Logan school district and did a great deal of good in that position. Over the years she remained our close friend and a member of Thoughtless Thinkers.

After much turmoil, state and campus politics calmed down somewhat, but it had been a harrowing experience, and Wynne asked for and received a year's sabbatical leave. In September 1953 we headed for Knoxville, Tennessee, where for one year he was director of the fertilizer division of the Tennessee Valley Authority. We drove our car, pulling behind it a 1928 Essex trailer, a two-wheeled, tarp-covered affair that held essential clothing and household items. The trailer lacked a functioning tail light, so we could travel only during daylight hours. We drove four hundred miles a day and it took five days.

In Knoxville we rented an unfurnished house, a block from a commercial street and quite close to the University of Tennessee. No one would rent a furnished place to a family with five children, so we bought some cheap furniture and managed. There were schools for Kip and Barrie nearby, and the other children were home with me. Sandra, Avril, and Lance were five, four, and two years old. There was no public kindergarten for Sandra, and in the brown notebook in which I wrote notes on my reading, I sometimes commented on our daily lives:

> Sandra, playing the other two were horses, with a long white elastic as reins.
>
> "Let's see what this booklet says to do to horses: Oh, you feed horses, you give them nosedrops."
>
> Avril: "You feed them booklets."
>
> Later, one child was in my old green house dress, another in apron, another in old pink chemise. They were galloping on broom, dust mop, and wet mop. "We'll fly to the sky, we'll fly to the sky!" All three sets of bare feet were black with soot that held them earthbound.
>
> There was always a fine dust of soot on the oak floors and linoleum of that house, despite my once-a-day wielding of broom and mop.[12]

In Knoxville, Tennessee 1953–54.

I continued to pursue my study of values, but I had not anticipated that the University of Tennessee library would refuse me permission to check out books because neither Wynne nor I had an official connection with the university. Consequently on weekdays, after the older children got home from school, or for several hours on a Saturday, I would dash over and sit in the reading room of the library, and read and take notes.

In the months before leaving for Tennessee, I was reading John Laird's book, *The Idea of Value,* because Charner Perry had said that every book on values referred to Laird's work. Elizabeth Hoyt also regarded Laird's book highly.[13] I have no idea who placed it in the Utah State Agricultural College library. As I read Laird in my kitchen in the square brick house, I took extensive notes in my brown notebook. I kept asking whether there was such a thing as intrinsic value, but never found a satisfactory answer in my attempt to relate philosophy and homemaking. Early on in Logan I had been part of a community Great Books course, for which I purchased and read Plato, Aristotle, and other works, but I failed to find the insight I sought.

Many years later another woman, much younger than I, would ask of philosophy some of the same questions I asked, but in relation to social work rather than homemakers' lives. This was Margaret Rhodes,

who spelled out her situation in *Ethical Dilemmas in Social Work Practice.*
She wrote:

> When I first studied philosophy, ethics was presented as an august,
> esoteric subject far removed from the concerns of daily life. My pro-
> fessors taught me to ask such questions as "if there is a good, how
> can we be sure it is?" . . . If students foolishly ventured to ask about
> the meaning of life or about how to act today, they were regarded
> with bemused condescension and sent over to the humanities or
> sociology department. I left philosophy after two years of graduate
> study and plunged into social work. For three years as a caseworker
> in a public child welfare agency, I found myself confronted daily
> with the most difficult ethical issues I had ever encountered.

This was in the 1960s. Later, when Rhodes completed part of a master's degree in social work, she found nothing there that addressed the
ethical issues that social workers regularly confront. She then returned to
graduate work in philosophy, completed her degree, and began teaching.

In her book, published in 1986, she reviewed strengths and shortcomings of utilitarianism, duty-based Kantianism, rights-based theories, Marxist-based ethical frameworks, intuitionist ethical theories,
and virtue-based frameworks. For purposes of social work she chose
virtue-based philosophy centered on human excellence, and suggested
that among the virtues for social workers are compassion, detached
caring, warmth, honesty, a certain kind of moral courage, hopefulness,
and humanity. She argued for an informed relativism, urging constant
re-evaluation of one's own position in light of other people's experience. Rhodes recognized that such re-evaluation is only possible if
there are some commonalities, including basic respect for human dignity, belief in equal opportunity, and desire for community.[14]

Rhodes' s position makes good sense to me today, and if her book
had existed in the 1950s, I would have saved myself a lot of fruitless
reading. While social workers face different problems than wife-mothers, in that they deal with strangers and in a setting of governmental
bureaucracy, both wife-mothers and social workers deal with human
beings and with the larger community.

In Tennessee, since I was unable to put together philosophy and
homemaking, I gave up on philosophy and increasingly read about personality, finding more answers there to my perpetual question, "What is
the good life?" In my shadow manuscript, I used the phrase "helping
family members develop their personalities," a phrase popular with
home economists and child development specialists in the 1940s and

1950s. I became interested in ideas about the nature of a healthy person-ality. While in Tennessee, I read Karen Horney's *Neurosis and Human Growth: The Struggle toward Self-realization* and was much taken with the idea of the real self, which I used in an adult class in the LDS Church when we returned to Logan. As time went on I read much on self-real-ization. Gordon Allport was one of my favorite authors.[15]

Thanks to a letter from Sterling McMurrin, I met Howard Parsons, who taught philosophy at the University of Tennessee.[16] He invited me to attend his seminar on values. The students were several young men and a married couple. At one point I asked and received permission to give a session on homemakers and values. Nobody attended my pres-entation except Parsons and the married couple.

As for social life during that year, our family depended mainly on the small branch of the Mormon church in Knoxville, which met upstairs in a labor hall near the center of town. It is hard work to keep a branch going, so everyone worked. I was nearly forty years old. All the other women were younger and were either pregnant or had babies, so I found myself teaching the children's Sunday school, followed by "Primary" immediately after. My major resource was the Knoxville public library. I checked out and made good use of *Blueberries for Sal, Make Way for Ducklings,* and other delightful books.

On hot Sundays a large window was open in the labor hall, with a fan filling part of it. I used to worry about children falling into that fan or out the open side of the window. It reminded me of the Mormon branch in Corvallis when I was small, and we met upstairs in the fire-house with the fire pole's hole in the floor as a frightening hazard.

In Knoxville when there was no Mormon Sunday school because of quarterly conference, I took the children with me to the Unitarian church, held in a large home on the street above our block. Imagine my delight the day the Unitarian program listed William James as scriptural reading!

Travels

Just as my own parents believed in travel as we were growing up, I was convinced that our offspring should travel. They certainly should see Washington, D.C. when old enough to appreciate it. Kip had already been there because, back in Logan when he was eleven years old, I sent him along on the train with Wynne when he had meetings in Washington. Kip stayed with our old friends, Emma and Paul Pearson, and their daughters showed him around the city. When the daughters got tired, their parents took over—a test of true friendship and every-one's feet.

Knoxville was quite close to Washington, and on a summer's day when Wynne was flying to meetings there, Barrie and I went along, the first plane flight for both of us. Over three days we saw national mon-uments, museums, and the national 4-H headquarters (in Logan Barrie had been a 4-H club member). Meanwhile back in Knoxville, Kip took care of the three little children, with noon and evening hamburgers and root beer, which he purchased from a stand on the commercial street. To pass the time, he took them to a movie each afternoon. The oppor-tunities of Knoxville should not be underrated.

On some weekends Wynne and I took the children on trips around the state. We visited Civil War battlegrounds and found them beauti-fully kept and heartbreaking. As a federal employee Wynne could not take much time off, so I traveled alone with the children during Easter week vacation. I farmed the three youngest out to Elaine in Detroit, by meeting her in Columbus, Ohio, where she took them off my hands. I drove to New York where Kip and Barrie had their first view of the United Nations, Empire State Building, Statue of Liberty, etc. Then on to New England where we saw Boston and visited Eleanor Parkhurst in Chelmsford. We saw Niagara Falls and then went on to Detroit, where I found Sandra and Avril ecstatic because Elaine had bought them white socks for Easter. Their practical mother always bought darker colors that would not show dirt.

Barrie's sixth grade teacher severely criticized me for taking Barrie on this trip because she was slated to represent her school in the city-wide spelling bee and had not finished memorizing spellings. Barrie spent hours learning the words in the spelling list. I helped her at night. Her teacher had her at her home from noon on Saturday till ten at night. We had taught her down through the "m's" and the contest actually fin-ished while on the "i's". Barrie placed second in the city and had her picture and a write-up in the *News-Sentinal*. Wynne and I did not attend, at Barrie's request, and so were much interested in this paragraph:

> Though the situation was tense, Barrie's cautiousness repeatedly
> brought laughs from the audience and officials. She requested def-
> initions, synonyms, repeat pronunciations and sometimes mispro-
> nounced the word more to her own satisfaction before spelling it
> in a slow cadence. The 11-year old runner-up always tapped her
> foot in time with her well-contemplated spelling. Oddly, however,
> she spelled ELEEMOSYNARY without asking any questions.[17]

Barrie also entered a Women's Christian Temperance Union oratory contest and won a silver medal . . .[18]

A surprising thing about the Knoxville schools was scripture reading at the beginning of school each day. Most students knew scripture by heart and easily quoted it when it was their turn. After all, this was the Bible belt. But Kip and Barrie had to memorize theirs the night before. Fundamentalist attitudes showed up in biology class. Although Kip's biology textbook had a chapter on evolution, the teacher said he could not discuss it in class. The Scopes trial had not been forgotten. On the basis of what he learned in Knoxville, Kip could never have become a biologist, but his achievement test score in math went clear off the chart.[19]

It was a terribly hot and humid summer in Knoxville. Although air conditioning was spreading rapidly across the country, we couldn't afford it. All we had was a small General Electric fan. In the summer of 1954, I sometimes piled the children into the car and drove into the Great Smoky Mountains, where we spent the day beside a stream that flowed turbulently among large rocks.

Political Events

The United States Supreme Court decision of 1954 to desegregate public schools shook the South. We knew 15 percent of the local population was colored (the word black was not in use). We had seen a parade of high school bands in which a colored high school had marched, and we knew these people were not allowed to use the public parks except on Thursday. We also knew that in the TVA building where Wynne worked, a colored woman who ran the elevator had a master's degree but this was the best job she could find. Wynne and I were appalled at the segregation we saw. Barrie recalls that our family visited a program held at an all black college and for the first time in her life experienced being a racial token.

All the members of our LDS branch were white. Three families had children in a small public school that had just acquired a new building. The PTA had recently helped paint it, and the parents were very proud of the facility—and also very determined that colored children would not be allowed in.

Another national political situation was the behavior of Senator Joseph McCarthy and the House Committee on UnAmerican Activities. By December 1954, the Senate had censured McCarthy, with Senator Arthur Watkins of Utah playing a strong part. We were appalled when

Utah voters failed to reelect Watkins to the Senate. Terrorizing those suspected of communism would continue, and ramifications in the lives of innocent victims would reach far beyond the 1950s. Some victims were students at the University of Chicago when I was there, students who had flirted with communism in the 1930s but later left it behind.[20]

As the summer ended it became obvious that, as a federal employee, Wynne could not leave in time to get the children back to Logan to start school, so we decided that I would drive to Logan without him. We packed up the ancient trailer, and he drove the first two hours of that first morning and then returned by bus to Knoxville. From then on I was on my own. Again, it took five days at four hundred miles per day. We bought hamburgers and root beer at noon and at night. Our breakfast was oranges and cornflakes with milk, eaten by the roadside. I could not back up the trailer for fear of snapping the tongue, so I chose motels with a layout permitting me to always move forward. "Forward in, and forward out" was my motto.

What a relief to escape the heat of the Midwest when we came into Wyoming's dry air and began to gain altitude! The three youngest were beside themselves with joy at the thought of being home again "down in Logan." As we pulled up to our house, we saw that our neighbors, the Kofoeds, had strung a long banner across the front, saying "Welcome!"

5 Conformity and Creativity

Some Views on Conformity

My shadow manuscript of the 1940s criticized conformity to perfect housekeeping standards and blind acceptance of advice. This was an uphill endeavor in the 1950s, which was a decade of considerable conformity. I looked again at Elizabeth Hoyt's approach. She began in the 1920s, as did my parents, by criticizing "keeping up with the Joneses," but she also wrote that emulation is important in introducing and diffusing interests.[1] In the 1950s the rapid spread of air conditioning and of television were examples of technological emulation.

Hoyt wrote that technology increases our opportunities for the good life but also increases our dangers, liabilities, and temptations. A trade association representing national advertisers arranged to check textbooks. When unfavorable comments on advertising occurred, the publishers were requested to get the authors to withdraw their statements. Publishers protested to presidents of colleges about faculty members even moderately critical of advertising practices.

Hoyt deplored the extent of government expenditure for technological research on instruments of human destruction, observing that we have hardly grasped the possibilities of our bombs and the still more terrible possibilities of the organized spread of the bacteria which bring death. She wrote of new fears that subversives were behind every lamp post, every hearth, and at every council table, so people must take no chances. It was considered better to destroy others who were innocent rather than risk everyone being destroyed. Hoyt's was not the only voice raised against this false reasoning. In 1955 the historian Henry Steel Commager wrote in an article published in Utah:

> A free society is a society where men and women are not afraid to speak their minds; to go to the church of their choice, or the assembly or meeting of their choice; to join such organizations as they fancy; to make their own friends and associates; to insist on their rights, even against officials . . .
> We must abandon the indignity of teachers' loyalty oaths and legislative investigations to discover subversives . . . A free society

does not humiliate its citizens . . . It does not intimidate them or permit officials, clothed with temporary authority, to humiliate them—not even if they are members of Congressional committees![2]

Neither Hoyt nor Commager named Joseph McCarthy and the House Committee on UnAmerican Activities, but serious readers could read between the lines.

As Hoyt analyzed conformity on national and international levels, she saw its impact on individual lives. Earlier she had developed the idea that a standard of living has three elements: the physiological, conventional, and personal. The personal requires individuality and courage, and a person of independent judgment tends to choose the individual and personal rather than the merely conventional.[3]

Oddly enough, some corporations were urging their own ideas of proper behavior onto executives' wives. William H. Whyte wrote two articles for *Fortune* and quoted an executive who said, "We control a man's environment in business and we lose it entirely when he crosses the threshold of his home . . . Management therefore, has a challenge and an obligation to deliberately plan and create a favorable, constructive attitude on the part of the wife that will liberate her husband's total energies for the job." The wife was cautioned not to drive a car better than her husband's superiors and not to be outstanding in personal ways. Intellectual pretensions should be avoided like the plague. When callers were expected, she should put *Harpers* and *Atlantic Monthly* under other magazines.[4]

Toward the end of the decade I became a member of the Logan Board of Education and was given a subscription to the *American School Board Journal*. Imagine my consternation when I read an article by a husband-wife team telling the wives of board members and the wives of superintendents how to behave. I promptly wrote a reply, called "Go Easy on Advice to Wives!" noting that the authors would not have told the *husband* of a board member how to behave.[5] Certainly Wynne would not put up with such nonsense.

Women and the Agricultural Experiment Station

In the 1950s I still faced the problem that, in Utah, women should conform to the ideal of staying at home and staying out of the labor force. And there was still the problem that the college did not want both husband and wife on its faculty.

A year after our return from Tennessee, Wynne became director of the Utah Agricultural Experiment Station and found some unanalyzed housing research done by home economists. Dean Ethelyn O. Greaves had died of cancer and the person who did the actual research had left the staff because of illness. Wynne conferred with the acting dean, Una Vermillion, and they asked me to analyze and write up the data, with help from Frances Taylor on the home economics staff. Frances and I became co-authors of two bulletins published in 1956, one on kitchen arrangements, and the other on use of kitchen shelf space by farm homes in the western region. Of course I could not be paid for my work, thanks to the anti-nepotism ruling, and for a time there was even debate over whether my name could appear on the bulletins, even though I was the principal writer. My name did appear.[6]

Women authors of Utah Agricultural Experiment Station bulletins were few and far between, although historically there was an auspicious beginning when Leah D. Widtsoe, wife of President John A. Widtsoe, spoke to the First International Congress of Farm Women, held in Colorado Springs in October 1911. Her paper, "Labor Saving Devices in the Farm Home," became Circular No. 6 of the Utah Agricultural Experiment Station and Extension Service. During the next eighteen years there were no women authors, until Almeda Perry Brown published four bulletins between 1929 and 1936 on the food habits of farm families and of school children in relation to physical wellbeing.[7] When Brown neared retirement in 1945, she was made a full professor and acting dean of home economics.

The woman to make the greatest mark on Experiment Station research in the 1940s and 1950s was Carmen Fredrickson of the sociology faculty, who taught and did research. She assisted Joseph A. Geddes, head of the department, with rural community studies. The anti-nepotism ruling did not apply to Fredrickson because her husband was not on the faculty. The fact that she had no children also fortified her position. Fredrickson was a remarkable person, active in community affairs, and especially in AAUW in which she held state and national offices. In 1950–51 she created a course called "Women Today," which she taught until her retirement. Both men and women took the course, which had this catalogue description: "The progress of women in American society from colonial days to the present. Some attention given to women's struggle for status in industry, politics, education, sex, religion, and the arts. Roles and contributions of outstanding women reviewed."

The content of Frederickson's course was remarkably similar to the content of the first women's studies course introduced into the USU curriculum in 1972. Without anyone realizing it, Fredrickson had begun women's studies at USU twenty years early. I knew at the time that some of her materials came from AAUW and from the Status of Women Committee of the American Council on Education.

In 1954 Geddes and Fredrickson published a bulletin on libraries as social institutions. Utah was the only state without a state library system, and many rural children had never seen a bookmobile. That same year the Sociology Department published research on the impact of urbanization on Davis county, including a section on the role of women, written by Frederickson. She next undertook a study of the impact of women leaders of Davis county on a changing order, published as an Agricultural Station bulletin in 1959. I regard this as a feminist document, making visible the experiences of the hundred women she interviewed. Because so few women were on commissions, boards, and in school principalships, Frederickson observed that women were not yet in full partnership with men. She was dismayed that no woman was on the Davis County School Board, no woman was a secondary school principal, and only one principal in the twenty-one elementary schools was a woman. Yet nationally at that time, in urban areas, about half of all elementary school principals were women.

Fredrickson recognized the increasing employment of women and wrote that more mothers in the labor force raised important public policy problems involving maternity leave, job security, and the use of public funds for child care—all vital questions today. By 1960 Fredrickson was researching the effects of the employment of mothers on the problems and problem-solving of families of northern Utah. She concluded that delinquency does not result from mothers being in the labor force. "The roots of delinquency are complicated and too numerous to be associated with a single cause."[8]

My Efforts to Help Others

My summers were filled with 4-H work, as leader of a club for Barrie and friends, and later for Sandra and Avril. I wrote an article for the *National 4-H News* about the high domestic standards upon which 4-H insisted and observed that sometimes conformity to standards of perfection does not make good sense. I wrote that during the summer of 4-H activity when Barrie set the table, we had a tablecloth, flowers in the center of the table, and plate, knife, fork, and spoon all in proper position. When school began in the fall, I fell into the old habit of bare table, no flowers, and tossed the silverware pell-mell onto the table. Our table was a wooden one. Formica would come later. In subsequent issues of the *National 4-H News* readers responded, referring to my article as "Silverware Pell-Mell." An interesting debate ensued, which I lost, according to the number of letters opposing my position.[9]

After writing up the housing research, I was at loose ends. Our college became Utah State University in 1957, and I was still ineligible for a faculty position. My mother's cousin, Pauline Udall Smith of Mesa, Arizona, asked me to help her write a book about our common ancestor, Captain Jefferson Hunt of the Mormon Battalion. When the Mormons left Nauvoo in early 1846 and started west, the Mexican War had begun. By the time they reached the Missouri River, President Polk had a proposition ready for Brigham Young—that five hundred Mormon volunteers should march against Santa Fe and across southern California with General Kearny's Army of the West. Although Young disliked losing this many able-bodied men, he realized it meant free food and transportation, and their pay would be sent back to the main body of Saints who desperately needed cash to buy supplies.

Jefferson Hunt was elected captain of Company A, consisting of a fifth of the men. The Battalion began its march in July 1846, went to Fort Leavenworth, and then on to Santa Fe. The Mormons never caught up with Kearny, did not actually fight any battles, suffered from illness and lack of water crossing the desert, laid out the first wagon road along the southern route, and finally arrived in San Diego in late January 1847.

Hunt led a colorful life. The next year he guided a party of fortyniners across the desert to southern California. Against his advice, some of them left the party to strike out on their own, looking for Walker Pass and giving Death Valley its name. Hunt served in the legislatures of California and Utah, founded Huntsville, and in his later years ranched and freighted in southern Idaho. A good family man, he had two plural wives and numerous progeny. He died in 1879.

Pauline composed the book out of family stories and other people's journals. Jefferson Hunt, himself, never kept a journal; when asked why not, he had replied, "Hell, I'm so busy making history, I don't have time to write it!" Although he did not write his history, his greatgranddaughter Pauline did, with firm hand and pen and ink on long sheets of lined yellow paper, which she mailed to me from Mesa. I typed, edited, sometimes rewrote, and mailed back. Two thousand copies of the completed book were published and immediately sold, mostly to descendants.[10] Pauline's son-in-law, historian George Ellsworth of the USU faculty, said to me, "You know, Alison, this is not really history." I replied, "I know it. A lot of it is family stories, but it's important to get them into print." He agreed.

While I was wrestling with Pauline's manuscript, Kip was a high school student. When he was seventeen years old, he entered the Science Talent Search. I wrote about his project:

> The Science Talent search was on. Our high school senior chose four-dimensional geometry as a project. He cut coat hangers into short strips and hung the corners together with modeling clay. The device which he created was large, angular, and occupied all the top of his desk. This meant his books moved to the floor. Scraps of paper with penciled mathematics lay scattered everywhere in the room. His clothes hung on the floor; his bed was perpetually unmade. Any real tidying-up was impossible for work was in progress, let the chips fall where they may. Just as he completed his paper two days before the deadline, he rushed downstairs, gave it to me and said, 'Type this for me, will you Mom?' and hur-ried out the door to join his friends on an overnight hike. Well, I typed it. He can type—all our children can type—but I make the fewest mistakes. There were seven pages. I understood the first two; his father understood the first four; I still wonder if the judges understood all seven. Anyway it won a placing.[11]

On the strength of this honor and doing well on the National Merit Scholarship exam, Kip received scholarships that would provide much of the funding of his undergraduate years at the California Institute of Technology, which he entered in the fall of 1958. He lived at home that summer and worked at Thiokol, where solid propellant rocket engines were being developed out in the desert beyond Brigham City. On June 24 I wrote to Wynne, who was out of the country, ". . . I don't understand much about his job, and he hesitates to write much, but yesterday when he was calculating the speed or something of the two different fuels, with different speeds, he discovered that they should be reversed in position, so he told the boss; a big test is coming up on Saturday, and the boss said 'Are you sure?' And he said, 'I'm quite sure.' So they switched the positions. Fifteen hundred employed at Thiokol now . . ."[12]

That first fall when Kip left for Caltech, I sent along thirteen cotton shirts, mostly short sleeved, many of them left over from his final year at Logan High. In my years at Iowa State I had watched men students mail their laundry home in cardboard suitcases for their mothers to do up and mail back. Did Kip mail home his laundry? No indeed. Did he wash his own shirts? No indeed. He discovered that the wrinkles hung out in the Pasadena climate, so he wore them over and over again, assuming that no wrinkles meant no dirt, a naive view for a budding physicist. The thirteen shirts accompanied him to Logan for Christmas and I washed them up in short order, giving stern instructions to get them washed regularly in Pasadena, instructions which I'm sure he disregarded.

Wynne's Trip to Iraq and the USSR

In the spring of 1958 Wynne had a phone call from the United States Department of Agriculture (USDA), asking if he would be interested in going to the Soviet Union as part of a team to look at soil and water. This would be one of the earliest United States' scientific teams allowed into the country, a country which we regarded as full of government enforced conformity. Wynne already had an invitation from the Iraqi government to look at their country's soil and water. As things worked out, he went to Iraq first, with the understanding that the USDA would inform where and when he would meet their team to enter Russia. Luckily for him, Burnell and Leora West were living in Baghdad and invited him to stay with them. Burnell was working for the United Nations as head of the Food and Agriculture Organization (FAO) mission in Iraq. Wynne had known the Wests at the AC when they were students together in the early 1930s.

Mail between the United States and Iraq was erratic, but enough of Wynne's letters came through so that we learned of heat, dust, poverty, isolation of women, and most of all, his evaluation of bureaucracy. He also described the historical and legendary places he saw. He visited the northern and southern parts of the country and went to Kuwait. Eager to learn the history of irrigation, he flew by helicopter over the faint edges of the ancient Nahrwan canal, 420 feet wide. The helicopter had a plexiglass front and no doors, because being closed in would have made it too hot. It was like flying through the air on a jiggling chair fifty to five hundred feet above the ground.[13]

In mid-June, the USDA notified me that the Russian trip was delayed a week. I sent word to Wynne by airmail, and the USDA sent a telegram from Beltsville to the United States embassy in Baghdad. Leora West happened to hear an embassy secretary say there was a telegram for Dr. Thorne about the trip to Russia, whereupon Wynne went to the embassy to inquire. He was told the telegram was classified and he couldn't have it. After much arguing he was allowed to look at it, but not take possession. The telegram said the team would leave Brussels for Moscow at noon on July 17. The team had his tickets and special passport.

In the remaining days of June, Wynne worked on the final report for the Iraqi government which included plans for a general soil fertility investigation. He wrote that the King's palace, whose magnificence he described, would be finished in November. On June 27 Wynne wrote that a new hotel had just opened, with bell hops in Arabian Nights costumes. Sixty people from Switzerland would run it for the first year. Wynne took the Wests and the J. B. Smiths to a farewell dinner there, just before he left Baghdad. Little did he, the Wests and Smiths, or the United States and British embassies realize that in a matter of days a revolution would topple the king's government, and two Americans staying at that very hotel would disappear. Together with Wynne's letters, I have a two-page appraisal of the revolution, written by Leora West, telling of the new government's plans for land reform and hoping they would materialize. Competent professional people continued on in their positions. And indeed, as we learned a few months later, the new government honored earlier commitments, including Wynne's pay for consulting.

Wynne met the soil-water team at the Brussels airport. They were C. E. Kellog, L. B. Nelson, Hub Allaway, Marline Cline of Cornell, Bill Donovan, and Joe Bulek (Foreign Agricultural Service, former agricultural attache in Moscow). Bulek was the only one who spoke Russian. They flew on a Russian jet to Moscow. Wynne had never been on a jet before. The luggage and freight were not tied down and slid violently up and down the aisle.

Wynne had a fascinating six weeks in the USSR. The Russian people were agog at seeing Americans, especially in the rural areas. Hospitality was warm, the food generous. Wynne sent airmail letters which I typed, sending a copy to close relatives and placing a copy at his office for everyone there to read. Interest was great. As I wrote Wynne, "Some think you are crazy to go to Russia and will never get out, and can't see why I am so calm about it."[14]

After his return, Wynne loaned the typed letters to a Federal Bureau of Investigations agent who came from Salt Lake City to ask for them, saying it was one of the ways the United States government could find out what was going on in Russia. Wynne told me there was no reason to withhold this information, and that the agent was an earnest young man who wanted to do well in his FBI career.

The Russians Come to Dinner

Wynne had not been home long when we got word that a Russian team of irrigation engineers would be traveling across the United States, with Logan as their westernmost stop. Wynne at once said we must have them to our house to dinner so they could see an American home. While in Russia, the United States team had not been inside a scientist's home. Although one scientist did invite them, he retracted the invitation and took them to a restaurant instead. Wynne wondered whether it was for fear of government retaliation, or because the Russian scientist felt that his home was far below American standards and wanted to prevent mutual embarrassment.

In the process of planning dinner for the Russians, I went downtown to Wilkinson's to buy a new pickle dish. When I said to the clerk, "I need this dish because a team of Russian scientists is coming to dinner," a complete silence fell across the store, and the other clerks and customers turned to stare at me. Americans were still paranoid about communists, because Senator Joseph McCarthy and his ilk had done their work well. When Wynne met the Russian scientific team at the Salt Lake City airport, and the Ukranian member dashed across the field to throw his arms around him, the first familiar face he had seen across the continent, one of the bystanders muttered "Communist!" at Wynne.

Later the Russian team said the most friendly place they visited was Logan. There had been hostility at all their other stops. They were not allowed to go on to California to see Disneyland, but by the time they reached Logan they were tired and glad to stop their journey westward. Originally there was a plan to take them to see Glen Canyon dam, still under construction, but knowing the anti-communist sentiment of construction workers, it was feared someone might take a pot shot at them, so that part of their tour was cancelled.

These men were no longer young. They had survived two world wars, with periods of near starvation. There were five of them: Aleksanor N. Askochensky, Sukhan Babaev, Ivan I. Budarin, Stephen M. Perekhrest, and Nuritdin Aliev. The United States government had sent along two interpreters, one a refugee from Russia. I noticed that when they sat in the back seat of our car, the refugee, on the outside edge, would turn rather sideways so his shoulder did not touch the Russian

The Russians came to dinner at our house, and they had lunch President Daryl Chase's. They are shown here with the president, Alice, and son Peter. Photo from *The Story of a House: The President's Home* by Alice Chase.

next to him. I am convinced he was a bona fide refugee. The other interpreter, we were told, was a retired United States Army officer.

When they arrived at our house for dinner, I had the table set. Other guests were Dean F. Peterson, dean of engineering at USU, and his wife Bess. Also present were Barrie and our three younger children. It was a summer weekend and Kip had driven to Yellowstone to visit his girl friend, which was just as well. We would not speak of Thiokol, Hill Field, or other installations. When they traveled in Russia, the United States team wore blindfolds as their car neared military installations.

Wynne came dashing into the kitchen with a bottle of vodka that our Russian guests had brought, and he thrust it into the freezer compartment of the refrigerator to chill. "The bottle will break!" I protested. "No it won't. It's 50 percent alcohol." And he dashed out to escort our guests around our vegetable garden (not in very good shape because Wynne had been out of the country most of the summer, and I am no gardener.) They saw our garage and asked if Wynne drove his own car. And they saw the new kittens.

Well, I had already poured fruit juice into our company glasses. When Wynne asked me where the little glasses were to put the vodka into, I said, "Oh, the kids broke those years ago." So we put the vodka, for adults only, into ordinary drinking glasses. Long toasts by the Russians and by Wynne had to ride on the inch or so of vodka in each glass. Now I knew that with this first toast it was absolutely necessary to drink the liquor down in one fell swoop. What I did not know was how strong vodka is. One sip and I was scalded all the way down my gullet. Etiquette or no etiquette, I hastily set down my glass.

The sharp-eyed young children, watching the guests, told me later that the retired United States Army officer did not drink his vodka. He poured it into his fruit juice and then never drank the juice during the meal. I noticed he didn't drink the juice, and assumed he was allergic to it. Not until two months later did we learn that he was with the Central Intelligence Agency, and being on duty, did not drink. When he found out, Wynne was outraged, feeling our own government had violated our integrity as citizens.

We did have a pleasant time visiting. The Russians were delighted with the two ceramic Russian dolls on the table, which Wynne had brought home with him. Three inches high, their wide dresses would swing from side to side when pushed with a finger. You could almost sense homesickness as the Russian visitors touched the dolls. They gave the youngsters small pins; one said "The 10,000th student of Turkmanian University." The man from Uzbekistan gave us square, embroidered caps. In return, the youngsters gave them sea shells from their collection.

In the living room afterwards, I showed the retired army officer a book of Russian rhymes for children that Wynne had brought home, and asked him to translate one of them. He did it half-heartedly because he was very busy listening to everything that was going on in the room. At one point the Ukranian began to speak German with Wynne, off in a corner, but the army officer stopped them, saying, "We speak only Russian or English." He himself, obviously, did not speak German.

The next day, USU President Daryl Chase and his wife Alice had the Russians to their home,[15] and in the evening some of the faculty held a picnic up the canyon for them. We all sat around a bonfire in the dark night, and four of the Russians sang songs. They had beautiful voices. The songs were all about rivers and were tragic. The Russians teased Wynne about his inability to sing, which he took in good humor, pleased they were friends enough so they dared tease him.

On their last day the head of the group, Askochensky, quietly shared pictures of his family with Wynne and me, an unusual thing for a Russian to do. And he presented a book to Wynne to give to Kip, saying, "I also have a son studying physics, and I hope some day they will meet under peaceful circumstances."

Inquiry into Creativity

Throughout the 1950s and 1960s, I continued to give talks to PTAs and women's groups, under the title of "Leave the Dishes in the Sink." Instead of dwelling on the shortcomings of perfect housekeeping, I shifted to the idea of creativity, as portrayed by Frank Barron in the September 1958 issue of the *Scientific American*. Barron and colleagues at the Institute for Personality Assessment and Research at the University of California, Berkeley, studied the characteristics of highly creative painters, writers, physicians, economists, and other professionals and found that highly creative people can stand more ambiguity and chaos than other people, because they find such chaos challenging and believe they can put their own kind of order onto it when they are ready.[16]

At our house we dwelt so often amidst physical chaos that I decided one reason we could stand the mess was being so engrossed in particular projects, let the chips fall where they may, that we were unaware of the chaos around us. Could it be, I wondered, that too perfect a house prevents the flowering of creativity? Not that Barron suggested this, but I would.

I spoke of the array of materials (I called it "stuff") with which children do creative things. I told about explaining carbon paper to our three young ones when we lived in Tennessee. I put the carbon on top of a piece of white paper and marked it with a pencil. We lifted the carbon and saw the mark. Then it occurred to us that one doesn't need a pencil, so I pressed with my thumbnail. When we lifted the carbon, there was a crescent mark. Sandra, five years old, ran from the room and came back with her hairbrush. She made several swirls on top of the carbon, and when we lifted it up, we found dozens of beautiful curved lines.

I called this an act of creativity because it was an unexpected combination of things. Carbon paper and a hairbrush usually do not end up together. Her idea was original; it was a surprise. The result was beautiful, and this made it worthwhile. But beauty is not the only kind of source of worth; there is also the delight of a child. It is wise to praise a child who creates something, but the real worth remains the child's own sense of pleasure.

Speaking to a roomful of mothers in Ogden, I asked for examples of something creative they had seen a child do. One told of an episode that happened in the home next door. The mother had given her little girl a pretty pink nylon umbrella. One day when she came home she found her daughter under the dining room table making doll dresses out of the pink material. "If it had been my child," said the woman telling the story, "I would have spanked her for cutting up the umbrella. But my neighbor was wiser. She realized her daughter wanted to make doll clothes, and there were no pretty scraps in the house. So she went out and bought remnants and turned the child loose with them."

It was pleasant to experience the frequent humor that emerged in my audiences. At the Ladies' Literary Club of Hyde Park when we discussed how to get children to work, one mother made the sage observation, "When trying to get work out of your girls, if you have one girl, you have one girl. If you have two girls, you have half a girl. If you have three girls, you have no girl at all."[17]

In 1959 a group of parents asked Wynne and me to join them in exploring matters related to giftedness. An informal group at first, it subsequently incorporated as the Northern Utah Association for the Gifted. Ray Nelson of the Logan *Herald-Journal* wrote of our members: "They have no objection to the status given athletic superiority, which everyone does enjoy having and watching, and the status given the superior money maker, another superiority we all appreciate. But they deplore the tendency to call efforts to cultivate superiority of talent or intellect, snobbish . . . They are not, they maintain, malcontents out to reorganize a whole system." Among the activities begun for children and youth were a summer creative dance program, and a class in German that went through the year, sponsored by Sigma Xi and the College of Education.[18]

Through this group I became acquainted with *The Gifted Child Quarterly*, which published an article of mine, later reprinted in a book edited by John Curtis Gowen, et al, *Creativity: Its Educational Implications*. Mine was the only article written by a housewife; it was awkward being a writer without professional affiliation. Here are some excerpts:

> Neither *Perfect Housekeeping* nor *House Beautiful* dominates our home. We live in a university town in a high, square, old-fashioned house. The upstairs bathroom contains an immense closet with wide shelves for quilts and blankets, but we don't keep our extra bedding there. Instead we keep stacks of *National Geographic*, all the art work and notebooks which our five children have lugged home from school and wanted saved, lots of maps, and a stack of very large envelopes containing pictures and clippings about American history, English history, Renaissance art, religion, plants, animals, etc. . . .

By way of further inventory let us consider the kitchen cupboards. The glassed-in shelves intended for lovely china and glassware are filled instead with games, puzzles, stamp collections, two decorated cans which contain embroidery floss and half-completed dishtowels, two sets of knitting in progress—I think they are to be bedroom slippers. My silverware box does not contain silverware; it has been subdivided for a sea shell collection which has overflowed into Christmas card boxes. There are tennis and badminton rackets and three cameras.

Scattered in various other places are scratch paper, type paper, pencils, crayons, scissors, water colors in small jars, three kinds of glue, chalk, compass, rulers, three kinds of tape, balls of string, and ink. At this very moment two children are at the kitchen table writing with a pheasant feather and ink, just to see how it might have felt to be a scribe in colonial days.

As for books, we have them on stars, birds, trees, flowers, shells, history, and the usual childhood classics. Our history books include one of our local valley, telling of ancient Lake Bonneville, which once covered the entire valley floor and reached into the canyons of our mountains. The two older children brought home their geology texts from Cal Tech and Stanford, and the local geology professor gave us an excellent source book written for elementary and secondary schools. Our nearby canyons are Paleozoic, and we find such books valuable.

We also own, as a traveling companion, the WPA guidebook for our state. We studied about the fallen ghost town of Silver Reef as we walked over its rocks and picked up rusty square nails and bits of bottles turned violet by the desert sun. Nails and glass now lie in the drawer of my dressing table after several excursions to school to be "shared."

We take the *Scientific American*. Its advertising has magnificent pictures of rockets, satellites and other matters dear to the heart of the young devotee of space. Its articles need translation for the small fry but often the puzzle pages are entrancing. We did the Chinese tangrams and wrestled with the Japanese art of paper folding.[19]

One consequence of my article was that Ann Isaacs, editor of *The Gifted Child Quarterly*, invited me to write the "Parents' Page," which I did, without pay, from autumn 1964 to summer 1968. These were brief articles with examples of encouraging learning and creativity in children, and questioning some attitudes of our society.

Over the years I accumulated a lot of information about creativity. I particularly liked Carl Rogers's observation that the potentially creative person has three qualities, which I illustrated with my own examples:[20]

First is openness to experience, meaning one can see in the usual categories, but also sees much more. At the New York World's Fair I was standing in the Indian Pavilion, looking at a jeweled rug lying on the floor of the exhibit case, so exquisite a rug that it took my breath away. Flower stems were of small entwined pearls. Flower centers were amethyst, topaz, and beryl. A little girl stood beside me as entranced as I was. Turning to her mother she said in wonder, "Will it fly?" Her eyes reflected the enchantment of stories of flying carpets. She saw more than what was in the showcase. "Don't be silly!" said her mother sharply, and hauled her off to the next exhibit.[21]

Second is the ability to toy with elements and concepts, to play spontaneously with ideas, colors, shapes, relationships. This is the ability to connect things that most people would not consider connect-able, such as Sandra's combining a hair brush with carbon paper. I also remembered when Avril found dry bean pods in the garden, shelled out the multi-colored beans, and strung them to make a necklace.

Third is an internal locus of evaluation. The value of what is created is decided by the person, not by praise or criticism of others. This is independence. Frank Barron's article, using Solomon Asch's research and published in the 1958 *Scientific American,* concluded that highly creative people, besides being able to stand chaos, were also independent. I also made good use of Asch in my talks, holding up a sheet of paper showing lines of unequal length, as he had done in a now-famous experiment with a class, in which some members were told ahead of time to lie about the unequal lines and say they were the same length. Three-fourths of the "innocent victims" said the lines were equal in length, and only one-fourth said they were different, preferring to believe their own senses rather than conforming to the answer given by the majority.[22]

In the 1950s psychologists and the schools emphasized social adjustment, which to me was another word for conformity. It did not give scope to the human desire to be alone for periods of time, or to the capacity to stand up against society when one feels society is wrong. At one point I went dashing up to the campus to ask the department of child development and parent education how I could rear my children to be independent, to stand on their own two feet, and to defend their ideas of what is right. I was told there was nothing they could give me on such things, but they did have a lot of good information on social adjustment. This I declined.

Then I discovered that Jacob Getzels and Philip Jackson had dealt with this problem. These two researchers at the training school of the University of Chicago tested students from sixth grade through high school on intelligence, creativity, social adjustment, and moral character. There were plenty of tests for intelligence and social adjustment, but they had to invent tests for creativity and for moral character. Getzels and Jackson wrote that current educational literature gave greater welcome to the adjusted student than to the one with character, and this should be a matter of serious concern. "The question here, as with the highly creative and the highly intelligent students, is not which is better but how can we provide for both." I especially appreciated their description of a home that produced a highly creative adolescent:

> The father is a well-known biologist. The mother edited a small newspaper until the birth of her first child . . . The most striking characteristic of the apartment is the litter of books and magazines. Books by the hundreds are seen in the living room and in the hall, and they are veritably jammed into several of the other rooms.
>
> Mrs. Black is a large handsome woman quite at ease with herself and the world, even in a house-dress split at the seams.[23]

Wynne also wrote about creativity; I have carbon copies of three of his papers. In "Education for Research" he wrote, "In order for the gifted child to get enough course load in our average high school to challenge his abilities, he must have the courage of a gladiator and the hide of a rhinoceros plus the vigorous support of an irate parent."

Wynne's three papers dealt primarily with scientific research, and his favorite quotation was from Pareto: "Give me a good fruitful error any time, full of seeds, bursting with its own convictions. You can keep your sterile truth for yourself." Quoting from Whyte's *Organization Man,* Wynne went on to say, "The emphasis placed in our schools and industrial research laboratories on the social adjustment of the individual and on cooperative projects tend to crowd out the lonely genius of the past. After all, thinking is a lonely art and we must not eliminate the brilliant mind from research in our present stress on collective activity."[24]

We both liked to use famous examples of creative inspiration brought together by Brewster Ghiselin in his book *The Creative Process.* There was Kekule who saw the benzene molecule as a ring because he dreamed of a snake that swallowed its tail. Poincare was just stepping into an omnibus when he realized the nature of Fuschian functions. Coleridge wrote Kubla Khan from a dream. Mozart could hear the parts of a new composition not successively, but all at once.[25]

Ghiselin was a poet on the faculty of the University of Utah. We met him when he came to Logan to speak to Thoughtless Thinkers. I saw him again when he spoke at Calvin Taylor's "Workshop on Creativity" at the University of Utah in June 1963. Ghiselin never felt that research on creativity would hamper his poetry writing. Indeed, he was helping Taylor and his researchers set up tests to try to identify possible scientific talent in young people. A wide spectrum of people spoke at Taylor's workshop, including Virginia Tanner who created the early courses on children's dance at the University of Utah. Frank Barron came from California and told about his institute's research on personality. I told him how much I had used his September 1958 article in the *Scientific American*. For three days I attended the workshop, sleeping in a dorm at night. I was the only individual there in capacity of wife and mother. Everyone else had a salaried profession: teaching, business, art, and engineering.

Avril had her fourteenth birthday while I was at the workshop, and I wished her happy birthday over the phone. Truth is stranger than fiction, because years later Avril took her Ph.D. at Berkeley, doing her research on personality, at the Institute for Personality Assessment and Research. Still later, she joined the psychology faculty at the University of California, Santa Cruz, replacing Barron after he retired.

With ideas I got at the workshop and from my wide range of reading, and at invitation of Norma Compton of our faculty, I wrote a paper, "Homemaking and the Idea of Creativity," and presented it at a conference of college teachers of clothing, textiles, and related arts.[26] I quoted the anthropologist Dorothy Lee, who, in an analysis of home economics manuals, found more emphasis on getting along with others than on the inner experience.[27] I went back to Carl Rogers's idea of an internal locus of evaluation, and I gave Roy Heath's description of Reasonable Adventurers (1964) as people who are curious and critical, capable of close friendships and independent value judgments, and tolerant of ambiguity because of their stable self image. They evince a breath of interest even in the commonplace, and they have a sense of humor.[28]

I assumed that women as well as men could be Reasonable Adventurers, although the fact that Heath's study was of Princeton students, all male, made me uneasy. Years later it dawned on me that the Reasonable Adventurer did no volunteer community work, and caregiving certainly was not part of his description. However, the Reasonable

Adventurer never captured public attention anyway. Flower children and hippies did. On Mother's Day I received a homemade card of heavy purple construction paper with this hand-written verse:[29]

> Our Mom ain't got no bells or beads
> A 'jangling on her neck and knees
> And doesn't go to yoga class
> And don't dance nude upon the grass.
> We dig her.
> She's a nonconformist!
> Hippy Momma's Day!
>
> Love, Sandra, Avril, Lance

6 Social Justice: The 1960s

Liberal Tendencies

Over the years my liberal tendencies moved against the conservatism of Cache Valley, Utah, a conservatism far older than I.

Historian Charles S. Peterson, researching Cache Valley between 1890 and 1915, found it to be homogeneous with two-thirds of its population by birth being British, Scandinavian, or Swiss. They were little given to change because of the Mormon tradition and a strong sense of the family farm. Farm families were large and did the work so that itinerant workers and labor organizations were almost totally excluded. Even though hard times hit and mortgage debt grew, Cache Valley's people sought to conform to the system rather than reform it, as did Great Plains farmers and Oregon's Progressives.[1]

Wynne grew up in a small Utah farm town twenty-five miles south of Logan, in a family of Democrats more liberal than their neighbors. Together, Wynne and I expanded our horizons by reading *Harpers, The Saturday Review*, and the Sunday *New York Times*, the latter being a heavy burden on the mail carrier. We were Democrats, but as a university administrator Wynne had to be more circumspect than I, so I worked in the party for both of us. In the early 1960s one of the programs we favored was subsidized medical care for the elderly.

It happened one November that a talk was to be given on our campus by Dr. George Fister of Ogden, who was then president of the American Medical Association. He refused to divulge his subject ahead of time, but we speculated that he would speak either about quackery, or else about socialized medicine, which the AMA opposed. He would address Town and Gown, an informal gathering open to everyone, preceded by dinner. Town and Gown was invented by USU President Daryl Chase in an effort to ease tensions between townspeople and faculty. I suspected Fister's talk would not ease the tension between me and the medical profession.

Wynne and I went to the dinner, bringing with us several visitors from the United States Department of Agriculture who had come from Washington, D.C. for the dedication of the new Crops and Entomology

Labs. I said to our guests, ahead of time, that if it turned out that Dr. Fister was speaking against socialized medicine, I would not stay to listen. The large campus dining room was packed. I swear every medical doctor in Cache Valley was there, and I wondered who was minding the store. It was certainly no evening for medical emergencies.

After we ate, Fister rose to speak, and I realized in his first few sentences that he was there to argue against socialized medicine. I rose and departed. But Wynne and guests remained, trapped by people who had shoved their chairs about to get a better view. Afterwards the guests told me the speaker had made them more firmly convinced than ever that elderly people should have socialized medicine tied to Social Security.[2] Four years later, on July 30, 1965, President Lyndon Johnson went to Independence, Missouri to sign the new Medicare bill in the presence of former President Harry S. Truman, who had proposed such a program twenty year earlier.

At another Town and Gown meeting that same month I did stay to hear the speaker. I wrote about it in my family letter and also told about Kip at Caltech. We heard Judd Harmon, a young political scientist, wade into John Birch societies and their ilk. He didn't pull any punches and called arch-conservatives Cleon Skouson and Ernest Wilkinson by name.[3] I was astonished when the wife of a Board of Trustees' member said, "Wasn't Judd Harmon disgusting? I kept hoping he was drunk and not responsible for those horrible things that he said."

A similar thing happened when Esther Peterson came to campus to speak on employment for women. She was the Utah native newly appointed assistant secretary of labor and head of the Women's Bureau. The wife of a university official said to me, "Esther Peterson is a terrible woman. She thinks all women should leave their homes and go to work. I hear she's an atheist, too."

That was quite a family letter. I also wrote the following:

Kip is tackling the Supreme Court. He is protesting the loyalty oath required for applicants for the National Science Foundation fellowships. Wrote an editorial for the Caltech paper. Organized "CODA," which coordinates similar efforts by graduate students on other campuses. He will attach a disclaimer to his own applications and ask others to do so also. Then Linus Pauling's lawyer will take Kip's case to the Supreme Court. This lawyer has argued a good many cases before the Court. Kip will become a controversial figure if the case is accepted by the Court. Wynne thinks it is ok to try, but Kip's father-in-law is not so sure and thinks he may end up a martyr for nothing. Kip's scientific abilities ought to enable him to get a fellowship whether he is involved in this sort of business or not.

As matters turned out, the case did not go to the Supreme Court, and though denied at first, Kip did receive fellowships.

Conservatism always showed up at the annual November dinner of the State Farm Bureau, held in Salt Lake City. Because Wynne was director of the Utah Agricultural Experiment Station, he and I attended. I remarked in a family letter that the national president of the Farm Bureau, who spoke at the annual dinner, ranted against socialism in his talk. I also said that Wynne had attended national meetings in Washington and was elected chairman of all directors of agricultural experiment stations.[4] Other letters indicate that the Farm Bureau and the Cache County Commission were against mosquito abatement, and against more funding for the public library. I had discovered that more money was appropriated for weed control than for the library, and I said so in public, whereupon the county government ceased indicating on our tax notices how much went to what programs.

Proposals to fluoridate Logan's water supply always met hostility, even though Preston, Idaho, twenty-five miles north of us, had been fluoridating its water supply for ten years. In February 1964, Sandra and her teeth appeared on educational television as an example of what lack of fluoridation could do, as compared to the teeth of a Preston girl of the same age. Both girls and their dental charts were shown, with Sandra having two-and-one-half times as many fillings as the Preston girl. Four dentists on the program pointed out that Utah ranked fiftieth among the states with regard to correct amount of fluoridation in drinking water.[5]

As for the broader world, it touched our community when Peace Corps recruits began coming to USU for training. While people vaguely hoped the Peace Corps would increase chances of world peace, local authorities were busy stocking basements of various public buildings as bomb shelters. Wynne and I cleaned up our coal room, the furnace having been converted to natural gas, and put in shelves and some supplies, figuring that in an emergency we could drink water from our hot water tank and hot water radiators. We would strengthen our bomb shelter ceiling by stacking books on the living room floor directly above us. We thought we knew what we were doing, and then the Paulings entered our lives.

In the fall of 1961 Wynne learned that Edward Teller, inventor of the hydrogen bomb, was scheduled to speak on campus the next February. He insisted that Linus Pauling be invited to speak so the public could hear both sides. As events turned out, Pauling spoke early in February and Teller later that month.

Pauling and his wife arrived in Utah in a heavy fog. We didn't know where they had landed. Certainly not at the Salt Lake airport, which had no planes land all week and none that day. As matters turned out the Paulings landed in Ogden, and Wynne drove down to pick them up.

We had invited guests to Sunday night supper, and lots of people for an open house afterwards. It was a very lively evening. We found the Paulings delightful, friendly, full of ideas, and both with twinkling, large blue eyes, his more gray than hers which were almost lavender. He remembered my father from the Oregon State campus; he himself went to the campus in 1917. His wife Ava was also born in the Willamette Valley. I learned that she used to work as a judge at elections because she was very good at figures and because she was one of those rare persons, a Democrat, in that district. But when a loyalty oath was demanded she resigned.[6]

The next morning I took Mrs. Pauling and my friends Corda Bauer and Dorothy Lewis up Blacksmith Fork canyon to get above the fog and to see the elk herd at Hardware Ranch.[7] That evening, Old Main auditorium was packed with people waiting to hear Pauling. People said it was the largest audience ever, except for the time when Eleanor Roosevelt spoke. Pauling got off some good cracks against Edward Teller, and his humor, irony, and lilting voice charmed the audience. The next day there was a seminar, Pauling did a television program on tape, and in the afternoon Wynne and I drove the Paulings to Salt Lake.

On our way, with our guests in the back seat, Pauling told his wife that while he did a Public Pulse program in the evening, she was to send a telegram to the *Saturday Evening Post* in which he demanded the right to provide the *Post* with an article in response to one that Edward Teller had written, and he outlined some major points. She sighed and said, "Oh, Linus, you know how much I hate to send long telegrams!" But she did it.

When Teller came to town, Wynne was away. The auditorium was as packed as it had been for Pauling. Teller was as vigorous in attacking Pauling as Pauling had been in attacking him. Teller spoke with a thick accent but was an excellent speaker and held the audience spellbound. He was sure we needed the information from more atmospheric tests, and he encouraged shelters, saying they would save a good percent of the population. In contrast, Pauling had said we have plenty of information, more than Russia has. And shelters just made more possible the occurrence of a war, which very few would survive.

Over thirty years later, Harden McConnell, a chemist at Stanford University, reviewing three new books about Pauling, commented:

> It is hard for anyone who has not experienced such events to appreciate the truly oppressive political environment in the United States during the 1950s and '60s. I signed Pauling's 1957 petition against nuclear bomb testing with apprehension concerning possible adverse consquences to me. In my opinion Pauling had a major impact in the international decision to stop atmospheric nuclear bomb tests, to the benefit of everyone.[8]

Community Work

As the children grew older I had more time to give to community work. Kip left to become an undergraduate at Caltech in 1958, and four years later he went on to Princeton for graduate work in theoretical physics. Barrie left for Stanford in 1960, where she majored in anthropology. When the Pauling and Teller talks occurred, I was forty-seven years old; Wynne was fifty-three; Sandra, thirteen; Avril, twelve; and Lance, ten.

In Logan, a continuing local issue was the need for a sewage disposal system because raw sewage was flowing down into the west fields and out into Bear River. When there was a very cold early winter without snow, the children and I went ice skating on the sloughs west of town, and they said they could see feces under the shallow ice, but feces was not the word they used.

Women's groups had been trying very hard to get a sewer bond passed. We all knew each other and had worked together for good causes through the local Women's Legislative Council. Despite its name, this council was not composed of women in the legislature, of which there were, and still are, painfully few. Rather, the council represented many women's groups, and when the state legislature was in session a handful of local council members drove to the Capitol in Salt Lake City on Thursdays to attend a State Women's Legislative Council meeting and to observe the legislature. Sometimes there were pre-legislative meetings.

Mostly, however, our council met once a month in the Cache County courthouse to discuss current local issues, with its members reporting back to their own organizations. An amazingly large number of women's groups belonged to the council including civic, religious, school, political, professional, literary, and study clubs. We were unaware that this Council would be for us the final phase of the women's club movement that began in America in the nineteenth century and kept Progressive issues alive before and after the turn of the century.[9]

On December 3, 1962, while I was at a meeting on strategy to get the sewer bond passed, a dramatic power outage occurred in our neighborhood, leading me to write an article for the *Herald Journal* which appeared next day under the heading, "Some Things That Happened Last Evening":

We live across the street south from the First Ward Church, and at 5:40 by our kitchen clock, there was an explosion and the electricity went off.

My son on an errand to Tim's grocery had paused to watch insulation burning on the wires. Burning material had been falling into trees. And then came the explosion 'and it was light as day,' he said.

About this time the AC Women's Club had concluded their regular Monday meeting and had been discussing what they should do, as citizens, about the sewer bond. They voted unanimously to support it. (Later in the evening Eleanor Van Orden would phone to tell me this.)

Where was I in the meantime? Not at home to see the burning insulation and the explosion. I had been called to a five o'clock meeting in the Chamber of Commerce rooms to help plan the taxpayers' meeting to be held Wednesday night in the Logan Junior High.

I was asked if the Women's Legislative Council would co-sponsor the meeting. Of course the Council would, said I, because they had voted on a resolution supporting the sewer bond . . .

Last evening I put in a call to Allie Burgoyne, president of the Logan chapter of AAUW [American Association of University Women]. Would they also co-sponsor the meeting? She phoned her officers and in a short while phoned me back. 'Yes, we would be glad to.'

At 6:30 I started driving home and found traffic directed at corners by men with flashing red lights because the semaphores were out. It was impossible for me to cross First South to my home. 'Wires are down.'

Not knowing what to do, I stopped by a house lighted by a candle and used a telephone, but got only busy signals. I didn't know whether the children were in a panic at home; I didn't know whether they had enough sense to stay out of the street, for some of the trouble was obviously directly in front of our house.

I drove down Center to Main and then came along First South, where by special dispensation, crewmen let me through the barricade to drive slowly home on the left hand side of the street.

The children, thrilled with living by candlelight, had fed supper to themselves and two neighbor boys. 'Let's go to the library,' I said. 'It will be light and warm and you can do your homework. Besides, I want to talk to the BPW [Business and Professional Women] officers; this is BPW meeting night at the library.'

We walked out in the darkness, gingerly, hugging our side of the street while trucks and men, and huge beams of light probed the transformers on the pole across from us.

Would the BPW members be willing to co-sponsor Wednesday's public meeting, I asked. They voted strongly in favor of doing so. One member said, 'Whenever I travel outside the state and people ask me where I'm from and I say Logan, they say 'You mean that awful town that still has its raw sewage out in the open?'

The BPW accepted a list of chairmen of ward areas of Logan who will distribute leaflets about the sewer bond next weekend. Would they volunteer to help the ward chairmen distribute these? Many were agreeable.

Home again to a fast cooling house. To bed. Trucks and men worked far into the night. Silence. At three A.M. a solitary truck drove up and a beam of light probed the transformer directly across from my bedroom.

Before dawn, trucks, men and voices in the street. In the darkness I grope my way about. Somehow I must find fuel to make a fire in the fireplace.

The whole experience makes me pause. How dependent we are on other people in an emergency such as this: The men who guarded the streets to prevent my entanglement with wires last night. The men who are now trying to fix the transformers. The men checking the fuses in our homes. And the coming sewer campaign.

Earnest men are trying to find wise solutions which will protect the people . . .[10]

I should have added, "and earnest women." In today's parlance, the sewer bond effort was an example of women's on-the-ground networking and mobilization.

Besides a sewage disposal system, we badly needed a better way of dealing with garbage. There were nineteen city dumps with at least two burning all the time. We were urging the city commission to set up a sanitary landfill or buy an incinerator. The local Women's Legislative Council sponsored a public meeting in the old junior high, and there was hidden amusement when one commissioner kept calling the proposed incinerator an "inseminator." I was chairing the meeting and hadn't the nerve to correct him. The sewer bond was defeated. We did get a sanitary landfill, and a few years later voters approved sewage lagoons which have proved a delight to water birds and a satisfaction to airplane pilots who immediately know they are in Cache county.

The Logan Board of Education

In 1959, still unable to get a professional position at USU, I decided to get myself onto the school board. One of the five members of the Logan Board of Education had moved out of the city, so I wrote a note saying I'd like to fill that vacancy and gave my qualifications. The board put me on, and I later won public reelection twice.

The four men board members belonged to Rotary club, considered to be the most powerful service club in the valley. Two had ties to the university: Milton R. Merrill, a political scientist who became academic vice president, and Norman Salisbury, a banker who was also on the USU Board of Trustees. The school superintendent was Sherman G. Eyre, a very capable person, and board relations with him were good because the board knew the difference between his duties and the board's. Board members took turns being president. Because their USU duties kept them so busy, Milt Merrill and Norm Salisbury chose to skip their turns at being president of the Logan Board, which explains how I came to be president four separate years out of the eleven I served on the Logan Board, in great contrast to the Cache Board which would not permit their solitary woman member, Doris Budge, to serve as president. The Cache district included farms and towns across the county and tended to be conservative.

One duty of the board president was to hand out diplomas at graduation. It was my turn to do the diplomas in 1969, when Lance was scheduled to graduate from high school. He knew how I greeted each graduate with my right hand extended to shake hands, and my left hand held slightly back with the diploma, ready at the last moment to thrust it into the recipient's left hand. The day before graduation, Lance and a friend were sitting on the couch in our front room, and he said with a grin, "Mom, you know what we're going to do when we go across the stand at graduation? We're not going to shake your hand." "That's fine," I said with a smile. "I'll kiss each of you instead." At graduation I noticed that Lance and friend each had a right hand extended the moment they hit the stand.

The high point of my early years on the board was the bond election that made possible a new junior high building, to be built all at once. Until then, the district's slim capital budget meant building schools only in stages. The PTA, women's groups, and business community cooperated beautifully and on May 10, 1961, a large headline on the front page of the *Herald Journal* proclaimed "City School Bond Issue Approved by 2589 to 69." This was a 97.5 percent vote. Although I was head of the residential drive for votes, the real work was done by a USU faculty wife, Edith Pedersen, who later died, much too young, of breast cancer.

Three years later we held another bond election, this time for improvements at several schools. It passed with a 96 percent affirmative vote. However, the capital budget was separate from the operating budget, and we continued to find it difficult to get enough operating money for schools. Each school board had power to tax property, a power which we used gingerly to prevent taxpayer revolt. A state uniform school fund helped poorer school districts, for which Logan qualified. Various state monies went into this fund, and I gave a great many talks to PTAs and to service clubs explaining this.

I spoke to the local Women's Legislative Council on school finance. And once, while George Dewey Clyde was governor, I spoke to the State Women's Legislative Council on the proposed finance program for Utah public schools. That was in November 1962.

The governor, a conservative Republican, an engineer, and former dean of engineering at USU, gave an hour long talk before my turn came. When he sat down I could see the Logan delegation tense up for fear he would remain for my talk, which they knew contained economics diametrically opposed to his. Fortunately the governor departed for what he considered more important matters.

In his talk Governor Clyde mentioned that he had had breakfast with Governor George Romney of Michigan, but Clyde did not tell what Romney had done to help Michigan schools get more funds. I knew that Romney set up citizens' committees because my sister Elaine chaired one. I told of the Romney plan and hoped the audience realized that Michigan had a Republican governor who believed in more money for schools, while Utah had a Republican governor who was pitting higher education and the public schools against each other.[11]

Insufficient operating money continued to plague Utah schools. The teachers called a two-day strike in May 1964, only they didn't call it a strike, but a "staying out of school." The Utah Education Association (UEA) voted to stay out of school Monday and Tuesday because Governor Clyde refused the advice of his own committee on schools that a special session of the legislature be called to consider putting six million more dollars into the uniform school fund. At one point the governor became so angry he threatened to call out the National Guard to force teachers to stay in school.

On Saturday evening, before the Monday when the strike would begin, all the local superintendents came together in Salt Lake City to hear Ted Bell, state superintendent of schools. Little did anyone realize that years later Bell would become United States commissioner of education under President Reagan and would literally save the cabinet status of education.

The next morning, Sunday, at ten, the presidents of all school boards came together with the superintendents to hear Bell. The Utah School Boards Association voted thirty to six in favor of a resolution that every school district should make an honest effort to hold school Monday and Tuesday. I spoke briefly at that meeting before television lights and several microphones, and said that the real power to make a decision lay with local boards, and the real work would be done after we left the meeting and went home. A Salt Lake board member in a long speech accused the UEA of subversive leadership and implied they might even be communists. "So much hokum!" I wrote my family.

That Sunday evening we held a Logan Board of Education meeting in the Woodruff school, the one behind our home. After half an hour of deliberation we voted unanimously to offer a compromise to our teachers: that they stay on the job as usual on Monday, but we would declare school closed on Tuesday, and they could all go down to the UEA meeting in Salt Lake if this was their desire. Since 180 days of school, by law, must be conducted in order to get our state money for operation, we declared Saturday of this week a school day, to replace Tuesday.

The Logan Education Association representatives came in at seven o'clock. We talked for some time, and they accepted the compromise, though with some misgivings for fear the UEA would chastise them for not staying away from school two days. At eight P.M. in the Woodruff school, a Logan Education Association meeting of all teachers took place, with three of us from our board present at their invitation. The vote was 118 to nineteen to accept the compromise. When the announcement was made of school on Monday (rumors had been rife that there would be no school) there was a commotion outside the open door and we heard boys' voices saying, "Ugh!" and then running feet. (Lance was one of the eavesdroppers.) The teachers burst into laughter.

Box Elder school district and a small number of others did as we did, but Cache district did not, nor did the big school districts. They announced that school was open. Most teachers stayed away, and there was some attempt to use substitute teachers, parents, and others. Some vandalism occurred and the national press capitalized on the situation.

Years later a school official observed, "It was the first time in the nation's history teachers had actually withheld services. People were shocked that Utah teachers would be such rebel rousers."[12] The good that came out of the teachers' action was that the school boards association set up a cooperative agreement with the school superintendents' association, UEA, and PTA to work together in preparing school finance legislation.[13] Change was in the air whereby there would soon be official negotiations within school districts. I noticed that a *Herald Journal* reporter began coming to our board meetings. Our superintendent's usual written report sent over to the newspaper office was no longer sufficient.

The May of the teachers' "staying out of school" strike also saw dedication of the new junior high building for which the bond vote had been 97.5 percent in favor. That summer, in cooperation with the city government, Logan school district held another bond election, this time for a municipal swimming pool to be built next to the new junior high. The campaign was spearheaded by the Logan Recreation Board, which included representatives of the city government and the school board. I chaired the recreation board, and City Commissioner Nephi Bott was vice chairman.

Bott opposed the muncipal pool. He wrote letters to the newspaper and gave talks using interesting arguments: Swimming is dangerous and spreads disease; and anyhow our young people should be working in the beet fields not swimming; and anyhow Logan can't afford a pool; and besides it is taking the bread and butter out of the mouth of the Logana swimming pool owner (a public pool privately owned).

Women's organizations, the PTA, and businessmen set up the usual block campaign. I wrote my family that I had bet the school board we would win by 65 percent. They doubted it. The vote was 67 percent in favor, and by November the pool was completed and dedicated. Bott reluctantly came to the dedication but stood smiling beside me in the newspaper picture.[14]

Also that November, Calvin Rampton, a Democrat, defeated Governor Clyde. During the campaign, Rampton stopped by our home to see me, and to congratulate me on the successful school bond votes in Logan. He asked me to vote for him, and I said of course I would. He said he knew I had an advanced degree, and that his own wife was working on an advanced degree at the University of Utah. After his election, Rampton appointed me to the State Building Board, a powerful five-person board, which oversaw building at all state institutions, including the prison, mental hospital, colleges, and universities.[15] I held this position for twelve years, the same length of time that Rampton remained in office. After I joined the board, one of its first acts was to recommend to the legislature a large bonding bill for buildings. This bill passed. One reason Rampton appointed me was because I favored bonding, in contrast to Merle Hyer, a Cache Valley farmer and conservative Republican, whose place I took on the board.

So now I belonged to two boards with power, the State Building Board and the Logan School Board. Each had funds and a staff. Each had five members, with me as the only woman. Yet I was never treated as lesser because of my gender, I assumed because the men were gentlemen in the true sense of the word, and because I was a competent person with the added prestige of holding a Ph.D. in economics.

The War on Poverty

I helped create two new organizations in the 1960s. It is difficult to create a new organization that possesses any semblance of power, especially when compared to the two boards to which I already belonged. One of the new creations was the Governor's Committee on the Status of Women, which I will discuss in the next chapter because it was a forerunner of contemporary feminism in Utah. The other creation was the Northern Utah Community Action Program (NUCAP), federally funded under the Economic Opportunity Act, an act which undergirded President Lyndon Johnson's War on Poverty, part of his Great Society Program. But I can't tell about NUCAP until I tell about its forerunner, a little migrant school on the south edge of Logan.[16]

In 1962 the United Church Women, composed of women in the local Presbyterian and Episcopal churches, set up a summer class for the children of Spanish-American migrant workers who came from Texas each May to work in the sugar beet fields, stayed to work on beans, and then in August went north to harvest apples and other crops, before returning to Texas in the middle of November. Today we would call them Hispanics, but "Spanish-American" was the term then in use.

Joyce Davis and Adelaide Bohart, representing United Church Women, went out to the camp on the south edge of Logan where ten migrant families lived, crowded into abandoned quonset huts near the old Amalgamated Sugar factory. They took with them Elizabeth Rodriguez, a Presbyterian who was a former migrant worker. She spoke Spanish, understood migrants' problems, and convinced the families of the importance of a summer class for children while parents were working in the fields. At home in Texas these youngsters received only five months of regular school, and the church women thought a summer class could help with English, arithmetic, and health habits. The local Catholics also became involved in this project for humanitarian reasons and because most of the migrant workers were Catholic. Women from the Baptist and Lutheran churches also volunteered help. The LDS Church was never directly a sponsor, but individual Mormon women, especially Angelyn Wadley and Lucile Burgoyne, became involved.

This little summer class, held in an old garage, lasted almost eight weeks. It was taught by Lucile Burgoyne, an excellent teacher in the regular school system. She taught without pay, assisted by Elizabeth Rodriguez and other volunteers. Although Lucile Burgoyne spoke no Spanish, other volunteers did. The children found the hours pleasant and were safely out of the fields.

The second summer, the National Council of Churches gave some financial help to United Church Women to pay the teacher's expenses and lay linoleum on the floor of the garage. It did not close on one side, and swirls of dust settled over table and chairs as large trucks passed, hauling limestone. This time the teacher was Donna Rose, a returned LDS missionary who spoke Spanish. Volunteer women still helped.

During neither of these first two summers was there publicity about the little school. The public welfare department knew nothing of its existence. Why should it? Migrants were transients and ineligible for welfare. The third summer the little school moved into a brick storage room with an electric light hanging from the ceiling, and a door that could close. The school district donated school desks. It was not an ideal environment. For one thing, there were rats. But the housing that the migrants lived in wasn't ideal either. Sanitary facilities were poor.

Enter the federal government in the form of the Economic Opportunity Act of 1964. Always well informed on social legislation and now involved with the migrant program in Box Elder county as well as in our county, Joyce Davis told me we needed a Community Action Program to be an umbrella over Head Start, Neighborhood Youth Corps, and the migrant programs. If I would work on getting a CAP, Joyce said she would work with the migrant programs. I had already persuaded the Logan Board of Education to apply for a Head Start grant.

Carol Clay, who had always lived in Cache Valley, realized that getting a CAP would take a countywide effort, and at this time she was urging creation of a community chest, which didn't need federal funding but did require a broad county effort. I still remember when Carol and I were walking across campus toward the extension service's annual women's leadership conference; we stopped and decided that she would do the community chest and I would do CAP. We would work together under auspices of the Cache Women's Legislative Council, of which Carol was president. Here again was the Women's Legislative Council taking action in the spirit of the Progressive era, just as women's clubs of our country had done in earlier years. This time we would have allies among low-income and ethnic groups.

First we laid groundwork with those we considered vital to our plans, including the school superintendents, County Commission, and Cooperative Extension Service. The Women's Legislative Council invited a broad spectrum of community leaders to attend an organizing meeting. This meeting, held on January 19, 1965, led to creation of the Cache Community Council, which we hoped could apply for OEO money. There were also committees appointed including one which, under Carol Clay, quite quickly made the community chest a reality.

Early that spring, rather unexpectedly, two consultants from the San Francisco office of the United States Department of Labor showed up to help us fill in the forms of a migrant proposal. They urged us to think big: not just a four-week class for the youngsters, but eight weeks; have some evening adult education in auto mechanics for the men; have a pre-kindergarten program such as Head Start for the young children. Migrant mothers could help with the school lunch and at the day care center, learning nutrition and wise ways of child care, and earning the minimum wage of $1.25 at the same time. And do it for all three migrant camps in the valley, not just for the one on the edge of town.

We found ourselves getting acquainted with people we had never known before, and laying big plans. That was how it came about that we prepared a twenty-eight-page migrant proposal. Eight copies were required in a hurry by the Office of Economic Opportunity in Washington. The local Job Service office said I could use the Xerox machine in the state's Department of Employment Security in Salt Lake City, eighty miles away. There was not a single Xerox machine in all of Cache Valley.

The day I left for Salt Lake City to photocopy, I was racing against time. First I picked up letters of support written by various officials. By noon I was in Salt Lake City. Employment Security ran off the pages for me—224 sheets of paper, unsorted. I hurried to the Capitol to the small office of the state Office of Economic Opportunity coordinator, tucked in a bit of space off the governor's waiting room. The coordinator was not in.

"I need to sort out all these pages and staple each copy of this proposal," I said breathlessly to the governor's secretary. "Can I spread these papers on the rug in the waiting room?" I gazed longingly at the broad expanse of superb carpeting in the waiting room. After all, nobody was waiting to see the governor, for the governor was out of town. "Of course not!" replied the governor's secretary briskly.

"Even though I'm a good Democrat and the governor is a friend of mine?" I ventured, saying to myself: that's the advantage of living in a state with small population. If you enter politics it's easy to get to the top; and when your party is in power, the governor calls you by your first name. True, it had taken sixteen years for my party to get into power, but now I intended to make hay while the sun shone.

"The governor doesn't want clutter in his waiting room," said the secretary firmly.

"Well," I said, willing to compromise, "could I just sort this stuff in a corner of your office, behind this armchair?"

She said yes, and so I knelt down and began sorting and stacking and stapling twenty-eight sheets to compile eight copies. I was surrounded by CAP sheets of all sorts, letters of consent, estimates of cost, a civil rights sheet, etc. As I finished, I thought my knees would never unfold so I could stand upright. The secretary let me make a long distance call to the Office of Economic Opportunity in Washington saying that the proposal was coming, airmail. The call reached there just before five P.M., Washington time, but I need not have hurried so fast, because the office worked late into the night.

Weeks went by. We didn't get federal funding that summer. Church women raised some money. Joyce Davis and the Migrant Council found a director for the project, a young sociology student just graduated, who could spare a summer. Also a young woman social worker, just graduated. Both would work without pay.

When the migrants arrived in May the weather was bad, there was no work for them, and red tape kept them off food stamps. Monsignor Jerome Stoffel donated six hundred dollars from the Catholic Church to tide them over. Fortunately, the Cache County Board of Education offered use of the little Hyde Park school building without charge, and provided books and materials. Two regular school teachers taught for a pittance. The public health service provided a part-time nurse. Bessie Lemon, extension home agent, coordinated transportation, as local women with their cars brought children from three camps, the one south of Logan, one in Lewiston, and a smaller one in Amalga. Women in Hyde Park, mostly LDS, made noon lunches for the children.

One beautiful summer morning I went out to visit the school. Of a potential forty students, there were thirty brown-eyed youngsters, clean, shining, enthusiastic, in two rooms, one for the first and second grade, and the other for third to sixth. At the end of the four weeks, the teachers and their aides reported that the children had made good progress. The newspapers were lyrical in their accounts of the school, and the pictures of the children would melt your heart.[17]

It had taken 150 volunteers to make this school possible, an average of five adults for each child. Is there any "proper" ratio in a project like this? The residents of Cache Valley learned more about the migrant families than they had ever known before. The women who took the children to and from school in their cars realized for the first time under what primitive conditions the migrants lived.

Finally, in 1966, our grant applications began producing Office of Economic Opportunity funds. Money came for migrant programs. The first CAP money came in my name until the county commissioners could get used to the idea of accepting federal money. When the Head Start money arrived, I promptly turned it over to Superintendent Sherman Eyre. That summer both Head Start and the migrant school were held in the Woodruff School across from Logan High School. Soon the Cache School District took responsibility for migrant education with funds from Title I of the Elementary, Secondary Education Act, and still does today. It was Joyce Davis who insisted from the very beginning that migrant education belonged in the public schools.

Our Northern Utah CAP encompassed Box Elder, Cache, and Rich counties, and one-third of its board consisted of low income people who learned to deal with county commissioners and other officials, fulfilling, in a way, the mandate of poverty programs of "maximum feasible participation of the poor."

Office of Economic Opportunity funding could also be secured for projects for senior citizens. At the suggestion of the state's councils on aging and tourism, the local chamber of commerce, and the county commissioners, I wrote a supplementary project to fund eleven low income senior citizens as information aides in a tourist program.[18]

Five years later we were in a battle to keep NUCAP. Across the country protests over civil rights and the Vietnamese war intensified. Suspecting that organizers in community programs fueled the fires of revolt, President Richard Nixon wanted all CAPs ended. Ours was the first one slated for demise in the western region of six states. I think we were chosen because we were small, semi-rural, and presumed to lack political clout.

When we sensed this danger, the county commissioner who was president of our NUCAP Board suggested he step down and that I take his place. The board duly elected me president in January 1971. The picture in the *Herald-Journal* shows me seated with my second vice-president, Neil Leatham, head of the Head Start Advisory Council.[19] What I like about the picture is that I am wearing a pantsuit, the first local woman in relatively high office to be seen wearing a pantsuit in the pages of the *Herald Journal.*

On April 18 my picture was again in the newspaper, on the front page, reading a letter from the Denver regional office saying that our CAP was being de-funded. The preceding Saturday our NUCAP Board had met with Bill Bruhn of the State Office of Community Affairs, who said this was a political matter and we should ask our congressional delegation for help. Immediately our Cache and Box Elder Migrant Councils wrote letters. I sent an official NUCAP letter to the congressional delegation and to Governor Rampton, and persuaded County Commissioner William Hyde to phone the delegation, telling them that Cache County wanted the CAP office kept. If our CAP folded, Head Start, Neighborhood Youth Corps, and the Emergency Food Program would need to find other sponsors, and this would be difficult. Then I wrote a letter to the regional Office of Economic Opportunity office in Denver requesting a hearing.

On May 9, which was my birthday, I wrote my folks that every few years my birthday and Mothers Day hit together and this was the day. It was a beautiful time of year in Logan, with crab apple trees in full bloom.

IN THEIR REORGANIZATION Thursday the Northern Utah Community Action Agency reconstituted itself with one-third low-income representatives, one-third private representatives, and one-third public agency representatives. Alison Thorne and Neal Leatham, above, were chosen as chairman and second vice-chairman, respectively. Hyrum Olsen was chosen as first vice-chairman.

Wynne had been in Washington D.C. the previous week and saw the Vietnam war protesters. Many were arrested, including bystanders. Half the doctors who cared for the wounded were also arrested.

I was happy to report to my folks that our county Democratic convention passed a resolution, which I helped write, reading, "Be it resolved that this convention calls for the setting by the U.S. Congress of a date certain for their withdrawal of all U.S. Military Forces from Indochina and that this resolution be transmitted to the Utah Congressional Delegation so that they may know our concern in this matter."

The CAP hearings were May 21–22. Two men came from OEO to present the case against us. James L. Young, deputy director of the Seattle region, conducted. We sat at the middle of the long side of the ping pong table. The other regional OEO man, Morris Lewis of Denver, sat to Young's right and I sat to his left, with our Board members seated in two long lines at right angle to me. This was in the old knitting mill on south Main Street, which had become the Cache Opportunity Center. Logan High art classes had painted the walls with murals on a white background, so the room appeared large, light, and airy. The Woodruff school loaned us a hundred folding chairs.

Gunn McKay, Democratic congressman, was not there but sent Robert Higginson who read McKay's very fine two page letter favoring re-funding. Brent Cameron of Frank Moss's staff (Democratic senator), made strong remarks. Wallace Bennett, (Republican senator), did not come, but, in Washington D.C., he went to the head of the Office of Economic Opportunity to defend us. Sherman Lloyd, (Republican congressman), said if the decision went against us, he would swing into action. The governor, though not present, indicated his firm support.

Spanish Americans from our migrant councils testified. Roland Chico, a tall and broad American Indian who was a member of the Utah Migrant Council, made a strong statement in our favor. The state Office of Economic Opportunity director, who originally told Denver it was all right to de-fund us, lost his job immediately. His successor, a young lawyer who attended our meetings, wrote Denver a strong letter urging re-funding. He took me to dinner after the second meeting closed and was very curious about who was coaching me. I didn't tell him that Wynne, Brent Cameron, and Ronald Chico coached me. He couldn't understand how a non-lawyer could work out such a good case. Actually Denver could have nailed us to the wall several times, but the two regional men refrained. I believe they hesitated because the governor and the congressional delegation wanted us re-funded. At the end of the meetings Denver phoned me saying we were re-funded.

Other Matters

In my early work with CAP, I unexpectedly received an invitation from the USU Department of Sociology to teach their longstanding course on rural community organization and leadership. I think the Civil Rights Act of 1964 caused the demise of the anti-nepotism rulings. I accepted this invitation, beginning in 1966 and continued for several years, using examples from local community work, from the Peace Corps, and from scholarly writings on community organization.

The summer of 1966 I taught a workshop for teachers of disadvantaged (meaning low-income) children. A Head Start grant paid my salary. This proved to be a strenuous period because Wynne had his second heart attack. While he was in intensive care at the Logan hospital, his doctor Merrill Daines, who was also a Logan School Board member, told me that I could not take Wynne home to our house with all its bedrooms upstairs. This time Wynne needed a first floor bedroom.

Wynne's recovery from his first heart attack, in 1963, was on a single bed in the large, sunny kitchen, next to the old fashioned radiator, only a few steps away from a half-bathroom under the stairs. But such primitive living arrangements would not do in 1966. Fortunately we had been talking with Carol and John Clay about their home that was for sale, one-half block from the hospital and near where we had lived during the war. Carol told me they wouldn't sell to anyone else while we waited to be sure that Wynne was out of danger.

With Wynne safely out of intensive care, I signed a check for the down payment, and the children and their friends helped me move. Wynne came home to a first floor bedroom and a very long telephone cord, because he insisted on carrying on university business to the extent that the doctor allowed, and then some. He absolutely refused to be an invalid, and we never treated him as one.

I have always believed that Wynne's first heart attack was brought on by the shock of his father's death from a heart attack, followed soon after by his brother Leland's death from a heart attack. Leland was four years younger than Wynne. Their two older sisters developed heart symptoms at this time. Wynne's third heart attack occurred February 8, 1971. I have no theories about the cause. Earlier, on January 14, an avalanche in Logan canyon swept away the end of our cabin, filling it with debris-laden snow. Wynne was careful not to go up to see the damage. Instead, he sent Sandra and her friend, Sue Lusowski. On their return, we gathered around the kitchen table, and Sue sketched the appearance of the cabin. Just then the local newspaper arrived, and there was a picture of our cabin on the front page, looking much as Sue had sketched it. By May, when enough snow had melted so we could begin clearing up the place, Wynne was giving instructions, but leaving the heavy work to the rest of us. He delegated the rebuilding to Lance, our competent nineteen-year old.

In early June, Wynne did not endure commencement well. He was on the platform with other dignitaries, and I was in the audience. He stood too long as the graduates all filed out. But I didn't realize this, and I had climbed the stairs to the upper concourse when I suddenly heard President Taggart call through the loudspeaker, "Is Alison Thorne in the audience?" I turned and saw that Wynne had collapsed. I ran down those

In Santa Barbara with Elaine, August 1968.
Back row, left to right: Lance, Grandpop Comish, Kip, Kares, Avril.
Front row: Sandra, Wynne, Bret, Alison, Barrie, Linda, Elaine,
Grandmother Comish.

steps with my heart in my mouth. Wynne's face was as white as his shirt.
He smiled weakly and said, "I seem to have fainted." We got him into an
ambulance, and after staying overnight in the hospital, he was released.
It was not an attack. He had taken a nitroglycerin pill as he stood for the
graduates to file out, and the blood had rushed to his feet instead of his
head, where he needed it. He took the nitroglycerin because he planned
to walk over to the building where Sandra's college, Natural Resources,
was holding its ceremony. He didn't get there, and neither did she.

That summer, when I was sure that CAP funding would be
renewed, I resigned from the board, citing concern over Wynne's
health. Considerable infighting ensued, but ultimately Marvin Fifield,
a USU faculty member in special education, became board chairman
and piloted CAP safely into sponsorship by the Bear River Association
of Governments, a newly created three-county organization empow-
ered to secure federal grants.[20]

7 Feminist Straws in the Wind

Betty Friedan's *Feminine Mystique* came out in 1963. Her message was that women are trapped as housewives and are unhappy, but no one pays attention. By sheer coincidence that year, for a few days in May, I kept track of what I did beyond my usual routine household work:

May 22. Wednesday
    Made salad for [LDS] stake dinner
    Made angel food cake, frosted, for Burgoynes [1]
    Wrote six family letters [same letter to all, using carbons]
    Set water going on the lawn
    Studied
    Read in two books, took notes, read *NY Times*

May 23. Thursday
    Went to mortuary for Lucile Burgoyne
    Attended graduation of Jr. High
    Read Carmen Fredrickson's paper

May 24. Friday
    Wrote notes to Charlene Cardon, Ila McAllister on origami
    Attended Lucile Burgoyne's funeral
    Typed notes on Jahoda's mental health book
    Visited Carmen and talked
    Went to H.S. graduation
    Chauffered Wynne from college

May 25. Saturday
    Moved Lance's possessions to sleeping porch, first step in
        upstairs spring cleaning
    Studied
    Gave Sandra a permanent

May 26. Sunday
    Prepared and taught adult Sunday School class
    Went with Wynne to Ogden to visit his mother
    Attended discussion group [Thoughtless Thinkers] on
        existentialism

May 27. Monday
Did extra big washing and ironing
Gave permanent to Avril
Typed article, and studied

It was a busy life, not entirely domestic, and I doubted that I was suffering from what Friedan called "the problem with no name." I disagreed with her belief that every woman needs a no-nonsense nine-to-five job,[2] but I continued to wish for a steady faculty position teaching a class or two.

A couple of years earlier, Wynne expressed his view of my life when we appeared with several family life faculty on a television program called "Women and Education," in the USU series "Man and His World." None of us questioned the appropriateness of generic man in the series title. Yet the 1960s would prove to be a decade that asked hard questions about females and educational opportunities, questions that would help generate the new wave of feminism.[3] Wynne and I introduced the television program with a dialogue, for which I still have his handwritten notes.[4]

> *Wynne*: My place on this program was attained through marriage and living with Alison for 24 years. I never know what I will find when I come home. Taffy, telegraph wires . . . projects take precedent over a neat house.
> *Alison*: I don't believe in being a perfect housekeeper.
> *Wynne*: Projects. Astronomy. Ideas are adventure. Learning belongs to everyone.
> *Alison*: I gave up a career of teaching consumer economics, taught myself philosophy. It's real nice to be married to a man who doesn't object to how much I spend on typewriter ribbons, paper, and books.
> *Wynne*: Your professors at Iowa State chided me for taking you away from a promising career. Talents in public service and with family gave rewards? But I have felt that you have had just as stimulating and full a life with your family, writing, and community service. You have been able to lead in worthy causes that you could not have done with a full time job.
> *Alison*: Without mothers as leaders, certain community activities would fold right up: Cub Scouts, Girl Scouts, 4-H and PTA. Then there are organizations for women, regardless of profession. Work together for better government. Women's Legislative Council. I think right now the community work I enjoy most is serving on the Logan Board of Education.
> *Wynne*: I'll bet I'm the only man in the state of Utah who wears shirts ironed by a school board president.

Wynne was right, about his shirts and about my varied career. Yet it was disconcerting that, because I was a homemaker living in the state of Utah, many males treated me as though I were under my husband's thumb. William Bennett, director of the USU Extension Service and also high in the LDS Church hierarchy, asked Wynne if it would be all right if the extension service invited me to speak to the Emery County Teachers' Institute. Afterwards Wynne told me that he replied by saying, "You don't need to ask me. It's up to her. They'll be lucky to get her because she's the best speaker in the State of Utah."

Ten years later when I was temporarily teaching an elementary economics class, and there was heavy statewide argument over the Equal Rights Amendment, word leaked to my class that I would be debating on television, in Salt Lake City, in favor of the ERA. A young man on the front row asked, seriously, "Do you have your husband's permission to do this?" Again, the assumption in Utah, particularly among Mormons, was that men led and their women followed.

In the early 1960s, when the campus was gradually fumbling its way toward a women's movement, the Associated Women Students organized a Women's Week assembly honoring various women, including Evelyn Rothwell, renowned oboe player, who appeared in the evening with the university band. Jaqueline Kennedy and Esther Peterson were also honored, in absentia. I was one of several local women honored, along with Edna Baker of the Utah State Board of Education, whose husband was USU basketball coach; and Alice Chase, wife of the university president. Although she had enjoyed her own career in teaching school, Mrs. Chase was honored as "the woman behind the man."

Afterwards Alice said to me, "I may be the woman behind the man, but you were the only woman with a man behind you." I was quite startled because, in the dimly lighted auditorium, I had not seen that Wynne was there.[5] Yet this was wholly in character. As I recall the boyfriends of my college years, he was the only one who went out of his way to attend any occasion on which I was honored. When the State School Boards Association awarded me their Distinguished Service Award—a complete surprise to me—Wynne was there. I thought he was in Chicago attending professional meetings, but Superintendent Sherman Eyre alerted him, and he flew back early.[6]

In 1963 Dean Phyllis Snow of the College of Family Life very much wanted me on her faculty, and Milt Merrill, academic vice president and also a member of the Logan School Board, was amenable. But President Chase upheld the anti-nepotism ruling. I wrote my family that if I couldn't get onto the USU faculty, I would apply to the University of Utah.[7]

Dean Snow wanted a new research project in her college and suggested that I develop one with Don Carter, head of the Department of Family and Child Development. We were to write a proposal to send to the National Institutes of Health (NIH), using my ideas on women's style of commitment to homemaking. We reasoned that if federal money paid my salary, the anti-nepotism ruling could be circumvented. I would need an academic title to give credibility to our proposal. My contract with the university, approved by the board of trustees, listed my title as assistant professor and associate in research. The contract also stipulated "No salary."

After months of work, during which our colleagues teased us about our "black market research," our proposal was ready to send to NIH. Because Wynne directed University Research, he signed off on it, but the proposal never left the campus. The vice president for business stopped it cold with a letter saying that, even if federal money were obtained, I could not receive any of it. He sent the letter to Wynne, not to me, and a nasty letter it was.[8] He sent the proposal back to Don Carter.

Carter's reaction was to say to me, "Even though you can't do research because of your husband's position, you can teach for me any time, and be paid for it. Teaching does not come under Wynne." So, in March 1965, I began teaching a new course that I designed and called, "Family in Its Social Setting." I never knew why President Chase relented on the issue of anti-nepotism, but the Civil Rights Act of 1964 did contain Title VII prohibiting discrimination against women in employment.

As soon as the university began paying me, my title dropped from assistant professor to lecturer. I didn't think to ask why. Vice President Milt Merrill, with no precedent for paying a part-time woman with a Ph.D., set my pay at what retired faculty men received when they taught an occasional class. It was very low. When I took on the additional course, "Rural Community Organization," in sociology, my teaching still did not amount to half time during any one year, so I was ineligible for tenure. I would remain a lecturer for more than twenty years.

Today one can ask feminist questions of our proposal on commitment to homemaking. We assumed that women were the primary homemakers, and we looked at a great many studies of how families used their time. I wrestled with classifications; in fact that's why I kept track of my own activities during those six days in May 1963. Categories of domestic activity, such as "work," "nonwork," and "leisure," may each contain caring relationships and self-fulfilling activities, but exactly what fits where? Feminist economists are asking these questions today.[9]

Don Carter's work on the proposal was not wasted. He presented a Faculty Honor Lecture, "Commitments in Marriage," lifting the concept of commitment from our proposal but developing it differently. Although he had a section on women as human beings, and quoted from Simone de Beauvoir, Ibsen's *The Doll House*, Betty Friedan, and Alice Rossi, his was not a feminist approach.[10]

Feminist Glimmerings in Higher Education

By 1960 some universities and colleges offered continuing education "plans" for women who wanted to renew their education. The University of Minnesota, Radcliffe, and Sarah Lawrence were among the earliest to do this. Programs for "rusty ladies" these were sometimes irreverently called, but they did point to institutional barriers to women's higher education and led to the rescue of much real talent.

University conferences on changing roles of women, with invitations to women of many walks of life, were another straw in the wind. Initially fueled by 1960 census figures that showed a great increase in employment of women, these conferences also included other aspects of women's lives. The University of Utah held its first women's conference in September 1962, and other annual conferences followed. Esther Landa, director of women's programs in the Division of Continuing Education, was chief architect of these women's conferences. I already knew her because she was on the Salt Lake City Board of Education. Esther invited several of us from USU, as well as other women from across the state, to help plan these conferences.

On one occasion Virginia Harder, director of our program in home economics education, drove her car. Dean Phyllis Snow and I were with her. While we were gone, Virginia's son, John, sprained his shoulder in an accident at Logan High School. A desperate attempt was made to reach Virginia, and someone remembered she had gone to a meeting at the U. of U. with Alison Thorne. A quick phone call to Wynne brought forth this remark, "Oh, they've gone to one of those meetings about women, the poor things." The high school seemed to know what he meant because they reached Virginia through a call to Esther Landa's office.[11]

Land grant colleges are no strangers to women's conferences. After all, their Cooperative Extension Service held annual women's leadership meetings for fifty years. Although such meetings were not overtly feminist, they should be analyzed for clues to the gender consciousness which was a prelude to explicit feminism.

The USU Women's Annual Leadership Conference of October 1961 was especially illuminating. It dealt with the "outlook for women's employment" as well as more traditional topics of spiritual values and gracious living. Bessie Lemon, our county extension home economist, and I each spoke on our lives as "working mothers." We carefully explained this was not a debate. I said I was a working mother even though not paid, and told of my domestic and community work. Bessie Lemon told how she managed to hold her full-time paid position because her children and husband helped at home, and he helped the children with their extracurricular activities. Because of poor health, he was unemployed.

The keynote speaker was Esther Peterson who, under President Kennedy, was assistant secretary of labor and head of the Women's Bureau. At that time she held the highest position of any woman in the federal government. The daughter of a school superintendent, she grew up in Provo, Utah. After marrying Oliver A. Peterson she worked with labor unions, and then went with him to Sweden where he was with the United States Embassy. They had a long-time housekeeper who helped with their four children and made it possible for Esther to combine family and career. Her talk at our extension conference held only one reference to feminism. "I sort of myself don't feel like a feminist. I think we are persons."[12] In reality, she always remained a strong advocate of women.

The Woman Question in the Media

That was October 1961. Two months later, on December first, Kennedy announced appointment of a President's Commission on the Status of Women, with Eleanor Roosevelt as honorary chairman, and Esther Peterson as executive vice-chairman. Historians now recognize that one of several purposes of this commission was to counteract forces favoring the Equal Rights Amendment (ERA), which stated that equality of rights under the law should not be denied because of sex. There was fear that the ERA would undermine the protective legislation for employed women that women's groups had fought so hard to secure. But that was only one aspect of the commission's work, and a hidden one at that. The commission gathered information on women's education, civil and political rights, social insurance and taxes, employment opportunities, volunteer work, and the way women were portrayed in the media.

In a special consultation on images of women in the mass media done for the president's commission, cartoonist Al Capp strongly defended as an ideal the kind of woman shown in advertising. But author and columnist Marya Mannes saw the unpardonable degree to which the media neglected "the full-time working wife, the wife who supports the family, the single working woman, the career woman with a husband and family, the professional intellectual, and the Negro woman . . ."[13]

As the 1960s wore on, the media gave increasing attention to women's interests because women were voicing dissatisfaction with their lives. Yet the image of woman as sex object persisted. The October 1962 and July 1965 issues of *Harper's* contained some serious articles, but across the top of the initial page was a woman lying on her side, looking out at the reader. In 1962 this reclining figure had curves more exaggerated than those of Mae West, and instead of a dress she wore across her body the words, "The American Female." She had a very young face, and a large bow ribbon in her hair. In 1965 the same figure again appeared, except that her curves had smoothed down a bit, and she wore a yellow dress with no wording. The face was the same, but the ribbon was gone, and she wore spectacles. A sure sign of intelligence, I presume. But if she was so intelligent, why was she still lying down in public?

Yet in that inimitable way of American media, the seriousness of some of the articles belied the sex pot. The 1962 issue had a large section of several articles, which the editors introduced by saying that women were re-examining their roles as wives, mothers, earners, and members of the human race. "However, it is happening so privately, and with such an unmilitant air, that one must look to the statistics [on employed women] for perspective . . . Crypto-feminism, it would appear, is a mass movement."[14] The fourteen authors with essays in this section ranged from Bruno Bettelheim to Anne Sexton. Beneath Sexton's poem is an editor's note: "Last year, she was one of the pioneer group of twenty-two women scholars at Radcliffe College's new Institute for Independent Study."[15]

Marion K. Sanders, one of *Harper's* editors, showed in a satire how difficult it was for women to secure high rank in federal employment, saying the administration wanted only beautiful, young women. Sanders paid tribute to the Very Important Wife with white gloves and mentioned Very Important Wives who were Eminent Economists and Accomplished Painters.

Three years later Sanders wrote the lead article of in the July 1965 issue of *Harper's*, entitled "The New American Female: Demi-Feminism

Takes Over." This title was emblazoned on the deep pink front cover, below the toned-down sex pot who had gained eyeglasses. Sanders paid tribute to women's volunteer civic work, especially Project Head Start. She noted that some women combined career and family, but were careful not to compete with their husbands and readily consented to move if his career took him elsewhere. Sanders still saw no militancy, but noted a contrast between Betty Friedan's *Feminine Mystique* and Phyllis McGinley's *Sixpence in Her Shoe,* a warm-hearted description of the home-keeping wife. A footnote observed that Friedan's book sold 650,000 copies and McGinley's not quite 100,000.[16] A feminist straw in the wind?

The Governor's Committee on the
Status of Women in Utah

Although the President's Commission on the Status of Women was quietly anti-ERA, it provided a framework for bringing women together, ultimately leading to overt feminism. Upon release of the commission report, *American Women,* the National Federation of Business and Professional Women met in Washington D.C., and urged their state presidents to put pressure on governors to create similar state commissions.

Utah's BPW president was Edith Shaw, associate professor of education at USU. I first knew her when she taught at the Whittier school and then became the principal. Edith took seriously the matter of forming a Utah commission on the status of women. She also attended the Rose Garden meeting called by President Lyndon Johnson to urge creation of Head Start programs across the country. Edith, along with Esther Landa, who was also at the Rose Garden meeting, made Head Start a reality in Utah.

Republican Governor Clyde was not enthusiastic about establishing a Commission on the Status of Women in Utah. In the first place, only the legislature could create commissions. Well then, it could be a governor's committee, Edith said. He wasn't enthusiastic about that either, but he was under pressure from twenty-five organizations, most of them women's groups carrying on a tradition of civic interest.[17] In January 1964 Clyde appointed an all-women Governor's Committee on the Status of Women in Utah, with Edith Shaw as chairman. As one of six members, I was assigned to the subject of women's employment. Although Edith and the governor were Republicans and I was a Democrat, I was chosen because they both knew me and appreciated my Ph.D. in economics.

At the end of the year we were ready to give Governor Clyde a mimeographed progress report dated December 16, 1964. We made an appointment to present it to him, expecting to get good newspaper coverage. Unfortunately the worst snowstorm of the season struck, and Edith Shaw, after sliding down my street, left her car in a snow bank, and we walked to the bus station. The bus was delayed in Idaho, and when it finally came and we reached Salt Lake, the streets were unplowed, and no one was at the Capitol. Fortunately our Salt Lake City members had made the presentation without us. Yet the press gave our report just a few lines. Nobody, but nobody, it seemed, cared about the status of women in Utah in 1964. The following month, January, Democrat Calvin Rampton became governor and reappointed us. He asked for a report in 1966, after which he would consider our work finished and would dissolve the committee.

The Governor's Committee on Status of Women had no budget. We used money out of our own pockets for travel to meetings. I kept minutes, typing them with numerous carbons, and mailing them out at my own expense. I took my car when we held a hearing in Price for employed women. We fought our way out of the Salt Lake Valley toward Soldier Summit in a thick brown dust storm, as night fell and tumbleweeds hurtled toward us.

We appointed subcommittees to help us gather material for our final report.[18] When it was completed, Edith arranged for it to be printed in Logan. The six hundred dollars raised by BPW clubs across the state was not enough to cover the cost of our thousand copies, so Edith and I went to Milt Merrill and asked if USU would put up an additional four hundred dollars. He agreed. We mailed copies to high school and college libraries in Utah, to women's groups, to Commissions on Status of Women of other states, and to the Women's Bureau of the United States Department of Labor. The President's Commission report had a slick white cover with a design in black and red. So we also gave our report a slick white cover, but with our own design in black and red. Our title page read *Utah Women, Opportunities, Responsibilities, Report of the Governor's Committee on the Status of Women in Utah, June 15, 1966.* I wrote the sections on employment of women and on poverty.

Upon receiving our report, Rampton dissolved us, as promised. But pressure from the original women's groups, plus others, led him to create a new committee of twelve women of diverse backgrounds, with me (a Democrat) as chair. I suggested a different name because I had found that very conservative women in the state did not like the term "status of women." To placate them, I suggested the Governor's Advisory Committee on Women's Programs, and this became our name for one year. I now think this was too conciliatory.

The governor's secretary, Pat King, became our secretary, too, and the governor gave us some of his own funds. We met monthly in the governor's board room of the Capitol. We studied state and federal labor laws as they affected women and supported several proposed state laws, most of which failed. The Fair Housing Bill, the Human Rights Commission, and the Therapeutic Abortion Bill did not pass. Ten of our twelve members favored the abortion bill; our two Catholic members abstained from voting.[19]

It was a time of increasing concern about the adverse effects of over-population, a concern felt on our campus and nationally. I recall standing at the back of the Sunburst Lounge of the USU Student Union, listening to a panel of six faculty men discuss overpopulation. In the question period, I asked why no woman was on the panel. After all, women are the people who give birth. It had never crossed their minds to invite a woman, and they promptly suggested I join them, but I was on my way to another appointment. I did stay long enough to tell the audience that the Governor's Committee on Women had voted overwhelmingly in favor of therapeutic abortion. Four years later, in 1973, the United States Supreme Court legalized abortion with *Roe v. Wade*, but ever since, the Utah legislature has tried to limit women's rights to legal abortion.

In the summer of 1969, after a year with the Governor's Committee, I decided to resign because of other obligations. Barbara Burnett, sister of Esther Landa and active in League of Women Voters, took over the chair and restored the Status of Women title. She provided excellent leadership, and the committee had strong members. In 1973 the Utah Legislature made the committee into a commission with an appropriation.

Conferences in Washington D. C.

From time to time, the Women's Bureau of the Department of Labor held conferences for state Commissions on the Status of Women. I attended two of these, both held in Washington, D.C. Looking back, I can see that the conference of July 28–30, 1965[20] laid the groundwork of my conversion to the women's movement in two ways. First, I heard what was probably the final debate between proponents of protective legislation for women in employment, and proponents of the Equal Rights Amendment. The ERA had the strongest arguments. Second, I heard Franklin D. Roosevelt, Jr., chairman of the Equal Employment Opportunity Commission, indicate a lukewarm approach to enforcing Title VII of the Civil Rights Act. I was appalled. Had his mother been alive, I believe she would have been appalled too, but Eleanor Roosevelt died in 1962.

Betty Friedan attended that conference, arriving in Washington to find "a seething underground of women in the government, the press, and the labor unions who felt powerless to stop the sabotage of this law. Several women gathered around her luncheon table to form an organization to support enforcement of anti-discrimination legislation, and Friedan wrote the letters NOW on her paper napkin, standing for National Organization for Women."[21] I was completely unaware that this was happening, even though I was at the same luncheon, but it was a very large room with lots of tables.

In 1968 I again attended a conference of status of women commissions, held June 20–22. It was a time of much turmoil in Washington, D.C., as described in my family letter:

I stayed with Gertrude Gronbech in Washington, out on the edge of George Washington University, not far from Washington circle, and could walk to and from the Washington Hilton where the meetings were held. There were people at the meetings from almost every state in the union. Many important people spoke; one evening it was Mrs. Martin Luther King (fragile looking, with great dignity, and yet wistfulness), the mayor of D.C. who is named Washington and is Negro, and his wife who is head of all the girls' Job Corps in the country. Eight Negro girls from the Charleston Job Corps sang for us; it was a moving experience. The Negro woman who is head of WICS [Women, Infant, Children Services] was there. At luncheons and dinners we sat at large round tables and I met remarkable women, including one 80 who is still in government work; she was the first person in the 1920's to set up classes for girls from factories; they came to Bryn Mawr in the summer and learned economics and English . . . Hilda Smith, now 80, was dean of women at Bryn Mawr; and then during the depression she continued working with the education of people, especially the unemployed. I became acquainted with the Negro head of the medical service at Howard University, a woman with a degree from Tufts. And the one who really took me under her wing when I first arrived, late, and saw her on the elevator, and was lost in the vast hotel—was a Negro woman from Indiana, whose way is paid by the Department of Labor every year; she has children, and a job in a factory, and went to college when she could find time and money, and graduated from college. She had arrived this time in Washington in a bus load of men representing labor, from Indiana, to take part on Solidarity Day, and after that had come on to the hotel for this conference in blue jeans and muddy shoes (because she was one who waded through the Reflecting Pool in front of Lincoln Monument).

We saw Resurrection City, from a bus, but did not go into it. There seems to be an air of uneasiness at night in Washington; I found myself locked out of Gertrude's apartment house when I was a few minutes after 11, getting home; I was in a taxi. It took considerable talking over a telephone, to convince the front desk they ought to open the door (an electric lock of some kind) and let me in.[22]

My View of Women and Higher Education

Daryl Chase retired as president of USU in 1968, and was succeeded by Glen L. Taggart. Both Taggart and his wife, Phyllis Paulsen Taggert, grew up in Cache Valley, but had lived elsewhere for years. They came here from Michigan State University. At a reception for the Taggarts, held in the Sunburst Lounge, I met Phyllis' s brother, F. Robert Paulsen, dean of education at the University of Arizona. He told me he was editing a book on higher education, but realized there was nothing in it specifically about women. Would I be willing to write a chapter on women and higher education? I would, and I did, and I was the only woman author among twelve.

A chief difference between my chapter and the others was that I used down-to-earth examples from women's lives, and had the audacity to describe women from behind the scenes, and who were considered marginal in college classrooms. I wrote:

> Each June, part of the commencement ritual at Utah State
> University is the PHT (Putting Hubby Through) ceremony. If the
> graduating man wants his wife to receive this certificate, he fills in
> the proper form at the Dean of Students' office. The afternoon
> before commencement, the ceremony of PHT takes place in the
> auditorium of Old Main, with the center section filled with the
> women candidates, and the outer section and balcony overflowing
> with husbands, babies, small children, and parents of the candi-
> dates. Each recipient walks over the stand to receive her certificate.
> Some are far gone in pregnancy, but each walks with dignity.

They are a courageous lot. They have lived on a shoestring, typed their husbands' papers, and shushed the children while their husbands studied. They have sometimes earned money by typing for others, tending babies for others, working in stores downtown, waiting tables, nursing at night in the hospital, and in countless other ways. Their wages have been low, unless they already had their own college degree and are nursing or teaching. But night nursing is tiring, and some of these would settle for part-time nursing with less pay and more sleep. There are not enough teaching jobs to go around, and some holders of teaching certificates end up in unskilled jobs. There are so many student wives seeking employment that the law of supply and demand operates to keep the wage structure low.

There is something else about the PHT ceremony that should be mentioned. There are a few, but growing number of young women who walk over the stand to receive the PHT, who appear the next morning capped and gowned in the commencement line to receive in their own right an earned bachelor's degree. 'In their own right' is a phrase that speaks volumes about the nature of marriage in our society.[23]

I also wrote about the kinds of women I had in my own classes, telling of mothers in their twenties or thirties, widowed or divorced, trying to get a teaching certificate so they can fend for themselves; the women who look tired and worn, often with no help with their children, yet they are impelled to take a heavy class load so they can get out quickly and start supporting themselves and their children.

Before I went into my down-to-earth approach, I gave facts showing that in the United States women's educational status, relative to men's, declined between 1930 and 1965. Only 32 percent of master's degrees went to women in 1965, compared with 40 percent in 1930. Only 11 percent of doctoral and equivalent degrees went to women in 1965 compared with 15 percent in 1930. A National Academy of Sciences report showed women to be slower than men in achieving full professorships, taking two to five years longer in the biological sciences, and as much as a decade in the social sciences. Three percent of lawyers, 1 percent of engineers, and 6.7 percent of physicians were women.[24]

I quoted from an NIH study that urged more women in biomedical areas, and recommended ways of enabling women to combine the rigors of graduate study with home and family responsibilities. The NIH study urged changes in employment practices so women could work on a part-time basis during the years of pressing family responsibilities.

The final recommendation suggested attitudinal reasons for women's poor showing in numbers in professional fields:

> Action programs should be initiated to dispel the 'inferiority myth,' and the concept that women must make a *choice* between career and domesticity. A fourth of the women in the study said being a research scientist and physician would restrict chance for marriage. A third said parents discourage daughters from training in such fields. It was suggested there be greater recognition of women successful in these fields, and programs to foster career aspirations.[25]

In today's terms, this was a call for role models and mentoring. But the NIH study didn't say outright there was discrimination against women as they sought education and employment in the professions. It did not mention sexism and male domination, arguments that a vigorous women's movement would soon make. From the 1940s to 1972 there was unconscious as well as overt discrimination in the sciences and other professions, and not until the data were accumulated and women banded together to name the problems and take action would there be a change.[26]

Concern Over Women's Low Pay

Our subcommittee on employment, within the Governor's Committee on Status of Women, knew that fear was the real reason that working women in Logan's downtown did not come to our hearings. They were afraid of losing their jobs if they showed even a breath of militancy. The hearings in Logan and in Price (which had a better attendance) were held with help from Carlyle Gronning of the State Industrial Commission, who explained the state labor laws.[27] Later we had another ally in Elizabeth Vance who headed the state Anti-discrimination Office under Governor Rampton. She was a Democratic national committeewoman, and had managed, somehow, to get nurses' salaries raised in Utah.

When the Neighborhood Youth Corps for high school students was paying the federal minimum wage of $1.25 an hour, their mothers who cooked in restaurants downtown were getting only eighty cents. We shrugged off employers' criticism by saying that students had to attend one hour of counseling for every three hours worked, making their pay ninety-four cents. But this was still more than women cooks made, and we saw little prospect of change. For some occupations, union membership might have been feasible. When Pat Woodruff, on our Status of

Women Subcommittee, tried to find out how many Utah women belonged to unions, the male members of the union she belonged to dumped the contents of her office desk drawers onto the floor. However, with time, some unions became more hospitable toward women.

When the State Industrial Commission appointed me to the advisory council of the State Department of Employment Security (Work Force Services), I hoped to have some influence. The advisory council was formed in the 1940s to monitor and write appropriate state legislation for the unemployment insurance fund. In 1965 when I joined, the state office had also taken on responsibility with regard to some Office of Economic Opportunity (OEO) programs. In fact, Theodore Maughan of the state office was one of the four men who helped me write the proposal that brought in our first Northern Utah Community Action Program funding.[28] At advisory council meetings, six union men sat on one side of the table and six corporation officials sat on the other. Three public representatives sat at the ends and had no vote. I was one of these and, of course, was the only woman. The council promptly made me vice chairman.[29] Ogden attorney Dave Holther had been chairman from the time that the council was first formed. When he became terminally ill, I succeeded him.

From the very first, I let the advisory council know that I was concerned about women's low pay. When restaurant owners came to ask exemption from including waitress's tips in their pay, for purposes of calculating unemployment insurance payments, both sides of the table acted as one in refusing exemption; and when the owners left, council members spoke out against the disgracefully low wages of waitresses. But of course we had no real influence on those wages.

One day, while waiting for council meeting to begin, two of the union men said to me that they thought unions could get women's wages up. This indicated a softening. However, the Utah legislature continued its strong support of the right-to-work law, and the Mormon Church maintained a constant anti-union stance, as well as an insistent view that women belonged in the home, not out in the labor force. Utah was and is a conservative state.

Our Daughters and the Women's Movement

Barrie, Sandra, and Avril arrived at the women's movement on paths different from mine. Barrie was a graduate student in sociology at Brandeis University and lived in Cambridge, Massachusetts. After she came home for a visit the summer of 1966, she went to Washington D.C., to attend the wedding of Margy McNamara and Barry Carter, friends from Stanford University days. Barrie took along my white gloves, the ones I occasionally wore to Faculty Women's League. I was awestruck that my gloves were going to the wedding of the daughter of Secretary of Defense Robert McNamara. In her letter home, Barrie wrote that after the wedding, held in the Washington Cathedral,

> . . . We walked out past rows of tourists, who had noted that above the entrance was carved in stone, 'The Way of Peace' (a little irony for the Sec. of Defense).
>   Walking towards the car, we passed the Kennedy brothers who were chatting with Alice Roosevelt Longworth (in her eternal broad-brimmed black hat). We followed the rows of chauffeured limousines from the church to the McNamara's home in Georgetown . . . Handshake with LBJ (who was warm and fatherly and looked like a slightly shabby Rotarian in dress and manner—while at the same time appearing kingly and slightly formidable); Conversation with Fulbright (who stood alone more than once in the chess game—I walked up, introduced myself, and said I appreciated his courage and position on the Vietnam issue; he seemed to appreciate my comment, and replied 'Thank you; we need all the help we can get') . . .
>   I'm mailing back your gloves, Mom, under separate cover. Any minor stains on them (will wash out) are the finest champagne. So don't complain. As it turned out, only about half the women wore hats to the wedding—I joined the hat-less lot, as did Mrs. McNamara.[30]

In May 1967 Barrie wrote of Vietnam Summer, a Cambridge project against the Vietnam war. She belonged to two different draft resistance groups and did draft counseling. A year later she wrote that she had met Dr. Benjamin Spock. Barrie attended Resist, the adult support organization for draft resistance that raised money for the legal defense fund for the indicted Boston Five, which included Spock.[31] Her letter of January 19, 1969, told of civil rights protests at Brandeis. She was still in the draft resistance movement. She ended her letter by saying: "Also enclosed is a bibliography on women from my women's liberation study group. Will write more later about this new activity. Tally ho." She wrote a long letter in May telling of the Female Liberation Conference, which was organized in part by Bread and Roses.[32]

> Bread and Roses was formed when a number of separate consciousness-raising groups, some out of SDS (Students for a Democratic

Society) and others out of the anti-war movement joined together in early 1969. The regional Female Liberation Conference that I wrote about in May 1969 was partly sponsored by Bread and Roses [which] took its name from the famous 1911 strike of women textile workers in Lawrence, Mass.; they sang a song about 'give us bread, but give us roses too.' We had a sense of ourselves as socialist-feminists, though we used the term 'women's liberation,' not 'feminism.' There was another radical women's liberation group in Boston, Cell 16, which was explicitly radical feminist (though I wonder if they used the term feminism—I don't think that term became widespread until the mid 1970s when we became more aware of women's history of protest.) Bread and Roses was quite large at its peak—certainly at least 1000 members. Among the many activities: a women's health group that developed *Our Bodies, Ourselves*; zap actions—we pasted little signs that said 'this offends women' over sexist ads; rape education work; a speakers' bureau (Donna Hulse and I went to various churches and school groups, including a sociology class at Harvard, to explain 'women's liberation').[33]

Boston was hot and sticky the weekend of Labor Day 1969, and I was visiting Barrie before flying to Austria to meet Ione Bennion and proceed on a round-the-world trip of six weeks, during which Ione and I would meet Wynne briefly in India and in Tokyo. Sandra was holding fort in Logan, and Barrie wrote to her on September 16, telling what was going on in Cambridge.

The Women's Liberation movement is big stuff around these parts. Is there any wind of it in Utah?

When Mother was here en route to Europe she met a lot of my friends, who told me afterwards, 'She's got quite a woman's lib rap herself' (an ultimate kind of compliment) . . .

I noticed in a big compendium of educational statistics for the U.S. that in 1965–66 only 3 women got BA's in forestry, nationwide (I think there were over 300 men, maybe more). I circled that figure and thought proudly of you.[34]

Sandra was the only one of our offspring to attend Utah State University, and was one of four women students in the College of Natural Resources.[35] Forestry students were required to attend a six weeks' summer camp up Logan canyon, and she would have gone except it would have required daily driving back and forth from Logan because there were no "facilities" for women. Male students were housed at camp. She chose not to attend under those conditions.

Women's facilities were made available the following summer, but by then Sandra had essentially completed her bachelors degree.

During the summer of 1969, Sandra worked as a United States Forest Service research technician in the Uintah Primitive Area. She worked alone in the mountains, traveling about in a tiny Volkswagon Bug. If the roads were muddy, she rode a horse provided by a private wilderness outfitter. Before she departed Logan to take up this job, her boyfriend Robert Brown gave her a two-bladed axe for chopping wood and for protection. But that particular axe sent mixed signals because he painted its handle pink and inserted rhinestones just above the blade. Today I wonder if that axe could be called androgynous, but more likely it suffered a case of split personality.

The Forest Service's only uniform for women was a gabardine skirt and jacket, and Sandra, wearing knee high socks with the skirt, was often mistaken for a Girl Scout.[36] When she received Barrie's September 16 letter asking if there was any wind of women's liberation in Utah, Sandra was living her own version by entering a male-dominated field and demanding equal opportunity.

Avril, in the meantime, had entered the University of Utah in 1967 and by 1969 was majoring in sociology. That spring she attended Christian Albrechts University in Kiel, Germany, on the Baltic. In this exchange program she learned German well enough to get credit in political science and philosophy. Back at the U. of U. that fall, she helped develop a drug referral center on campus. She wrote in October:

> It looks like our suicide, school freak-outer, drug referral center on campus is really getting going. Dean [Virginia] Frobes is really hot on the idea and Ballif Hall has given us a room in the basement. I'm the official secretary and am trying to maneuver my time schedule to avoid flunking a few classes. Lance is also helping with this.[37]

Lance had entered the U. of U. as a freshman that fall. Avril wrote her October letter on the letterhead of *"Channing Club,* Affiliated with Student Religious Liberals, 318 Union Building." In February 1970, Avril's letter home said that she and Joni were going to start a "women's liberation thing" in the dorm, and that a Students for a Democratic Society (SDS)) conference was being held that weekend in Los Angeles. They planned to go, and she added, "Barrie wants a report on women's lib from the coast."[38]

Things were hopping everywhere, and the women's movement was only one of several movements of the 1970s.

8 Activism in the 1970s

The Year 1970

Three movements claimed our family's attention during the year 1970: the antiwar movement, the environmental movement, and women's liberation. The thread of civil rights ran through all of them.

Avril went off to the Students for a Democratic Society (SDS) conference in Los Angeles in February, and on her return to the University of Utah, sent us a letter which began, "Have no fears that sibling #4 is becoming a true revolutionary. My hopes have been dashed. At least as far as SDS goes." At an early session, Avril sat down in a corner and kept hearing mumbling sounds from a stranger next to her. She wrote, "I glanced over to check this one out and summed him up with the label 'Oriental Hippy'—8" long hair, wide-brimmed hat, mustache, cowboy boots, safari jacket." He asked her if she would mind going to bed with him after the meeting, and she replied briskly, "Go to hell, male chauvinist." She wrote that male SDSers regarded women's liberation as '"crap." They did have concern for women's low pay scale, but in psychological liberation they were sexist. Avril was appalled at the totally abstract arguments against democracy and capitalism, two concepts which she found that SDS equated, and she observed that, in reality, workers detested revolutionary college students.[1]

Back at the University of Utah campus Avril continued classes and her work with the drug crisis referral center. Before the year was out, the center became Helpline, headquartered in the student union with Avril as codirector. Sixty undergraduate volunteers did double shifts on the phone, with twelve graduate students as semi-professional backup, and with one "shrink" on call at all hours.[2]

Early in 1970, Barbi Ellefson, an editor at the *Salt Lake Tribune*, interviewed Avril and me on our views of the women's liberation movement, but nothing appeared in its pages; I supposed it was because so much else was being printed those days about the women's movement. The *Chronicle of Higher Education* had an article on "Faculty Women View Their Status," and when Wynne came home from meetings in

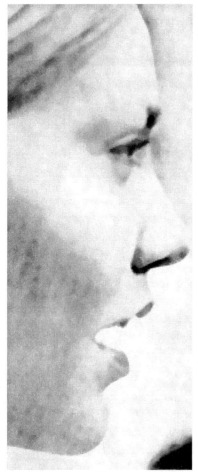 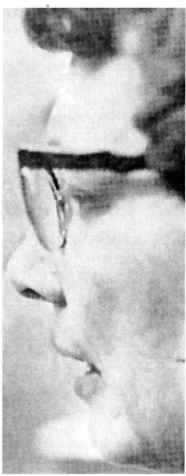

Avril Thorne   Dr. Alison Thorne
From the Salt Lake Tribune May 3, 1970.

Washington, D.C., he brought a news clipping about NOW (National Organization of Women) marchers.[3]

On May 3 the *Salt Lake Tribune* interview bore fruit. Avril and I appeared on the front page of the "For Women" section of the Sunday paper with a headline, "Mother, Daughter Cite Roles in Today's World." Avril's profile was on the left edge of the article, and mine was on the right edge. We were marginal women, not only because we were literally on the margins, but also because we were at the bottom of the page, the top half being given over to a male historian and his young son—and their opinions on women's liberation.

In the interview, Avril said she was more a psychological liberationist than a movement one, feeling if she got caught up in a movement she would get sucked into all sorts of things she really was not committed to. I told of my concern for women in poverty, and my hope to see all people, men and women, have a fair shake. I wanted more women in better paying positions, and more women lawyers and scientists. Avril said, "I think Mom's more for hitting the normative structure, and I'm for hitting the psychological structure." Avril criticized stereotypical roles of both men and women.[4]

Yet in the eyes of Cache Valley it was not women's liberation but the antiwar movement that transformed me into a radical. Upset over the Cambodian invasion and the death of four students on the Kent State University campus, several USU students and faculty arranged for a peace march through town on May 15.

I joined the march in town. A block and a half before we reached the high school, I went up to the front and took a corner of the banner from a young bearded man. I had heard rumors of possible violence when we came to the high school. Ahead of time Allen Stokes had gone with two USU campus leaders to get permission from Mayor Richard Chambers and the city commission to hold a peaceful march. The course was charted so it went past the First Presbyterian church, up to Mr. Tims' Grocery Store corner (which had become a parking lot), turned and proceeded east without going onto high school property. Mayor Chambers let it be known in a news release that he was against what the peace march stood for, but had consented to a peaceful march and police would be kept in the background. Matter of fact, he had promised police protection. When Allen said to me, as I walked with him and we reached Main Street, "Where is the police protection we were promised?" that was the moment I decided to move toward the front.

As we came toward the corner of Mr. Tims', there across the street beside the high school stood a burly policeman, legs apart, arms folded, daring us to come across. Several faculty stood by him. Actually the high school ROTC was down on Crimson Field having its spring review and school was out, and I imagine a great many people were down there out of sight. But not all students were there. Over near the high school entrance were lots of students, some of whom wanted to cross and join. I learned as I walked in the march that the faculty and administration had forbidden students to join, but somehow six or eight had joined us along Main Street, or even earlier, and they were right behind me. As we came opposite the crowd across the street, student Clair

PART OF THE MORE than 200 Utah State University students and Logan townspeople participating in Friday afternoon's peaceful march for peace are shown above. The group marched from the campus, through the business area, to Central Park, where a short meeting was held. Participants carried placards with slogans and admonitions. Herald Journal photo.

Kofoed, behind me, said, "Let's shout for them to come on over!" I turned around and said, "Be quiet, don't say a word." They didn't.

Clair, a good friend of Lance's, grew up across the street from us. Having known him all his life I could turn around and say briskly, "Be quiet, don't say a word," and depend on him to obey. So we got peacefully to the corner of the block, turned toward Center Street, then went down to Central Park, known as Merlin Olsen Park today.

We had worried about intersections for fear somebody might try to run us down. Right behind me were college students with wives and babies, and somehow a baby in a stroller doesn't seem a good target even for extreme rightists. Quite a number of USU faculty marched and their wives. Sandra, too, marched. A total of 250 left the campus after memorial services on the lawn, at the top of the open air amphitheater, honoring the Kent students, those who had been killed the day before in Mississippi, and those who died in the Indochina war. A peaceful assembly was held in Central Park where 250 more people joined us.[5]

The march was on Friday. The following Sunday the *Herald Journal* carried the story and a picture on the front page of me at the head of the march, holding the banner. The invasion of Cambodia by United States forces triggered my participation in this peace march. The previous

November, I had been in Cambodia with Ione Bennion to see Angkor Wat, one of the stops on our six weeks round-the-world trip together. We were impressed with the gentleness of the people we met in that small country, and we were subsequently appalled that our own nation had invaded it.

Logan High School graduation occurred soon after the peace march. Fortunately it was not my year as president and I had only to sit on the stand, but I could feel crackling hostility. There were exceptions. A young woman student body officer came to my home to give me a beautiful handkerchief and to say she appreciated what I had done. In my view, it was ridiculous to educate young men only to send them overseas to be killed. Furthermore, being a school board member should not deprive me of my citizen's right to protest war.

That same month, student antiwar sentiment was reaching a high pitch on the University of Utah campus. Lance and Avril took part in campus sit-ins, and I recognized them on a television newscast. Avril wrote that, on one occasion, they left a sit-in when informed that if they got arrested the bail was a thousand dollars. Eighty students were arrested.

Wynne and I sent telegrams protesting the war to the four men of Utah's congressional delegation. Senator Frank Moss was the only one to send a favorable reply. I helped write an antiwar plank for the platform of the Cache County Democratic party.[6]

Kip, by then an associate professor of theoretical physics at Caltech, came to USU to give a talk on the nature of the universe and spoke to a packed auditorium. Before he arrived, the *Herald Journal* published Kip's open letter against the Vietnam War, telling of concern over the needless loss of life of young men. He suggested that the Caltech faculty have a day of mourning and political education, and that the university's academic calendar be rearranged so that, for the two weeks in November before the election, there would be no classes, allowing faculty and students to campaign vigorously for candidates who were against the war.

Kip's letter ended: "It is not just a radical minority of the young who are being alienated from our government and society. It is the majority of the young. I see it even on the normally apathetic Caltech campus. It frightens me; it frightens the entire faculty of Caltech; it frightens the leading universities of America; and it should frighten you." In answer to this letter (which was also published in Pasadena, where Caltech is located), three open letters of opposition and two in favor appeared in the *Herald Journal*.[7]

My part in the local peace march continued to have repercussions. I received a handwritten letter, unsigned, that said, "For heavens sake Allison Thorne—have you lost your buttons? We might expect more from a 'so-called educator.' Haven't we enough problems with our youth and communism which is at the bottom of it all; without people like you making a spectacle of yourself and trying to help the problem makers. This is your last stupid mistake. Vote time is coming and don't you forget it."[8] There were petitions against me and, sure enough, I lost the school board primary election. Everett Harris received 240 votes, Dean Porter 143, and I had only ninety-seven.[9]

In spite of this turmoil, life went on during the summer of 1970. Lance worked for John Hunt in forest recreation, interviewing tourists, just as Sandra had done earlier. Lance was seeking conscientious objector status, and Barrie sent him and his friends materials from her draft counseling project in Boston. Lance's draft call number was thirty, a number so low that it meant he could be called up by early 1971.[10] As a member of the LDS Church, he could not claim conscientious objector status because ostensibly the church prided itself on patriotism and endorsed the Vietnam War. But the LDS Church called so many eligible young men on missions, urging college enrollment and marriage immediately afterwards, that in Utah the risk of being drafted was greatly increased for inactive and non-Mormons. Lance was an inactive Mormon. Ultimately when his number was called and he took the physical exam, the doctor found a heart murmur and Lance was deferred.

While Lance worked for John Hunt during the summer, Sandra worked at the Bear River Bird Refuge west of Brigham City, under a male supervisor who had strong opinions on appropriate female dress. Not only did he require that she wear a skirt, but he told her to kneel so he could determine if it was too short. This was the type of behavior one expected of Brigham Young University but not of the United States Fish and Wildlife Service.[11]

Sandra and Robert Brown planned to be married on August 22, in a garden wedding at our home, and in the fall they would enroll again at USU, he to complete his bachelor's degree, delayed because of two years of military service which was spent in the United States. She would begin a master's in forest recreation.

Avril went to Boston for the summer, at Barrie's invitation, and worked with Dean Mitchell, a Utahn who directed the conscientious objector program of the international office of the Unitarian Universalist Service Committee. As codirector, Avril edited a letter listing possible jobs for alternative service, and answered letters from conscientious objectors who wanted jobs. She took charge of the office when Dean went to Seattle to a conference on problems of young American men fleeing to Canada to escape the draft. At age twenty-five, Dean was, himself, under indictment for evading the draft. He claimed conscientious objector status on religious grounds, although he didn't believe in a supreme being. At the Seattle conference, Dean found that forty Americans a day were moving into the Vancouver, British Columbia, area, and estimated that from fifty to sixty thousand Americans were living in Canada. With help from Quakers, Mennonites, and Vancouver physicians, the Unitarian Universalist program assisted these "refugees" in finding jobs and housing, and in communicating with their families in the United States.[12]

On August 22 our whole family gathered in Logan for Sandra and Bob's wedding, a wonderful affair, if I do say so myself, as one with a hand in the arrangements. The newlyweds moved into a duplex across town.[13]

Back in Boston to complete her summer's work, Avril wrote that the American exiles in Canada preferred to be called expatriates, and women's liberation preferred the term "sexist" to "chauvinist." It was becoming clear that within movements, the choice of names and labels was an important matter.

During the summer Barrie worked for her major professor, Everett Hughes, a warm person and a distinguished sociologist. He was by then in his seventies, had retired from Brandeis, and now held a position at Boston College. Barrie had an office there and was writing her doctoral dissertation on the draft resistance movement. She was also working with Hughes on a book about education in the medical and legal professions, which included a section on student culture, unrest, and activism. I was interested in what she wrote of the relation of these professions to Office of Economic Opportunity anti-poverty programs, and of the need to recruit women to medicine and law.[14]

Alienation of youth continued to be on many people's minds, not just those of Kip and Caltech. During the summer and fall of 1970, Utah was preparing for the White House Conference on Children and Youth. White House Conferences on Children had been held every ten years since 1909, and this particular one, because of the unrest of young people, included youth defined as ages eighteen to twenty-four.

Governor Rampton appointed task forces on various topics, and meetings were held across the state to outline problems and get young people's opinions. Among the topics were health and drugs, civil and legal rights, national service and the draft, and economy and employment. I chaired the urban-rural task force.[15] My assignment included holding a regional conference with a broad spectrum of young people in attendance, and with dialogue between them and receptive adults on topics of concern to youth. We held this conference in the Logan Junior High School with attendance from Rich, Box Elder, and Cache counties.

Two hundred youth attended along with a sprinkling of adults to carry on dialogue. We had university students including some who were in the peace march, 4-H youth council members who were college freshmen, the high school Neighborhood Youth Corps members, and youngsters selected by their high school principals from all the high schools. There were ten discussion groups, and by and large they spoke up freely, and in fact asked for more such dialogues. The group talking about the draft agreed unanimously on abolishing the draft and having a volunteer army instead. In school matters, all agreed that students should have more voice in decisions, but appeared to doubt that changes would be made. The results of this meeting were combined with results of fourteen other regional conferences held across the state, and the summary was to go with Utah delegates to the White House Conference on Children and Youth in March.[16]

By including them in our conference at Logan Junior High, I had legitimated the youth who were in the peace march, and the youth of the Neighborhood Youth Corps. As matters turned out, President Nixon was afraid to have a national gathering of youth, so regional meetings were held instead and our Utah delegates went to Denver.

In preparing for the White House conference, our urban-rural task force had among its thirteen members two men who listed themselves as architect/planners, and one who was a community planner. They, with a sociologist, emphasized the findings of a Utah survey that 84 percent of urban youth worried about pollution, but far fewer adults cared. They noted various national writings on the environment, and the movement of hippies into rural areas. At one point they proposed changing the title of our task force to "philosophy of youth toward environment."

At USU, Tom Lyon of the English Department founded the Earth People, which held a meeting in January 1970. Sandra attended. This group had gathered up litter in Logan canyon the year before, and now came together to hear the views of the Forest Service on further widening of the Logan Canyon highway. Sandra returned to say that the Earth

People mostly dressed way-far-out. But there were also some clean-shaven, neat haircut types, and a considerable number of faculty.[17]

The county commission acted to keep smoke stack industry out of Cache County, and a new sawmill was not permitted to burn its waste. In April a campus teach-in week focused on the population explosion and on pollution. Edward Abbey spoke on campus to a large crowd, with Earth People prominently present. Allen Stokes, ornithologist, Quaker, and chief sponsor of local anti-draft counseling, spoke to our Sunday night discussion group on the Earth People movement and attitudes toward nature.[18]

In June, Wynne invited to dinner at our cabin the faculty involved in seeking an ecology grant: Dean Thad Box of Natural Resources and his wife Jenny, John and Ruth Neuhold, Fred and Marilyn Wagner, and Austin and Alta Fife. Carolyn Steel also came. She held a new Ph.D. from the University of Chicago in systems research, and was associate dean of our College of Education. The Rockefeller Foundation was interested in this project and would send a three person team for an on-site visit October 21–22. Before the visit, Wynne sent Al Boyce, one of the team members, a copy of Austin and Alta's latest book, on western ballads.[19] In November a $600,000 Rockefeller Grant on environmental planning was secured, and plans for an Ecology Center at USU went forward. Faculty Women's League had a program on the environment, with USU faculty as speakers. Locally, the environmental movement had begun.

I used environmental material in my classes and insisted that my community organization students attend environmental hearings. I used Elizabeth Hoyt's concept of basic cultural interests, with emphasis on the aesthetic and empathetic, and one of my students wrote a lyrical account of her experiences in the hidden areas of Mt. Jardine north of us. In class my sociology students wore casual attire, while the family life and home economics students wore "appropriate" clothing, but with time the difference lessened.

Sandra's Environmental Career

In the summer of 1971, Sandra was employed as forest ranger up Logan Canyon, the first woman to hold this position. She was in charge of six camp grounds and the Guinevah Amphitheater programs. Sandra bought Forest Service male trousers and altered them to fit, but for amphitheater programs she was listed as "Interpretive Rangerette," and was required to wear a skirt. The next year, however, Sandra had the company of three more women forest rangers, and the Forest Service had finally come out with a women's uniform—pants and vest in double knit polyester of a yellowish pea green color. Sandra declared it "horrendous" and didn't buy it.[20]

Sandra's favorite episode in her Logan Canyon work was the time she was cleaning out a stall in the women's side of a restroom and heard a mother and small girl enter. The mother went into a stall, telling the child to wait. Suddenly the little girl saw a ranger jacket backing out and shouted in alarm, "There's a forest ranger in here!" Sandra's head emerged as she said sweetly, "But I'm a female ranger."

For her master's at USU, Sandra created guides for environmental education field trips, completing her degree in December. Bob Brown completed his degree in business, and in January 1973 they moved to Houston to look for work. Things were booming in Texas because of the oil shortage and Bob found a management position with SIP, Inc., a corporation that did construction for oil companies.

Sandra, too, tried the oil companies, hoping they had a position dealing with the environment. They didn't, and she wrote in discouragement, "My kind of a job is not created yet." So she tried the schools, but they didn't have environmental education positions. Next she tried local parks, and wrote that the Houston Citizen's Environmental Coalition was helping her, "the only outfit willing to help a misfit girl."[21] Her luck turned when she tried the district office of the Soil Conservation Service. She was hired and became the first woman soil conservationist in that district, and one of only three in Texas. An article in the *Houston Chronicle* shows her paddling a canoe with her director, looking at flood levels of Armand Bayou.[22]

Sandra was placed on the Environmental Educational Council for Southeast Texas Schools, and completed conservation plans for three elementary schools, as well as for two county parks.[23] She designed outdoor learning classrooms, wrote a Nature Trail Tour for Armand Bayou, and trained two hundred members of the League of Women Voters and American Association of University Women to be volunteer guides. She also created a new kind of woodland contest for members of 4-H and Future Farmers of America clubs. But all was not sweetness and light. Sandra wrote:

> Had a rotten experience at my talk to the Daughters of the
> American Revolution. I gave a slide talk on conservation problems
> in Houston touching on destruction and channelization of streams
> and bayous, lack of silt and sedimentation control, unscrupulous

developers, lack of flood plain management and land use planning (which is absolutely non-existent in Houston). Had many favorable comments afterwards and then a woman came up and really laid into me! Said how she hated me, my beliefs and everything I stood for. That her forefathers came here in 1610 so no one could tell them how to use their land, etc. She wouldn't discuss anything but screamed at me with more hate than I've ever seen directed at one person! Don't know how but I kept my cool and eased out, ran to the car and swore all the way back to the office.[24]

Here again are women's organizations: LWV, AAUW, and DAR. Sandra joined the Federal Employed Women, which urged opportunities for women and opposed discrimination. In 1975 there were only five women Soil Conservation Service professionals in all of Texas, but they started a statewide annual women's seminar for women SCS employees of all levels.

League of Women Voters of Cache County

Losing my place on the school board was not the end of the world. Another avenue for community work opened up in the newly organized League of Women Voters of Cache County (LWVCC). Anne Hatch was the impetus behind this new organization. She had belonged to the League of Women Voters in Ames, Iowa, before moving to Logan with her husband, Eastman Hatch, who joined the USU physics faculty. Both grew up in Salt Lake City. Anne wanted to associate with up-and-coming women while working for the common good, and she had been particularly prodded by her friend, Norma Matheson, an active LWV member in Salt Lake City. Norma's husband Scott would later become governor of the state, succeeding Rampton. Anne Hatch's liberal leanings were already showing, because when she was in a supermarket back on May 15 and saw the peace march moving past, she promptly put down her groceries and came out and joined us.

In November, Anne invited state LWV officers to an organizational meeting in the Cache Chamber of Commerce meeting room. Reggie Benowitz of Ogden spoke on how to create a league. I remember her well because Reggie wore a pantsuit. Soon afterwards I went out and bought two pantsuits and wore them when I taught, a radical innovation in campus dress of faculty women. The BYU didn't permit women to wear pants on their campus, nor would the LDS Church-owned hospitals let nurses wear pants.

Word of mouth brought in our first LWV members. Some, like Anne Hatch, had belonged elsewhere. Jenny Box had belonged in Lubbock, Texas, where she helped register Blacks to vote, much to the consternation of conservatives. Her husband, Thad Box, dean of Natural Resources at USU, was very much a liberal too. Dorothy Lewis, who taught child development at USU, had belonged to LWV chapters in the early 1950s when she was a graduate student with two young children, first at the University of New Mexico and later at Iowa State University. Our new LWV chapter included other women faculty, mostly single. Some of our younger members were nonemployed faculty wives with young children. A few members were not attached to the university in any way. Ione Bennion, I, and a few others were former members of the Women's Legislative Council, but we had become disillusioned with the council when a change in its policies narrowed its possible actions.

One requirement to form a LWV was twenty-five paid-up members, and dues were $7.50, a lot of money in those days. Recalling the first membership meeting, Anne Hatch said there were twenty-four paid up members, and they needed one more. Phyllis Snow, dean of the College of Family Life, rose to leave, and paid her $7.50 before going out the door. A general sigh of relief ensued. At its height LWVCC had seventy-five members. A democratic organization with the goal of educating voters, LWV invited anyone interested to join. Leagues made studies of problems which might be solved by government action, discussed their studies, and if consensus was reached, worked for change.

Among the young faculty wives who belonged were Janet Osborne, Elki Powers, Carol Windham, and Mary Farley. They had young children and in order to get their LWV work done, they formed a baby-sitting cooperative. Janet also arranged for baby sitting at the 1971–72 meetings of Faculty Women's League, an innovation. Today we speak of child care, not baby sitting, and eventually the state LWV produced an excellent child care study that influenced state legislation, and which I used in teaching women's studies at USU.

Janet Osborne recalls with laughter that she and Elki Powers came to those early LWV meetings together, wearing long white boots, fancy hair-dos, and jingling earrings. Janet's children said of LWV, "You are a bunch of hippies!" which prompted Anne Hatch to report that her sons complained, "Do you have to join every radical organization that comes along?"[25] Our provisional League of Women Voters of Cache County was formed on November 12, 1970. A brief history of LWV written in 1972 says:

Now the real work began. For a Provisional League to achieve full recognition, it must fulfill a number of requirements. For example, a comprehensive Know Your County study was undertaken, in which almost every aspect of county government was investigated, officials interviewed, graphs prepared, charts and figures interpreted and so on. When we felt sufficiently well-informed to be able to ask intelligent questions, we invited the three county commissioners to attend a meeting, and spent an enjoyable and revealing morning picking their brains.

Our study was well done and qualified us to become a full fledged league on March 30, 1972. LWV regularly monitored Cache County Commission meetings and other public meetings as well. Jennie Christensen, reporter for the local newspaper, had attended the county commission meetings for some time and welcomed the presence of other women. Jennie and the League were appalled at how the commissioners did preliminary work and held LDS prayer behind locked doors, often failing to unlock them when the official meeting began. The women often had to knock loudly to gain entrance.

Convinced that the three-man commission form of government fails to separate legislative and executive functions and is not representative, LWV pushed for a change, but it would be fourteen long years before voters mandated an executive-council form of government for Cache County, in 1986. Success was due to the shrewd strategy of getting the mayors' association to spearhead the campaign for change. Our LWV member Helen Roth attended council meetings of all the towns and met often with the mayors, giving them basic facts from the LWV studies and insisting that they take the initiative.

Changing the Logan City government from a three-man commission proved easier than changing the county government. In 1974 the league produced "A Study of Alternate Forms of Local Government," and the next year voters mandated a change to a mayor-council form. Carol Clay, who worked very hard for the change, was voted in as a member of the new council. She was the only woman. No woman had ever served on the Logan or Cache County Commissions. Once when I asked a commissioner why this was the case, he replied that women are incapable of dealing with heads of departments, especially with regard to county roads and city streets. This was sexism, a term that didn't exist in the 1950s and 1960s.

League members made other studies during the 1970s, including of mosquitoes, low-income housing, Cache and Logan school districts, youth services, mental health, solid waste, and water resources. Our attempts to get a mosquito abatement district were foiled time and again. Jenny Box worked on the "Cache County Mosquitoes" study along with Cathy Schultz, Jeri Malouf, Janet Osborne, Elki Powers, and Carol Windham.

Jenny Box has described the successful petition drive for a mosquito abatement district, and how league members visited every one of the nineteen incorporated areas to speak to city councils. But for reasons unknown city council members began to withdraw support. The county commission put the issue on the November 1974 ballot hoping to kill it. Logan City and immediate towns around it were strongest in support. The vote was favorable, but the county commission refused to appropriate funds for mosquito abatement, giving as their reason that while individual voters might support mosquito control, their leaders did not.

Attempts were made again in 1975 and 1976, but opposition continued. One resident of College Ward who privately supported mosquito abatement, said, "Please don't let my neighbors know. Someone will run over my mailbox, cut off my water, shoot my dog."

It was with surprise that Jenny Box noted, many years later, that opposition in that area seemed to have collapsed. She wrote, "It was with some bemusement that League members read the April 19, 1989 headline in the *Herald Journal*: 'Mosquito Control Program Gets OK.' With the enthusiastic support of most of the residents of College Ward/Young Ward, the Cache County Council created a Mosquito Abatement District for that area."[26] However, countywide mosquito abatement has never come into being.

Public Library Funding

In addition to mosquitoes, another continuing problem was lack of adequate funding for local libraries. In the 1920s and 1930s, the library in Logan was supported with a small sum from both Logan and Cache governments, but the twenty thousand dollar annual budget did not begin to cover librarian Virginia Hanson's salary, the coal bill, and purchase of books. Only the generosity of Boyd Hatch, who lived elsewhere but sent money, kept the library afloat.

I knew part of the opposition to increased library funding was the county commissioners' dislike of Joseph Geddes and Carmen Fredrickson of the USU sociology faculty, who kept pressuring them in the 1950s for more library support. I discovered that, as new commissioners were elected, they carried on this animosity.[27]

In spite of abysmal funding, Virginia Hanson was a fantastic librarian. I could write reams about her many kindnesses to so many children, and of our visits to her home out in Cornish, where she had a fascinating attic room reached by a ladder that pulled down from the ceiling. Every New Year's Day she entertained international students at their farm, and invited us too. She called the home, where she lived with her sister Mae, "Dreary Acres." But it certainly was not dreary to any of us. Mae taught at the Lewiston elementary school. In 1973 Virginia retired from the library, and five years later, Virginia and Mae were killed when their car stalled on the railroad track that runs between their farm and the highway.[28]

There were state-operated bookmobiles in some areas, and local citizens wanted such service for Cache County. The state did offer a bookmobile for six months, free, to find out if the people really liked it. Yet the county commission refused this offer fearing people would like it and they would have to cough up money to supplement the state's payments for regular service. Finally public pressure forced the commission to pay twenty thousand dollars annually for bookmobile service, which began in July 1963, but the commissioners continued to refuse to put money into the city-county library in Logan. Several towns in our county have long had their own libraries, smaller than the one in Logan, and they understandably wanted a continuing existence. Anne Hatch wrote a history of local libraries in 1963, and the League of Women Voters of Cache County completed a library study the next year.[29]

The county and city commissioners lost the chance for $150,000 of federal funding to enlarge the public library in Logan, and an outraged public wanted to know why. In 1975, out of a large meeting of Friends of the Library, emerged the Committee of Fifty, chaired by Kathryn Gardner, an extremely capable person who worked in the USU Merrill Library. This committee traveled about looking at libraries and recommended a countywide system. The county commission remained opposed. A later Committee of Nine also failed. The county commission would fund only their portion of the bookmobile.

About this time Logan changed from the three-man city commission to the council form of government, with Carol Clay as an elected member. She arranged for a Committee of Five to study the library situation. Stewart Williams, retired USU geologist and chair of the Logan Library

Board, was helpful. It was my fate to serve on all three committees: Fifty, Nine, and now Five.

But I found that the Committee of Five posed an awkward situation because one of the members was Newell Olsen, who had attacked me in an open letter in the *Herald Journal* on February 17, 1974, when he was opposing the Logan School Board's leeway election to transfer three mills from capital outlay to maintenance and operation. I was no longer on the board, but I supported the transfer and was a victim of his animosity. He wrote in the 1974 letter, "Can any amount of scientific research or study nullify the rebellious conduct of teachers in picket lines who spurn court injunctions, court order and legal subpoenas? . . . Of faculty members who march in rebellious and violent demonstrations that, ofttimes, commit arson, looting and murder (witness Allison Thorn, Logan City's Supt. of schools of yesterday)."

I was angry, but I remembered that years earlier when a nasty letter against me showed up in the local paper, Wynne had one blunt piece of advice: "Never get in a pissing contest with a skunk." Where was Wynne now, when I needed him? Well, he was in New Mexico at meetings of Western Agricultural Experiment Station directors. My friends said to forget Wynne's advice. "Sue!" they said, and prepared to collect money to pay a lawyer. I wrote a reply which appeared in the paper of February 21 under the heading, "Falsehoods":

To Editor:

On February 17 the *Herald Journal* published a letter from Newell J. Olsen which contained several falsehoods about me. Contrary to Mr. Olsen's statements:

I have never been Superintendent of Logan City Schools.
I have never taken part in a rebellious and violent demonstration.
I have never committed arson, looting or murder.
Frankly, it appears to me that I have grounds for suit.

Alison Thorne

Three days later, two letters to the editor appeared. The first was from Arthur and Doris Holmgren about "the recent vicious letter written by Newell J. Olsen." It questioned the judgment of the editor in accepting Olsen's letter for publication because it appeared libelous to them. The second letter was headed, "An Apology," and was from Newell Olsen. He said his referral to violence, arson and murder was intended to refer to those hectic days at Berkeley, Stanford, Kent State, Harvard and many other universities. He wanted to bring attention that a member of Logan City's School Board had actually joined a demonstration march. "I sincerely apologize to Mrs. Alison Thorne."[30]

The school leeway election of 1974 passed by 83 percent, and this flurry of controversy may have helped us. Here I was, two years later, facing Newell Olsen across the table as the Committee of Five met. We got along amicably. Our committee hammered out a compromise between Logan and the county government, a compromise which lasted into the 1990s.[31]

Another issue was the LDS genealogical library that, for years, occupied part of the public library, with taxpayers paying for its space, heat, water, and lights. Both Anne Hatch's history of the library, and the League of Women Voters' library study, noted the situation. The American Civil Liberties Union threatened suit.[32] The LDS Church moved its library to the basement of the LDS Tabernacle across the street, which proved a better location for its purposes. However, many faithful LDS members viewed the ACLU and the league with a jaundiced eye. One of our officers reported that league was respected for doing things well and thoroughly researching issues. "We are perceived, however, as trouble-makers, somewhat liberal, and usually non-LDS."[33]

Through all this, the handful of us who were LDS and in the League of Women Voters of Cache County, sought to serve as bridges between Mormons and non-Mormons, just as we had done on the Governor's Committee on the Status of Women, and in the War on Poverty.

9 The Women's Movement at
Utah State University

One day in the fall of 1971, I received a sheet of information from the Women's Bureau of the United States Department of Labor indicating that women's groups should be consulted when affirmative action programs are written. I gave it to Carolyn Steel, associate dean of the College of Education. At about this same time, a woman student asked faculty member Phyllis Publicover if USU could offer a women's studies course. In 1972 women secured input into the USU affirmative action program, and the first women's studies course was taught spring quarter.

The Ad Hoc Committee on the Status of Women

Affirmative action violations could mean that federal money would be cut off, and USU received federal funds through both research and building contracts. As Carolyn and I read over the Women's Bureau sheet, I wondered if we should organize a women's group on campus to advise the administration, and Carolyn said of course we should. With help from home economist Jane Lott (McCullough) and others, we called a campus-wide meeting of women for February 28 at noon. Thirty-five faculty and staff women and several graduate and undergraduate students attended and, among other things, elected a representative steering committee of nine. The steering committee met frequently, at times negotiated with the administration, and reported back to the monthly campus-wide meeting of women. The larger group named itself the Ad Hoc Committee on the Status of Women at USU. A couple of years later, the nine-member steering committee took over this name, and campus wide meetings were held only once a quarter.

In the fall of 1971, a male member of the administration (practically all of the administration was male) had written an affirmative action program which came back from regional HEW (Health, Education and Welfare) in Denver with considerable criticism. In March, federal HEW representatives would be on campus to discuss a revised affirmative action plan and negotiate a compliance contract. Our steering commit-tee wanted a voice in these matters.

Carolyn Steel chaired both the Ad Hoc Status of Women Committee and the steering committee. I kept minutes. The university-wide meeting of March 8 concluded: "We are finally joining a movement that has been going on for some time on other campuses. We are not women's lib; we are for equal opportunity on this campus." In reality we thought of our-selves as part of the women's liberation movement, but we did not want to frighten the timid. I personally preferred the label "women's move-ment." Utah's conservative climate kept us cautious. Yet Utah had an Anti-discrimination Office, established by Governor Rampton in 1965, and bills introduced into the legislature on higher education included bans on discrimination against minorities and women.

Barrie, on the sociology faculty at Michigan State University, wrote me that Stanford had a good affirmative action plan. The steering com-mittee asked Richard Swenson, vice provost, to send for a copy, which he did, and after studying it, he gave it to us. We discussed it in our campus wide meeting of March 8. Swenson, the new vice provost, was the administrator with whom the steering committee dealt. Wynne had known him even before he came to USU because they were both agri-cultural scientists. When the steering committee learned that at the University of Utah and at Weber State College in Ogden there was an adversarial relationship between campus women and administration, Carolyn asked me quietly whether I thought we should go the adver-sarial route, or could we trust Swenson.[1] "Well," I said, "Wynne tells me that Richard Swenson is absolutely trustworthy." So trusting became our route.

Over the years I had been a bridge between Mormon and non-Mormon women in community work. Now I bridged between adminis-tration and campus women. I was also a bridge between administrators' wives and campus women, because I explained to the administrators' wives, at a social gathering at the president's home, what the steering committee was trying to do. They expressed understanding and support.

Early in the contemporary women's movement, someone observed that some women are married to the power structure. I was married to the vice president for research, but I had considerable power with the university administration in my own right because I was on the State Building Board. Yet my own professional position at USU was humble. I remained a one-fourth time lecturer, which made me professionally an "irregular," a term we picked up from the Stanford affirmative action document. "Irregular" always made me think of cheap silk stockings. Considering my pay, it was appropriate. Yet being one-fourth time made it possible for me to remain on the State Building Board without being accused of conflict of interest.[2] In pushing the women's movement, I did not run the risks of untenured and tenure track faculty women, and thanks to Wynne, who supported me both financially and morally, I had the latitude and resources to be an activist.

While our steering committee dealt primarily with Richard Swenson, it made good sense to visit President Glen Taggart to introduce ourselves and to present to him our recommendations concerning preparation of an affirmative action program acceptable to HEW. I was chosen to make the appointment for an April 4 meeting with President Taggart, because I knew him well. I also knew his secretary, Berniece Brumley, who gave us the appointment for April 4, after we provided her information on the nature of our group and a list of steering committee members. My minutes of this meeting indicate that President Taggart, Richard Swenson, and Evan Stevenson (author of the rejected affirmative action program) were present. The meeting was friendly and quite helpful. Carolyn Steel summarized it as follows:

> 1. Commitment from President Taggart that this is a serious matter.
> 2. The Ad Hoc Committee (on Status of Women at USU) is recognized as a viable organization.
> 3. The administration's Affirmative Action Program Committee is using the guidelines submitted by the Steering Committee for rewriting the University's Affirmative Action Program.

We were off and running. Our representatives met with HEW people who came to campus. We pushed for an affirmative action coordinator, rewrote the maternity leave policy, backed the move to get a campus day care center, and pushed for a Women's Center, although it did not materialize for another two years. Our members were placed on various university committees, especially search committees for candidates for administrative positions. Actually, there weren't enough women faculty to go around for all university committees and they came to feel burdened. Tenured women were particularly scarce. We also helped organize the statewide Consortium for Women in Higher Education, which kept us in touch with women and happenings on other campuses. We compared women's salaries and designed strategy for improving women's status.

Barrie and I constantly shared information. She belonged to the newly created Alliance to End Discrimination, which included faculty, staff, clerical workers, and students. The Michigan State administration refused to make public their affirmative action program. The alliance not only forced its release, but also circulated a copy of faculty salaries which had been published, thanks to "a feisty member of the Board of Trustees." Barrie sent me a copy of the salaries.[3]

Here in Utah we didn't try to get faculty salaries published, but we did urge equalization of men's and women's salaries, and in early 1973 the Utah Legislature appropriated money for equalization at USU, Weber State College, and the University of Utah. Swenson conferred with us on how this should be done on our campus, not only that year but in succeeding years. However, secretaries' salaries did not come under the line item because there were no men to compare with. Swenson initiated a study of USU secretaries' pay compared with neighboring institutions. USU was at the bottom.[4] A petition with one thousand names influenced the state legislature to make a line item appropriation for secretarial pay.

There was also the matter of matrons, who were the women doing custodial work. A representative of the Department of Labor arrived on campus to remind the administration of the provisions of the Equal Pay Act of 1963, whereupon the title "matron" was changed to "custodian," with women's pay made equal to that of men. When this matter was first considered, the men custodians said women would not shovel snow and get up on ladders to change fluorescent lights, but the women said they would. They did, and they still do.

In 1973 the Ad Hoc Status of Women Committee began a newsletter, mailed to women across campus. It was put together by Joan Shaw, editor for the College of Natural Resources who later became Agricultural Experiment Station editor. These newsletters, now in USU Special Collections, are a fine historical source of information on the early women's movement at USU.

Another early effort of the Status of Women Committee was the attempt to get part-time women faculty onto tenure track. Karen and Joe Morse were a faculty couple, both in the Chemistry Department, who had earned their doctorates at the University of Michigan. Because their two sons were very young, Karen was doing research and teaching half time. I asked Barrie if Michigan State had a tenure policy for part time people. She sent me the policy their women faculty had written and placed before their administration, which had refused

to adopt it. With slight modification, we presented it to our administration, who approved it. We could not foretell the future, but as things
turned out, Karen Morse became full time when her sons were older,
later became head of the Chemistry Department, then dean of science,
and in 1989 became provost of Utah State University. In 1993 she
became president of Western Washington University.

Barrie also helped us when we learned of sexual harassment on our
campus, in the form of male faculty who wanted female students to go
to bed to get a good grade. Barrie sent us the Michigan State sheet dealing with this and other aspects of sexism. Karen Morse, Jane Lott, and
Janice Pearce (in health education and also very active in Business and
Professional Women), worked over this statement. Our administration
promptly approved it and paid for its printing. Because it was on green
paper it became known as the "green sheet." We sent a copy to Barrie,
and the Michigan State women liked our revised wording so much that
they adopted it. This statement received national distribution in the
February 1981 issue of *On Campus with Women*, a newsletter published
by the Project on the Status of Women of the Association of American
Colleges.[5]

Another concern of our Status of Women Committee was recruit-
ment and fair treatment of women faculty. The affirmative action plan
provided for a grievance council, and Judith Gappa's was the first case
to be heard. Judy had completed her Ed.D. degree and applied for an
extension service position, which was given to a white LDS male. Then
suddenly a second extension position opened, and another male, of the
same description, was hired. Judy decided to go to the grievance council for a hearing, and our committee assigned me to accompany her. In
my view, the strongest person on the grievance council was Larzette
Hale. She was on the accounting faculty and, at the time, was the only
Black woman in the country both to hold a Ph.D. and be a CPA.
Larzette cut through the rambling statements of the extension administrator with terse questions, and she demanded terse answers.[6] The
upshot was that Judy won her case, became the new affirmative action
coordinator, and received an academic appointment.

For all the effort of our Status of Women Committee to get more
women hired onto the faculty, the score card got worse instead of better. Counting instructors through professors, matters stood as follows:[7]

> Jan 10, 1972: 487 men, 72 women, women approx. 13% of faculty
> Feb. 15, 1979: 503 men, 63 women, women approx. 11% of faculty

The First Women's Studies Course

Phyllis Publicover of the education faculty received a visit from a woman student in late fall 1971, who suggested that a women's studies course be created at USU. Phyllis concurred and sent the student to me to see what I thought. Several other women students showed interest, particularly Becque Stewart. These young women, who belonged to a consciousness-raising group, helped us plan the course. Carolyn Steel, Mary Anna Baden in sociology, Phyllis Publicover, and I were the teachers, without pay. We taught the course during spring quarter, 1972, calling it "Evolution of the Female Personality"—not a good title, we later decided, but we lacked imagination at the time and simply lifted the title of the women's studies course at Cornell. We organized the three credit course under the rubric of SILEX (Student Initiated Learning Experience).

As we got ready, we had to scramble for material. Daughters were a help. Phyllis Publicover's daughter, Alison Kaufman, compiled a bibliography of items on women and women's issues, which we handed out. My daughter Sandra took the course and was ready to share her experience of male-dominated education and employment. Barrie sent us the outline for "Sex Roles in a Changing Society," a new course she had created and was teaching at Michigan State. USU was still too conservative to permit use of the word "sex" in our title, but we made good use of Barrie's materials. Avril, at the University of Utah, sent a course outline on women, done up in purple ditto, that she developed for her sociology professor (male). She wrote it under the name of Avril Prunella Thorne. Our daughters had complained about not having middle names, and Wynne once said, "Well, you can put Prunella in the middle," and this whimsy evolved into their calling themselves Prunella I, II, and III, in birth order.

Student Life carried a story about the new course, under the headline: "Feminist Movement: Class Stresses Women." The article included this provocative sentence: "The course is intended to be an academic one, not a substitute for a 'do gooder' organization, or a rap session for frustrated females: though one from which relevant service organizations run by, and aiding women could grow.[8] To me it hinted of disdain for consciousness-raising groups, and disdain for "do-gooder" groups.

Four members of the new League of Women Voters were in the class, including Janet Osborne, who for her term project drew up a list of non-sexist books for young children, the first such list any of us had seen. We incorporated it into our teaching.[9] We met on Monday evenings from seven to ten, beginning with a formal presentation in the student senate chamber, which had a large oval table with an inside carpeted area. There were extra chairs along the wall which we needed because sixty people enrolled, thirty-five of them for credit. The second hour we broke into four discussion groups, then reconvened for a final hour. The course topics included the history of the women's movement in the United States, the socialization of women, female personality, human sexuality, women in literature and media, and women and work. We brought in Jan Tyler from Weber State College to teach the section on sexuality. I saw role playing for the first time, which was done inside the oval of the table, with participants vaulting over. (Not until much later did I discover there is a removable section of the table and one need not vault. After all, how did the custodian use the vacuum cleaner?)

The next time around, during spring 1973, we renamed the course "Evolution of Women in America," and had two distinguished visiting speakers: Mormon historian Juanita Brooks, and from out of state, Natalie Zemon Davis of the University of California, Berkeley, who spoke on women in European history. She told us how she got the Berkeley faculty women together to seek improved conditions. The most remarkable term project was an exquisite piece of jewelry created by student Judy Curtis. It was based on a female form and made of silver with a stone inset. I still remember my amazement as she dug it out of her jeans pocket to show the class.[10]

For sheer intellectual excitement and comaraderie, spring 1974 was the peak. By then the course was called "Alternatives for Women." Twenty-one took it for credit, plus twenty-two auditors. We met in the "pillow room" of the College of Natural Resources, a room without chairs that was carpeted on the floor and part way up the wall. People sat on the floor with and without pillows. Students kept journals and did term papers. Twelve women taught the course and attended every time in order to learn from each other and the students. They were determined to soak up this new knowledge as fast as possible. Because the History Department had no woman on its faculty, one of their graduate students, Gail Casterline, presented the topic, "Recreating a visible past for women: women in American history."[11] For the first time we learned about Fanny Fern, prolific and popular writer in the mid-1800s, who made more money than Nathaniel Hawthorne, leading him to complain bitterly about "those damned scribbling women." We learned of other women as well, and of the existence of the biographical volumes *Notable American Women*.

Besides Gail Casterline on history, other topics and instructors of the course included:

> Wives and mothers: Alison Thorne and Jane Lott
> Women as objects: Pat Gardner and Jane Lott.
> Women and health: Jan Pearce and Karen Draper
> Women and science: Karen Morse
> Genetic engineering: Eunice Cronin
> Women's emotional health: Marilynne Glatfelter
> A proposed women's center at USU: Helen Lundstrom, dean of
>   women, and Peggy Menlove, president of Associated Women
>   Students
> Women and the law: Connie Lundberg, attorney from Salt Lake City.
> Employment of women: Joan Shaw and Judy Gappa
> Self-identity: Pat Gardner

Throughout my fifteen year involvement with this introductory women's course I taught a session on wives and mothers and usually included a bit about Barrie's experience. When pregnant with her first child, she was teaching "Sex Roles" at Michigan State and discovered that some of her women students considered pregnancy to be treason to the feminist cause. Barrie argued otherwise. Shortly before the baby was due she called the hospital to make arrangements for the birth, explaining that she was Barrie Thorne and that her husband's name was Peter Lyman. The hospital told her she would have to register as Mrs. Peter Lyman and continued to insist, even when Barrie explained that her legal name was Barrie Thorne and that her health insurance was under that name.

Finally Barrie and Peter phoned a feminist attorney in Ann Arbor who arranged for an item in the "Action Line" column of the *Detroit News*. A short letter from "Barrie of East Lansing" explained the problem with the hospital and asked for help. It was followed by a response from the state attorney general's office, explaining that it was legal in the state of Michigan for a married woman to keep her "maiden" name. Sparrow Hospital relented and Barrie entered under her own name and gave birth to a son on June 25, 1973.

A day or so later a hospital clerk came with a form asking for the baby's name. Barrie said it was Andrew Lucian Thorne-Lyman. The clerk said that the child could only have the father's last name. No hyphenated creation allowed. Peter arrived for a visit and found Barrie in tears. Once again they called the feminist attorney in Ann Arbor, who said "You can legally call your baby anything you want." With that legal reassurance, Peter went home and put on a suit and tie, to give more authority to his mission, and proceeded to the office of a hospital administrator. As soon as he saw the name on the door, Ms. Hawkins, he knew he had it made, since any woman listed as Ms. must be a feminist. Ms. Hawkins assured Peter that, indeed, parents could name a baby anything they wanted.[12]

Barrie also quietly analyzed the hospital power structure. I'm sure the hospital did not realize the hazards of having, as a patient, an anthropologist-sociologist. She discovered that the lowliest of employees, licensed practical nurses, were the most skilled at getting a baby to nurse at its mother's breast. The regular nurses weren't nearly as good at it.

Here at USU by the time we were teaching in the pillow room, Carolyn Steel had left our campus for an administrative position at the Sturt College of Advanced Education in Adelaide, Australia. Before leaving she strongly advised our women without doctorates to go get one as soon as possible, from institutions other than USU. Jane Lott (McCullough) became chair of the Status of Women Committee and noted in the fall of 1973, that of the eighty-seven women on the USU faculty, only thirteen had doctoral degrees. The administration had a newly instituted program of special leaves for women faculty to pursue doctoral work and Jane urged women to apply for such leave.[13]

After three years of teaching the introductory course under the SILEX rubric, we decided it was time to get women's studies into the regular curriculum and to add more courses. That USU should even have a women's studies program was remarkable in some people's eyes, given the conservative environment. Judy Gappa, the affirmative action officer, and Nick Eastmond, of instructional development, wrote an article for *Liberal Education*, in which they described this conservative context.

> The campus is located in a rural community in northern Utah. The leadership of the Mormon church, the predominant religion of the area, opposes most aspects of the women's movement, including the Equal Rights Amendment, day care centers, working mothers, and abortion. In the words of the editor of the local newspaper, 'It is considered bad manners to question or challenge established authority.' The power structure in Cache Valley, again according to the local editor, is overwhelmingly male.

I should pause here to say that the local editor to whom they referred was Cliff Cheney, a very bright and capable person. Later Cliff took a position with the *Ogden Standard Examiner*. He and his wife died tragically in an auto accident on black ice between Hill Field and Ogden. Cliff's article on the power structure in Cache Valley, published in the *Herald Journal* on April 22, 1997, contained this paragraph:

> One noteworthy aspect of the local power structure is that women are not a part of it. Some might attribute this fact to the predominance of the LDS [Mormon] Church values here. At any rate, none of the ten Most Powerful individuals named in our survey are women. Among the top 50 most influential people in the valley are only two women: Carol Clay, Logan city councilwoman and organizer of the valley's first United Fund drive, and Alison Thorne, former city school board member, who has long been active in local social, civic and feminist causes.[14]

We did establish a women's studies program in spite of the conservative environment, and the introductory course became part of a regular and expanded curriculum. By 1976–77 about 280 were enrolled in USU women's studies courses, and 80 percent of USU faculty favored additional development of women's studies.[15]

From the very beginning, women's studies encouraged activism by its teachers and students. The campus health center was appallingly inadequate and our class produced a caustically humorous video. Through the summer students worked toward getting the health center improved.

When Planned Parenthood first established an office in Logan, the Cache County commissioners sought to close it down. Our class helped gather petition signatures to keep it open, but controversy went on for months. Not until the fall of 1975 was Planned Parenthood on sound footing.

Another focus of activism was Title IX, an amendment to the Civil Rights Act of 1964 prohibiting discrimination in education on the basis of sex. Joan Shaw, editor of the Status of Women Newsletter, who also taught our session on employment discrimination, had a daughter, Ethy, at Skyview High School. One day Ethy wore a nicely tailored pantsuit that happened to be made out of blue denim. The dress code prohibited jeans for girls. Ethy also had the audacity to complain that there were too few sports offerings for girls. She was suspended.

Joan Shaw joined her daughter in alerting regional Health, Education, and Welfare officials to these violations of Title IX, adding the charge that pregnant girls of the county high school, who were at the alternative learning center in Logan, could not receive the same kind of graduation diploma as other high school students. Joan's daughter won the right to wear her pantsuit, and the administration had to do something about women's sports and regularizing diplomas. The Health, Education, and Welfare officers who issued this ruling told Joan's daughter to carry a notebook and record any attempts by students or faculty to intimidate her, but she never had to write anything down. People at the high school were supportive or quiet. But the community was not quiet. There was a big hue and cry against the government ruling, with petitions passed in LDS Church houses telling the federal government to stay out of Cache Valley, and urging the congressional delegation to repeal Title IX because it was a communist plot. The State Board of Education went on record against Title IX and urged other states to join them—which they didn't.[16]

Logan High School's dress code was more sensible, but the new Logan School District superintendent, James Blair, made a statement that women were incapable of being good school administrators, which brought a strong response from the Consortium for Women in Higher Education in Utah, and a flurry of letters to state legislators. I recall going to Governor Rampton's office to talk with him about pending employment security legislation, and after we had talked about that for awhile, he leaned back in his chair and said, "Now, about the Logan superintendent. I have had a great many letters about his attitude against women in school administration."

Before leaving the subject of women's studies, I should mention that, early in 1976, there were two new sources of material. One was a recently published book, edited by Barrie Thorne and Nancy Henley, titled *Language and Sex: Difference and Dominance*, which was dedicated to their mothers. The other new source of material was *Signs: Journal of Women in Culture and Society*, the academic quarterly that began publication in autumn 1975 and continues today.

On a humorous note, I saw at the bottom of the society page of the *Herald Journal* an announcement that I would speak to AAUW on women, with the title, "Who are we and where are we going?" Just below appeared this ad: "Going to the cleaners? Come to Martinizing."[17]

Creation of the Women's Center

Dean of Women Helen Lundstrom attended a six weeks institute at Harvard in 1973 on establishment of campus women's centers. She came home enthusiastic despite opposition of Dean of Students Claude

Burtenshaw, who didn't want the dean of women to have any real power. Dean Lundstrom and women students and faculty persisted. Finally the university administration decided that the women's rest room on the second floor of the student center could be made over into a women's center. This room was at the head of the sun-filled south stairs, stairs which had a mural along the wall showing desert vegetation and birds, done by Everett Thorpe of the art faculty. At the top of the stairs the mural showed a tall blue-green saguaro cactus. Past the mural one turned into a long hall, or turned sharply left into the women's rest room. (Years later when the building underwent expansion, the south windows and stairs were removed and the desert and its birds and cactus were exposed to real sky and weather. No one had thought to remove the mural first.) The rest room had a large foyer with mirror and chairs furnished by Faculty Women's League. This became the main room of the Women's Center, and the toilet section became an office. Not a bad arrangement.

Here one must pause and wonder what factors made possible creation of the Women's Center. It could not have happened without the support of women students and faculty, and of faculty wives. The male administration needed convincing, and their wives convinced them, as did enrollment trends and needs of women. Federal requirements of affirmative action and Title IX were outside influences.

Dedication of the new center was planned for commencement of 1974, a time of much excitement since soon-to-be-President Gerald Ford was commencement speaker. Because his son Jack was a student at USU, Ford accepted the invitation. Betty Ford would speak at our dedication, and cut the ribbon at the door of the Women's Center for Lifelong Learning. The atmosphere of the entire commencement was electric because of security precautions. Ceiling panels of the Spectrum, the campus arena, were removed, and officers with guns were positioned there. Secret Service men dressed (so they thought) like ordinary people sat scattered about in the audience. But they didn't really look like your everyday Utah family members. The tower of Old Main, the campus administration building, had one of its round windows removed, so an officer and a gun could cover the commencement march from Old Main north toward the Spectrum. Fifteen years later the round window glass still had not been replaced.

After general commencement there was a gap of time for people to find their way across campus to separate college ceremonies. The Women's Center was dedicated during that open time, in the Sunburst

Lounge of the Student Center. It was by invitation only, and there were more photographers and secret service men than audience. Ione Bennion and I attended together and heard Betty Ford speak briefly. We saw her exchange a genuine loving look with her husband. Then people headed for the broad stairs, ascending past the desert, birds, and cactus. But Ione and I ran up a back flight of stairs, which the ubiquitous Secret Service had overlooked, and were within touching distance of Betty Ford as she cut the ribbon and smiled brightly. Those assembled didn't know that the furnishings were all borrowed, but the new wallpaper and carpeting did belong to the Women's Center.

Anne Hatch, who had led the effort to create a League of Women Voters, became coordinator of the Women's Center, jointly with Dean Lundstrom. On matters of funding the two of them went directly to Richard Swenson, the vice provost, with whom our Status of Women Committee also dealt. Nontraditional (now called reentry) students, particularly women, were an important focus of the Women's Center. These were persons who had been out of school for a period of time. Some were displaced homemakers, and some were single parents. Both groups needed to earn a better living than was possible without a college degree. There were also women who, though married, had married young and returned to complete a degree.

This was the beginning of a strong trend that Marilynne Glatfelter summarized when she spoke at the USU Centennial in 1988. She observed that in 1976 there were only 150 women over the age of thirty-four enrolled at USU. Some ten years later, in the fall of 1987, there were eight hundred.[18] The Women's Center also sent out listings of courses offered in women's studies and kept course materials in its reading area. Marilynne Glatfelter's courses on assertiveness training and personal assessment and Jane Post's math anxiety course were taught at the center itself.

There would be other evidences of strength of the campus women's movement as time went on.

10 The Widening Reach of the Women's Movement

The Equal Rights Amendment

March 1972 Congress passed the Equal Rights Amendment which read, "Equality of rights under the law shall not be denied or abridged by the United States or by any State on account of sex."

Women's groups across the country swung into action to try to persuade state legislatures to ratify it, and, in Utah the Governor's Committee on the Status of Women played a coordinating role. I was no longer on the committee, but I was on their subcommittee assigned to write a brochure to convince the public and the Utah legislature that the ERA should be ratified.

I saw a parallel between our ERA effort and the struggle of suffragists before the turn of the century to get votes for women written into the Utah constitution. The suffragists were successful and when Utah entered the union in 1896 the state constitution contained the following section:

> The rights of citizens of the State of Utah to vote and hold office shall not be denied or bridged on account of sex. Both male and female citizens of this State shall equally enjoy all civil, political and religious rights and privileges.

One wonders how that second sentence on equality of rights got in. I suppose it was because, over the years, the rhetoric for suffrage became tied in with equality. In any case, Utah lifted the wording from Wyoming, which had become a state six years earlier. Over time the wording of that second sentence proved to be empty. To my knowledge it has never been used in litigation and cannot be considered a state equal rights amendment.

Historian Jean Bickmore White has written about the way woman suffrage made its way into the Utah constitution. In 1870 a Mormon territorial legislature enfranchised Utah women. Women voted for seventeen years and nothing disastrous happened. But in 1887 Congress took away this right, and Utah suffragists tried to get the vote

back. In Utah these nineteenth century suffragists were not seen as rad-
icals. There was no militancy. There were no public spectacles.
Suffragists did not espouse other controversial reform measures that
might alienate supporters. The women supporting suffrage were predominantly from the respectable Mormon establishment. Suffrage was
frequently promoted through the Relief Society, and there was grass
roots support throughout the territory.[1]

In the 1970s those of us who worked for ratification of the ERA tried
not to appear radical. We eschewed the term "women libbers." We
sought grass roots support and hoped the Relief Society would honor
its history on suffrage and related matters of equality.

But as early as 1970, LDS Church authorities made pronouncements
against the women's movement. A headline in *The Salt Lake Tribune*
blared: "Shun Women's Lib, Relief Society Told." According to the article, a church apostle, after quoting from items in national publications
which expounded on "free child care, free abortions and equal employment," told sixty-five hundred women in the Tabernacle, "Such idiotic
and blatantly false philosophy must not be entertained or believed—
for God has spoken."[2]

At the same meeting Relief Society president Belle Spafford
announced that *The Relief Society Magazine* would be discontinued after
fifty-six years of publication. Historian Jill Mulvay Derr noted that the
LDS Church movement toward "correlation" brought all activities into a
system directed by priesthood offices, but this had unintended consequences for women, "further diminishing any sense of female leadership
and collective identity, and focusing even more narrowly on woman's
role in the home."[3] Proponents of the Equal Rights Amendment found
themselves up against a narrow focus on woman's role in the home to
the exclusion of other interests.

In September 1972 our little subcommittee of the Governor's Status
of Women Committee was meeting in the governor's office. He was out
of town and, although we usually met in his boardroom, it was otherwise occupied. Three of our four congressional delegates had already
voted against the ERA, but we included in our brochure a long list of
organizations favoring it, including League of Women Voters, Business
and Professional Women, General Federation of Women's Clubs, and
Church Women United. We gave pro-ERA arguments.

Apparently as we worked, rumor went out that a group of women's
libbers were writing something in the governor's office that would
undermine the families of Utah. A phone call to the governor's secretary

resulted in an invitation to the callers to come and see what we were doing. Two very frail-looking wives and mothers arrived. They were sure the ERA would do away with doctors who specialize in treatment of women. Women would be drafted into the army, or would have to go to work even if they had children. We talked with them at some length, but I doubt if we modified their view. They left with several pieces of our printed material.[4]

At the end of December 1972, I attended a meeting in the governor's boardroom on strategies for getting the ERA ratified. The state BPW president reported from a poll they had taken on the stand of each club. The state president of the Federated Women's Clubs reported where their member clubs stood. Two presidents in the Provo area had refused to poll their members or to have anything to do with the ERA. However some women in the Provo area favored the ERA, including Algie Ballif, former state legislator, and Virginia Cutler, former dean of Family Living at BYU. Carol Lynn Pearson, a noted author, was in favor, and another woman living in Provo had personally purchased a lot of our little leaflets and persuaded a fabric shop to put one in each woman's purchase of fabrics and patterns.

Homemakers, Incorporated, a group based in Arizona, sent all our legislators material against the ERA, much of it taken out of context from a *Yale Law Review* article. We suspected John Birch Society money was behind them. They were one reason that Arizona defeated the amendment, although Colorado and Idaho had ratified.[5]

January 1973 was a bitter cold month in Utah. Wynne was on a quick trip to Hyderabad, India, and then was going on to Ethiopia on behalf of the United Nations Development Programme. With one day's notice I had agreed to teach an elementary economics course with seventy-five students. This was the class in which, when I said I was going to Salt Lake to debate in favor of ERA on TV, a young man on the front row asked, "Does your husband approve of this?"

It was Friday, January 26, and a blizzard had come in early. My car slipped badly on college hill, so I went home and waited a half hour and tried again. Though I still slipped, I made it safely to the top and to my class. At eleven, I was due to leave for Salt Lake City for the debate. The highway patrol warned me over the phone that the canyon was snow packed and slick with zero visibility and would be that way all day. I phoned Channel Five and said I was not coming.

But the legislature was holding a hearing on ERA at four that afternoon. Dean Phyllis Snow said we had to be there, and she would drive.

Carl Johnson of the forestry faculty would go with us to represent the USU Faculty Association, which backed the amendment. Beth Gurrister, chair of the Governor's Committee on Status of Women, lived in Brigham City and we picked her up. In spite of the bad roads we made it safely, though the wind blew snow steadily and cars were off the road.

The auditorium was packed. The opposition was powered by the John Birch Society and similar movements, and I considered their arguments drivel. Pro and con speakers alternated. When my turn came, I gathered up the opposition's chief arguments and refuted them. As I went back to my seat, a little elderly lady told me I did just fine. I had heard her telling someone near her, before the meeting began, that she remembered when Utah women and Susan B. Anthony marched for women's vote and how people laughed at them, but they had been right.[6]

Interest in women's issues ran high. The annual University of Utah conference on women, in September 1973, drew people from across the state and seventy-five women attended from Salt Lake Trade Technical College. I was particularly struck by the women and law session, called "Legal Wilderness," which resulted in creation of a strong support group for divorced women.

In November the annual state social welfare conference included a workshop on women as consumers of health services, which I co-chaired with Jan Tyler of Weber College. We could not persuade any male medical doctor to be on our panel, but we had a young mother from Provo who had confronted the local hospital on its practices with regard to births. She had persuaded new mothers to write the hospital about what they liked and did not like, and real changes had occurred. She was working on a checklist for doctors to answer.

On our panel we also had Mildred Quinn, retiring head of nursing at the University of Utah, who told us about the long and honorable history of midwifery training at that institution. Even then, on the Navajo reservation, seven nurse midwives were at work, and the Navajo women preferred them to male doctors. Mildred Quinn had not heard of the Boston Women's Collective, and I told her about *Our Bodies Ourselves* which I knew was in the university bookstore. Barrie had sent me an early copy before it became a published book.[7]

In 1974 the Utah legislature voted down the ERA. Years later former Governor Calvin Rampton said:

> I was amazed, however, when the legislature refused to ratify the ERA . . . I guess I was rather naive because I stated I didn't see how

anyone was going to be against it . . . At that time the LDS Church had not [formally] taken their position against the amendment, and in view of the fact that Utah had a similar provision in the state constitution, I could see no reason why Utah legislators wouldn't ratify a similar addition to the federal constitution. Some Republicans voted for it, as did almost all of the Democrats, so it was defeated only narrowly. After that the LDS Church took a position against it, and I'm still appalled at the amount of damage and division that's been done in our state and elsewhere over what I regard as an innocuous and desirable change in our federal constitution.[8]

Polarization in Utah grew. The LDS Church tightened restrictions on women at the very time that the women's movement was growing nationally and globally.

Three Significant Women's Conferences in 1977

HANDS ACROSS THE VALLEY

In April 1977 the USU Women's Center sponsored a conference called "Hands Across the Valley." A principal mover of this event was Jean Christensen, wife of Boyd Christensen, vice president for business. The Christensens, who were LDS, had lived elsewhere for many years, and Jean had seen LDS women work with other women in bettering their communities, but she saw very little of this kind of cooperation in Cache Valley.[9]

Here again was the long standing problem of how Mormons and non-Mormons lived together. I knew, and others knew, that non-Mormon women moving into Cache Valley suffered cultural shock. Mormons had so many church duties that they kept mostly to themselves, unaware that people who were not LDS would like to be better acquainted without attempts at conversion. Many Mormon children made life miserable for non-Mormon children who didn't belong to "the only true church." Teachers in the public schools sometimes asked for a show of hands on religion, perhaps to determine who would be going to LDS Primary after school on Tuesdays. I recall Superintendent Eyre sending out instructions for teachers not to do this.

LDS young people were told by their church and families not to date outside the church. But if non-LDS attended LDS seminary, this ruling could be overlooked. Still another sore point was that Mormons had little understanding or appreciation of the rituals of other churches. For example, they could care less about Good Friday, or about a possible Easter vacation, because the LDS Church did not pay much attention to Easter. A spring vacation always occurred, but it didn't have to be at Easter time.

Jean Christensen and Anne Hatch called together a large group of women from all over the valley and discussed with them Emma Lou Thayne's talk of the previous year on "looking at our similarities in light of our differences." Emma Lou Thayne of Salt Lake City was a gifted, warm-hearted LDS woman who taught English at the University of Utah, an author of poetry and prose, and the mother of five children. I had attended her talk in 1976, held in Logan and sponsored by the USU Women's Center. I found truth in her statement that the presence of the LDS Church affects the environment just as the mountains affect the horizon.[10] There were two commentators after her talk. One of them was Judy MacMahon, new director of the Logan Library, who said that, after moving to Cache Valley, she had to search her roots in Ohio to come to terms with Mormon culture.

Now it was 1977, and Judy and Carolyn Cragun were chosen to co-chair the conference, "Hands Across the Valley." Carolyn was a home-maker, active in the LDS Church and in doing good deeds in the community. Elki Powers, who along with Judy was a LWV member, designed a logo for the conference, a series of hands reaching toward each other. They were all white hands. There were very few people of color in Cache Valley, and race was not yet an issue.

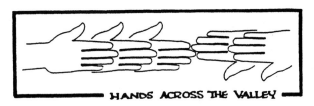

The conference began on Thursday night, April 7, with a keynote address by Emma Lou Thayne. The next morning Emma Lou joined the panel of local women, LDS and non-LDS, who had already met three times and had come to trust each other. They spoke on local issues. At one point the audience was asked to show by raising their hands how many were Mormon and how many not. It was evenly divided. On the question of who was native to the valley, it turned out that most were not. Even most of the Mormons were not valley natives.

At 12:30 Barrie Thorne and I discussed three generations. We had hoped my mother would come, but she and my father were living permanently in St. George. Louise Comish felt too old to attempt the trip, so Barrie had spent the night with them, coming on alone the next morning. We spoke of how Louise Comish reared her children and then gave our own views on family life. In making the point that parents should raise their children to be unafraid to take risks, Barrie said her favorite picture of me was the one on the front page of the *Herald Journal* leading the peace march, a remark that brought much applause and startled me. In the afternoon Barrie led a workshop, which the magazine *Utah Holiday* described as follows:

> . . . Mormon and non-Mormon women got together in a coopera-
> tive effort that some may not have guessed was possible . . . a
> women's conference at Utah State University in Logan. Called
> 'Hands Across the Valley,' the conference was created on the
> assumption that there were issues that mutually concerned all
> Cache Valley women.
>
> In a Student Union Lounge on a sunny April afternoon, the mix of
> women in the room for a seminar on Humanism and Feminism
> told the story. Pantsuits, levis and hiking boots sat alongside
> sweaters, dresses, blouses and skirts. Many of the women were in
> their 40's and 50's; students talked with mothers and grand-
> mothers; women who work inside the home talked with profes-
> sional women.
>
> 'Feminism can sound scary and shrill,' panel moderator Barrie
> Thorne began. Attractive, pregnant and unprepossessing, Thorne
> shatters feminist stereotypes by her very presence. She had ended
> the morning session with a generational discussion of her Mormon
> Cache Valley roots with her mother Alison Thorne. 'Historically
> and factually,' she continued, 'feminism is simply the freedom for
> women and men to make choices that affect their own lives. It
> stresses first of all that we are all human beings, that gender is sec-
> ondary. Obviously, it does not deny the facts of reproduction, but
> only that we can't rigidly channel individual lives on the basis of
> gender.'[11]

The baby that Barrie carried would be born September 7 and named Abigail Louise in honor of Abigail Adams and Louise Comish.

In her discussion, Barrie chose to define humanism simply as being human. Feminism of course was a suspect term, but she insisted on using it. Indeed, some of my LDS friends insisted on calling themselves both feminist and LDS.

Back in the auditorium there was reading of poetry written by Cache Valley women—marvelous pieces—especially "One Woman's Mecca Is Another Woman's Zion," by Sue Van Alfen. There was also an art exhibit on campus with works of five outstanding Cache Valley women artists.

The conference led to the creation of ten groups to meet in homes, three times before the next October, with hope of eventually forming a Women's Interfaith Council.[12] One of these groups met at my home, but I found, as did the others, that while there were non-LDS women eager to participate, it was hard to get LDS women to come. I prevailed on my immediate neighbors, and they came out of loyalty to me. I was also fortunate that Phyllis Taggart and Jerrilyn Black, both LDS, chose to attend my meetings. Extremely perceptive women, Phyllis was married to the president of USU and Jerrilyn was married to the head of the Sociology Department. Our non-LDS women were associated with other churches, and some but not all, were faculty wives.

In going over minutes of my meetings, I find we spoke of understanding religious practices of others that affect the community; adequacy and inadequacy of family services; knowledge of what agencies render what services; concern over child abuse and battered wives; questions on the mental health program and what can be done to prevent suicides; safety on the streets and campus; and why rapes were not reported in the local newspapers. We stayed away from ERA and abortion. [13]

THE SALT PALACE MEETINGS

Before I can describe the statewide women's meetings held June 24–25, 1977, in the Salt Palace, I must give the background that started it all, International Women's Year (IWY).

Whether called feminists or participants in the women's movement, activists across the world were concerned about women's poverty, poor education, poor health, overwork, lack of resources, and lack of political voice. The United Nations declared 1975 to be International Women's Year and urged countries to gather data on women's condition. The UN conference in Mexico City launched International Women's Year and the International Decade of Women. It drew thirteen hundred official delegates from 130 countries. Seven thousand others attended at their own expense, including thirty-seven women from Utah, some of them from BYU.

The IWY logo was a dove with the women's symbol and equality designed into it to represent the major goals of Equality, Development, and Peace. This logo appeared on IWY reports and on postage stamps issued by various countries. I have the IWY stamp of the People's Democratic Republic of Yemen, because Wynne sent me a letter from there while on a five-week consulting assignment for the United Nations Development Programme.

After the Mexico City meetings, Congress created the National Commission on the Observance of International Women's Year, which spent twelve months investigating issues affecting women and then published its findings and recommendations in the document, ". . . *To Form a More Perfect Union . . ." Justice for American Women*. Congress came forth with five million dollars for state conferences to consider these recommendations and to elect delegates to a national women's conference to be held in Houston, Texas, November 18–21, 1977.

In Utah the IWY Coordinating Committee, with forty-two members of diverse religious, ethnic, and political backgrounds planned the state conference with twenty-five thousand dollars from Congress, fourteen thousand dollars from the Utah Endowment for the Humanities, three thousand dollars from private companies, as well as many individual donations. They scheduled the IWY Conference for June 24–25 in the Salt Palace, a round, tan brick conference center not unlike a giant salt shaker. We came to call this gathering simply the Salt Palace meetings.

In May the coordinating committee held "mass meetings" across the state to consider issues important to women, but these were poorly attended. I was one of only a handful who attended the meeting, held in the cafeteria of Logan High School.

Enter the LDS Church. Apparently the LDS women's auxiliary, the Relief Society, thought that more Mormon women should show interest and they prevailed on Ezra Taft Benson, then of the First Presidency, to arrange phone calls to key church leaders telling them that each ward should send ten women to the state conference. The Relief Society followed up with instructions on how to participate and enclosed a list of candidates for election as delegates to the national meetings. These women were listed as "conservative patriots" dedicated to preserving the Constitution and traditional moral values. I noticed that the list of suggested delegates was short on Democrats and racial-ethnic minorities, and long on Republicans, the American Party, Eagle Forum, and right-to-life activists. The American Party and Eagle

> # "...TO FORM A MORE PERFECT UNION..."
> ## Justice for American Women
>
>
>
> *Report of the*
>
> NATIONAL COMMISSION ON THE
> OBSERVANCE OF INTERNATIONAL WOMEN'S YEAR
> 1976

The Report that the vast majority of Relief Society women did not read before they came to the Salt Palace meetings June 1977.

Forum were ultraconservative organizations. Right-to-lifers opposed the right to abortion.

What I did not know was that these conservatives held large "informational meetings" in Bountiful, Ogden, Kearns, Provo (two), Salt Lake City, and Logan. I was completely unaware of the meeting held in Logan. Conservatives supplied the speakers and told those assembled that the IWY conference was a plot by the federal government to take over people's lives, and that the delegates should vote down all the resolutions. Georgia Peterson, a Republican in the Utah legislature, was leader of one conservative group, and "Bishop" Dennis Ker, an ultra-conservative, led another group. It was not known if Ker was really a Mormon bishop, but he used religion in his arguments.

Early Friday morning, June 24, I drove to Salt Lake with Ione Bennion, Anne Hatch, and Vickie Coleman. Vickie was Black (the term African-American was not yet in use) and a member of our faculty. We had nominated her to be a delegate to the national meetings.

Three thousand had pre-registered, and thousands more registered as they arrived. The Salt Palace teemed with people, mostly but not entirely women. Later there were boasts that, with thirteen thousand in attendance, it was the largest of any state conference. The registration process was swamped, and the vast majority of attendees had not read the national report, '*To Form a More Perfect Union . . .*' I registered and pinned on my name tag, not realizing it was upside down, and wandered around in the crowd waiting for sessions to begin. The women milling about regarded me with suspicion until Leonard Arrington, the well-known Mormon historian, came along. He greeted me cheerily and loudly, "Hello, Alison. How are you?" Instantly the woman nearest me smiled and told me, kindly, that my name was upside down.

My general impressions were as follows: The ERA was shouted down (as a person who raised my hand for "yes" on ERA I was branded by all those around me as a package of evil); rudeness to those conducting; taking over of workshops, not permitting planned programs to take place; men with walkie-talkies walking along the edge, representing the Mormon priesthood and telling their wives and other women what to do. The ultraconservatives had control. Vickie, with her dark skin, stood out in the crowd. I wondered why more Black women had not come. Voting machines stood in a great hall. Women carried Phyllis Schlafly material and voted down every resolution the national commission had put forth—even voting down action against rape. Appalling to feel the hatred. Appalling to witness unquestioning obedience to male authority.[14]

The most thoughtful accounts of what happened were written by Linda Sillitoe and by Dixie Snow Huefner. They speculated over whether the LDS Church was duped by the ultraconservatives, or was it willing to be influenced, considering the fact that Ezra Taft Benson was highly sympathetic to far right views.[15]

There was an interval when I walked out of the Salt Palace and over to Temple Square to the Relief Society monument; my heart was full of sorrow. I knew in the depth of my being that my great-great-grandmother, Louisa Barnes Pratt, and my grandmother, May Hunt Larson, believed in equal rights for women. My loyalty to the church and to Relief Society was being shattered.

We stayed overnight with Anne Hatch's parents, wonderfully hospitable people, but we left the meetings early on Saturday afternoon because the atmosphere was chaotic and filled with hate. Emma Lou Thayne was heartsick, and in a column in the *Deseret News* she compared the Salt Palace meetings with "Hands Across the Valley."

> As in Logan, the steering committee was made up of honest, thoughtful women from all walks of life. Housewives, mothers, professional people, they had given hours and hours in months prior to the conference, attempting to isolate the credible concerns of all kinds of women in Utah. The whole thing was planned as an opportunity for women in the state to get to know each other and help each other . . .
>
> But there was no coming together, there was only an assembling . . .
>
> Much of the contingent that poured in for a last minute say in the proceedings came, unfortunately, armed with preconceptions, informed prejudice and a schooled determination to scuttle everything . . .
>
> And so much of the pillage was done in the name of God-fearing chastening . . . and everyone ended up losing (except perhaps the American party, who in a post conference flyer declared the sacking a victory!)
>
> . . . if we want to cradle freedom and respect for individual differences, we must find ways to come peaceably together for friendly persuasion.
>
> Logan did it. The hotbed that was Cache valley now teems with newly formed interfaith planning groups, downtown/university task committees, rural/urban discussion workshops preparing heartily for a better life together—and for another conference next year.
>
> Why can't that happen here?[16]

All my life I had assumed that the LDS Church urged members to vote, but left it up to individuals to decide for what or whom they would vote. I was horrified to learn that in the name of the church, Mormon women also sought to dominate and scuttle the IWY meetings in Texas, Washington, Idaho, Montana, and Hawaii.

In spite of, or perhaps because of the Salt Palace debacle, most Utah Democrats continued to favor the Equal Rights Amendment. Wynne and I attended the state Democratic convention in August because I helped write the human rights resolution which included the ERA, and we wanted to see it adopted. When each resolution came up for discussion, only one brief affirmative and one brief negative comment could be made from the floor.

I held my breath on the fifth resolution: Resolved that: ". . . equality of rights under the law shall not be abridged by the United States or any State on the basis of sex, race, age, religion or national origin, and that those laws presently in effect in the State of Utah to guarantee equal opportunity in employment all be vigorously enforced . . ." The negative comment from the floor was an attempt to take out the word "sex." I gave the affirmative comment by telling of the recent United States Supreme Court decision that General Electric and other private businesses could drop maternity benefits of employees, while still paying gender-related employee benefits such as men's hair transplants and vasectomies. I said this was discrimination against women. Had ERA existed, the Supreme Court could not have so ruled. Fortunately the Department of Health, Education, and Welfare's Office for Civil Rights ruled that this decision did not apply to Title IX regulations. This meant public schools and colleges could not drop maternity benefits because the Title IX regulations were signed by the president and reviewed by Congress in 1975. The Utah Democratic convention voted overwhelmingly in favor of the human rights resolution, keeping the word "sex" in it.[17]

National IWY Women's Conference, Houston

In the meantime, preparations went ahead for November's national women's conference in Houston. Thirteen of the fourteen Utah delegates elected to attend were Mormons, including Belle Spafford, former Relief Society president. There was only one ethnic minority. All were anti-ERA. However, they realized they could not go to Houston saddled with the votes against *all* national resolutions, so after holding hearings they modified their stand somewhat on such issues as credit, child abuse, rape, and battered women. The National IWY Commission had power to appoint delegates-at-large to "balance" representation, and in Utah's case, they did exactly that.

The commission appointed nine delegates-at-large for Utah to counterbalance the state-elected slate of fourteen, who were all against the

DELORIS BENNETT, Alison Thorne and Anne Hatch discuss the IWY national convention which opens in Houston today. The three are among the Utah women attending, Mrs. Bennett as one of the 14 state delegates, and Mrs. Thorne and Mrs. Hatch as observers. The three discussed their thoughts on the convention for The Herald Journal. (Herald Journal photo)

ERA. The delegates-at-large would sit in a separate section but would have the same voting privileges as the state-elected delegates. The national commission wanted to record their outrage that some states were not fair to their citizens, that in some states there was apparent control by right wing groups. Alabama, almost 30 percent black, had an all-white delegation.

Among Utah's delegates-at -large were Esther Landa, president of the National Association of Jewish Women, who conducted our state IWY meetings; Kathleen Flake who attended the international meetings in Mexico City and was now a law student at the University of Utah; Reba Keele, a BYU professor; and Lynne Van Dam, a writer and editor who defended ERA and was booed down at the state meetings.

The four of us who drove together to the Salt Palace meetings decided that we would go to Houston as observers, staying with my daughter Sandra, who lived there and also wanted to attend the meetings. But there were rumors of possible violence from far rightists, and Ione, who tended to have high blood pressure, decided not to go. Vicki Coleman was writing her doctoral dissertation for Rutgers University and felt she could not take the time. So that left Anne Hatch and me to make the trip.

To curb possible violence at the meetings, observer passes were required, and they were hard to come by. I managed to get one ahead of time from Gunn McKay, the Utah Congressman who was a conservative Democrat.[18] When we arrived at the conference, Utah friends gave us two more, so Anne Hatch, Sandra, and I became legitimate observers. Delores Bennett of Logan was one of the fourteen elected Utah delegates, and we had been friendly through years of community work. She was always strong in the Republican Party, but we had a habit of laying aside our party politics when they got in the way of community work. The *Herald Journal* interviewed Delores, Anne, and me about the coming Houston meetings and ran a picture of us.[19]

Before the meetings Delores gave me a flyer which outlined the position of the elected delegation on certain national issues, but the delegates-at-large in Salt Lake City had difficulty getting a copy. The elected delegates certainly were not happy that delegates-at-large existed. When the elected delegates passed candy during the flight to Houston, it stopped short of the delegates-at-large in the back of the plane.

At the Salt Palace meetings in Utah, the air had crackled with suspicion and 80 percent of attendees voted against the ERA. At Houston there was much more courtesy, and 80 percent of the delegates voted in favor of ERA. As a feminist and a liberal, I felt as though I had come home at last, and I heaved a sigh of relief. A nineteen-year old Smith College student who was a delegate to Houston from Maine said, "Now I know that all those other women feel the same way I do, if they call themselves feminists then that's what I am too."

The Texas delegation sat at the very front, to the left in the large hall of the Coliseum. The elected Utah delegation was directly behind them, bearing their "pro-family" standard, which irritated some of us because we had families too, and we cared deeply about them. Indeed, concern over legal rights of homemakers was one of the national resolutions. The delegates-at-large clustered at the back. Those of us in the slanting balconies could see better than the delegates-at-large, who were seated on the flat floor. Delores Bennett sometimes climbed the stairs to tell me how things were going because observers were not allowed on the floor. I was grateful for her kindness.

The one resolution that passed almost unanimously brought the Texas and Utah delegations to their feet to hug each other. It was the resolution on the rights of racial and ethnic minorities, which had been rewritten by the third of the delegates who were Black, Hispanic, Native American, and Asian American. It is important to note that these minorities were represented at the conference from one and a half to three times their occurrence in the general population. Gloria Steinem had worked with these women through two days and a sleepless night, helping them rewrite the resolution so it described their common experiences while preserving the special issues of each group. Later Steinem would look back on those two days as the emotional highpoint of her writing career.[20]

Resolutions came up in alphabetical order, which put the ERA fairly early on the agenda. Mary Ann Krupsak, lieutenant-governor of New York and a member of the national commission, was conducting the plenary session when the ERA came up. In fact, as a national commission member, she had attended our Salt Palace meetings, where she was not well treated. Krupsak called for the "aye's," and after an overwhelming vote in favor there were jubilant surges in the aisles and around the hall. Wisconsin delegates carried their banner, "Women's Rights, American as Apple Pie." Krupsak then turned the gavel over to her vice-chair, Esther Landa of Utah, who called for order. Esther was able to get the delegates back into their seats and called for the "no" vote, which was small. She brought down Susan B. Anthony's gavel, as she announced that the resolution favoring the ERA passed. The Smithsonian Institution had loaned the gavel that Anthony used at the 1896 conference on woman suffrage.

As expected, the other two most controversial issues were reproductive choice and sexual preference, which fortunately came toward the end of the alphabet, when some people were getting tired. Both resolutions passed. It was a historic moment when Betty Friedan, who had long argued that endorsing lesbian rights would hurt the women's movement, took a microphone to announce that lesbians are entitled to civil rights. After the conference we heard dire warnings that the issues of abortion and homosexual rights would be associated with ERA and prevent the ERA from getting the final three states needed for ratification. This would prove prophetic.

There were delightful moments at the conference: Great pleasure when the torch came in that had been carried twenty-six hundred miles from Seneca Falls, New York, through fourteen states, by runners who began September 29. They wore light blue T-shirts with "Women on the Move" above the IWY dove. We bought T-shirts for ourselves, and over the next few years on the day that I discussed the Houston meetings in women's studies class, I wore that T-shirt. On the stand at Houston were illustrious women, including the presidents' wives, Rosalynn Carter, Betty Ford, and Lady Bird Johnson. Among the luminaries who spoke were Barbara Jordan, Margaret Mead, and Jean Stapleton.

It was a colorful conference with tri-cornered hats worn by delegates from Washington D.C., Hawaiians in colorful long gowns, Californians waving yellow neck scarves, New Yorkers holding up apples. There were balloons and lapel pins of great variety. At various locations we saw women's art displays, women's studies meetings and materials, job placement booths, and a film festival. In the exhibition hall, Utah was the only state with two separate exhibits. The one organized by our IWY coordinating committee, with funds from the Utah Endowment for the Arts, showed a slide tape of women in Utah history. The exhibit set up by the elected delegation had brochures about Utah today, and flyers stating their position on national issues.

We were in meetings for a long time on Saturday. After the morning session, Anne, Sandra, and I went out to lunch, but then we returned and remained in the Coliseum from one until nearly midnight. Rumor had it that the radical right from the Astroarena were milling around the Coliseum, and we should keep our seats. This later turned out to be exaggerated.[21]

Gail Sheehy has compared the leadership and behavior at the conference with those of the counter rally held at the Astroarena. She wrote that the anti-feminists were a pro-family and pro-life coalition. "The signal feature of the audience was its white-bread homogeneity. . . . The striking feature of the leaders was that most of them were men. The only two Black faces noticeable in the entire assemblage were also up on the stage." Sheehy described Robert MacNeil's interview with Eleanor Smeal and Phyllis Schlafly for the MacNeil/Lehrer TV Report. MacNeil surprised both of them with a national Roper poll showing that only 20 percent of those polled identified with the anti-ERA movement and with Phyllis Schlafly. Smeal, who was president of NOW, thought for a moment and then smiled, because that was the percentage of opinion at the conference. Schlafly spent five minutes berating MacNeil, Lehrer, and the Roper poll. Afterwards, MacNeil was livid. "I've been reporting for many, many years," he said, his voice shaking with contempt, "and I just want to tell you that's one of the cheapest shots I've ever heard. I respect your right to say your piece, but there was a lot of meat in that poll, and we didn't get to it because of the time you took for your cheap accusations."[22]

In contrast to Schlafly, who epitomized anti-feminism, Bella Abzug was a guiding light. As congresswoman from New York she, along with Patsy Mink of Hawaii, had gained congressional support for Public Law 94-167, which funded the state conferences. I first saw Abzug before the national conference in Houston began, when she came in, through a light drizzling rain, with the runners who carried the torch. Someone said, when Abzug joined the run for the last couple of blocks, "Slow down, Bella can't keep up." But she more than kept up on the Coliseum platform, whether conducting or just sitting. At one point she lost her glasses and was poking about in her things and patting her pockets, when a Texas delegate motioned that they were lodged on top of her hat. A ripple of laughter went through the audience as Bella reached up, dislodged the glasses, and grinned. Her hats were her trademark at a time when women rarely wore hats.

Two years later, Abzug spoke on our campus, at convocation, which was held every Thursday in the large auditorium of the Fine Arts building. Before she went on stage, I urged a strong pitch for ERA. She did make a strong pitch—not that it did much good, because faithful Mormon sentiment was strongly against. Faculty member Dan Jones arranged for Abzug to speak to his large political science class and invited me to come, a pleasant enough invitation except that he warned me not to start controversy by speaking out in the question period. Oddly enough, Dan asked me for a bit of information in the question period. I gave the answer. No controversy resulted.[23]

Abzug chaired the National Advisory Commission on Women, created after the Houston meetings to advise President Jimmy Carter on legislation coming out of the National Plan of Action, which consisted of the twenty-five resolutions, ranging from arts to welfare, and passed at the Houston conference. But Abzug proved too outspoken for Carter, and he replaced her with Marjorie Bell Chambers, national president of AAUW.

I heard Chambers speak at Weber State College in Ogden when she said it was hopeless to pursue ERA in Utah and advised our AAUW branches to drop the effort. "If you must work for ERA," she said briskly, "go join the League of Women Voters." Here was the sensitive matter of the relationship of a national organization to its local members. AAUW had played an excellent coordinating role at the Houston conference and continued nationally to support all twenty-five resolutions.[24] All the eggs were not in one basket because ERA was only one of those resolutions, and feminism would persist along many fronts.

Sex and Gender in the Social Sciences

On campus our women's studies program found a home in the College of Humanities, Arts, and Social Sciences (HASS) when Dean William F. Lye offered us secretarial help, drawers in a filing cabinet, and funding for leaflets listing our courses. How pathetic, looking back, were those little bits of help for which we felt so grateful.

At the meeting where the amenities were offered, I was elected chair of the women's studies committee. We voted to accept the amenities, and we decided to try for a research grant from the Women's Educational Equity Act Program administered by the U.S. Department of Education. Dean Lye encouraged seeking such a grant and promised equipment, space, and other help if we got one. This act is another example of a national resource that could be used to make local headway in the women's movement and in women's studies.[25] Grants were the coin of legitimacy in higher education, as well as sanctions such as those of Title VII of the Civil Rights Act and Title IX of educational amendments to the act, which created affirmative action programs.

Over the summer we persuaded Judy Gappa and Jan Pearce to be codirectors of the project and major authors of the proposal. I wrote the justification, and Glenn Wilde, associate dean of HASS, worked out budget details. Our intent was to get women's issues into introductory courses in history, political science, and economics. Current classes would be reviewed, and then guidelines created for suggested curriculum content, and for making classroom interaction more equitable.

In April we received a Women's Educational Equity Act grant for $94,000, the largest grant the College of HASS had ever received. We were astonished when the Political Science and History Departments refused to participate in our project to mainstream women's issues. They assailed us in a joint department meeting, saying that if they let our representative sit in on their courses to look at course content and teaching methods, then they would have to let the John Birchers do it too. They never did come aboard. According to them we were a threat to academic freedom. We didn't argue. We simply asked the Sociology and the Psychology Departments if they would participate instead, and they said yes. The Economics Department had said yes from the very beginning.

The Sociology and Psychology Departments each appointed a graduate student to survey recent introductory texts, but the Economics Department was not so accommodating, so I did it myself. That was fine because I had the time, and I was wondering why it was so hard to bring women's issues into that particular field. I thought that reading current introductory texts might give me some clues.[26]

Codirectors Gappa and Pearce created a national advisory task force with a distinguished scholar from each field: Barbara B. Reagan, professor of economics, Southern Methodist University; Nancy F. Russo, administrative office for women's programs of the American Psychological Association; and Barrie Thorne, associate professor of sociology at Michigan State University. Also on this task force were two USU people: James P. Shaver, director of the Bureau of Educational Research in the College of Education; and Abelina N. Megill, director of special services for disadvantaged students. Marilynne Glatfelter, psychologist in the USU counseling service, and I, as an economist, were special consultants.

The task force and consultants met together on our campus in October 1979 and again in May of the next year, to discuss how to create gender sensitivity through course content and classroom interaction. These were tremendously exciting meetings. Barrie observed to me, with satisfaction, that Jim Shaver was not a sexist. I agreed with her.

By 1980 the guidelines were written and ready to be field tested. Judy Gappa had accepted a position as associate provost at San Francisco State University and arranged for testing to be done in eight colleges and universities in California. By December the testing was complete and the project took the final form of three loose leaf notebooks, one for sociology, one for psychology, and one for microeconomics. Each bore the title *Sex and Gender in the Social Sciences: Reassessing the Introductory Course.*[27]

The material on classroom interaction was the same in all three documents. The difference lay in suggested curriculum content. The content pages contained the best references that the task force knew, fitted into major topics of each field. In spite of Barbara Reagan's and my valiant attempt to pull together feminist content for microeconomics, it was obvious that the disciplines of sociology and psychology were more open to women's issues than economics. The sociology curriculum covered ninety-two pages; psychology, forty-eight pages; and microeconomics, only twenty-five. Even before we undertook this Women's Educational Equity Act project, the professions of sociology and psychology made position statements on sex and gender, but such a statement did not occur in the economics profession until 1990.[28]

Why was economics so far behind in this respect? The answer is complex. For one thing the percentage of women in the field was low. Also, economics claimed to be more scientific than other social sciences, but this claim hid subtle discrimination which eventually would be unveiled along with outright sexist bias and neglect.[29] And economics was dominated by one theory, the neoclassical, whereas sociology and psychology had many conflicting paradigms, theories, epistemologies, and methods. They were less bounded as disciplines and therefore more permeable.

Wynne's Death

It was a day in November when we finished writing the Women's Educational Equity proposal. Judy Gappa dropped me off at my house, stopping to join me where Wynne was busy planting daffodil and tulip bulbs under our front windows. He leaned on his shovel and the three of us visited together, unaware that Wynne would not live to see the tulips emerge the next spring. He came home ill from a trip to the Middle East in December, was diagnosed in late January as having cancer of the liver, and died February 15, 1979, at the age of seventy. Some of the family had come home for Christmas, but we did not know then how serious his condition was. Later each of our sons and daughters came and stayed for a time with me in Salt Lake City where he was hospitalized.

We were staggered by Wynne's death. I ached emotionally and physically. Yet I knew that hard work would get me through the shock better than anything else, and I knew that Wynne would not want me to go to pieces. His daffodils and tulips bloomed in the spring, a brave blooming against remnants of snow.

The first year after Wynne's death was rough for me, but letters went back and forth and I visited with various members of the family. I especially appreciated the October and May task force meetings when Barrie came to campus.

Sonia Johnson and the ERA

Sonia Johnson was twelve years old when her family moved to the First Ward of Logan. We moved to the First Ward three years later, and we, too, attended the LDS Church located just across the street from us, a church of red brick with white pillars on its wide front porch. The chapel has high arched windows, and at the front is Everett Thorpe's painting of a blue-gowned pioneer woman holding a baby. She stands beside a covered wagon that has a patchwork quilt smoothed over the bed inside. Seagulls circle above, and in the distance are gatherers of wheat. I always thought how very tired the woman looks, but Sonia saw more. Her poem about this woman ends: "and you, my pioneer sister/ with your grave and steady eyes/ who knew so well what there was to fear/ and feared not."[30]

When we moved to the First Ward, I began teaching the Sunday School class for young people. Sonia was in this class, and I found her warm and unusually intelligent. After her marriage she lived various places. It was while she was living in Virginia that the drama began that would sweep her along toward excommunication.

Her father, Alvin Harris, phoned me one evening to tell me that Sonia was on television. This regarded her verbal exchange with Senator Orrin Hatch in Washington, D.C. *The Salt Lake Tribune* of August 5, 1979, carried this story, which I paraphrased in a family letter.

> Sonia maintained that a substantial number of female members of the Mormon Church oppose the church's mandated opposition to the Equal Rights Amendment. They listed Sonia as being from Sterling, Virginia. Hatch said, 'You'll have to agree that in the Mormon Church almost 100 percent of the women are against the ERA.'
>
> Sonia: 'Oh my goodness, I don't have to admit that. It's simply not true.'
>
> Hatch: 'Yes it is. I'd be surprised if the Mormon women who are for ERA would constitute one-tenth of one percent.'
>
> They argued back and forth and Mrs. Johnson said she represents a loosely organized 'underground' group called 'Mormons for ERA' which has considerable support among Mormon women around the country. Many are willing to provide financial assistance but want to remain anonymous because they are afraid of what the church will do to them.
>
> Subcommittee chairman Senator Birch Bayh asked Mrs. Johnson whether she expected difficulty within the Mormon Church because of her strong statements on behalf of the ERA. 'I hope there won't be,' she replied. 'So do I,' Bayh said . . .[31]

Mormons for ERA grew even as LDS church spokesmen variously indicated that women would, and then would not, lose their temple recommends if they joined the organization. The *Salt Lake Tribune* of November 27, 1979, carried a large advertisement with 258 names on it, which said, in various sizes of print and capitals:

> This week we're thankful for our American freedom. Next week we might not be so lucky . . .

> On December 1, in Sterling, Virginia, Dr. Sonia Johnson will be tried in a Mormon Bishop's Court—a proceeding which could result in her excommunication. Sonia's bishop has charged her with influencing people to move away from the church's counsel, hampering church missionary effort and spreading false doctrine. It is stated that Sonia's words and actions on the Equal Rights Amendment are undermining the support of the Prophet.

> Sonia is only speaking her conscience!

> In denying free agency for Sonia, the Bishop's Court threatens the First Amendment freedom for all Mormons. When this freedom is suppressed by any group in our society, it affects everyone. Sonia doesn't want to leave her church. Nor will she abandon her principle. We believe she shouldn't have to make that choice. We urge the First Presidency of the Church of Jesus Christ of Latter-Day Saints to examine the issues in this case and

> Exonerate Sonia Johnson.

> The Following People Support the Review of the Sonia Johnson Case:

Then followed 258 names. Mine was one of them.[32]

Obviously we and other defenders of Sonia carried no weight with the church authorities. On December 1, Sonia Johnson was excommunicated. The next day a hundred people rallied in Salt Lake City at the federal building. Esther Landa was a particularly strong speaker, indicating among other arguments that many women's rights advocates across the country were outraged that Sonia was denied her right to freedom of speech or freedom of expression.[33]

Sonia wrote eloquently of her excommunication, and so did Linda Sillitoe and Paul Swenson in their article for *Utah Holiday*, which included a touching picture of Sonia, with her mother on one side and Esther Peterson on the other clasping her protectively on that bitter cold night in Virginia, on their way to the trial.[34] Sonia appealed, but the First Presidency in Salt Lake City turned down her appeal on June 30, 1980.

One evening three months later, I had a phone call from Sonia saying she would like to speak at USU and would do it without the regular fee. "People in Logan think I am of the devil," she said, "but if they can listen to me, they might find out that they are mistaken. I would like an opportunity to speak in my home town." So I approached a student body officer and a faculty member who were on the committee that arranged convocations, but they were not interested in facilitating any appearance of Sonia Johnson. USU might be a public institution but it has always been obvious to me that it listens to official Mormondom. Sonia was *persona non grata*. The support that I needed came from the women's movement on campus. We decided that I would arrange for a place, and on the stand would be Patricia Gardner, Marilyn Glatfelter, and me. One of our strong pro-ERA Mormon women offered to sit with us, but I said no, because I didn't want to jeopardize the high regard that Mormons had for her, and Mormons were essential to her work. I was inactive in the LDS church.

I wrote my family that Sonia Johnson blitzed Cache Valley. I was with her for two days. I introduced her to the Presbyterian adult Sunday school class on Sunday morning. Because her folks lived just across the street from the Presbyterian Church, and slightly east, we only had to walk a short distance.

Earlier there had been an article in *Savvy* magazine (women's executives' magazine) written by Chris Rigby Arrington. The Rigbys lived across the street west from the Presbyterian church. The article was about Sonia, and Sonia's mother loaned me her copy, so I could copy it for Chris's mother and for my own family. It included a description of fast meeting in the First Ward.

On Monday I took Sonia to two different sociology classes. We had lunch with several women feminists on campus and a woman reporter for the *Herald Journal*. At twenty minutes to five in the afternoon, I picked up Sonia and her mother, and another car took her son and brother Mike and her sister. We arrived at the business building to find the business auditorium jammed and people out in the halls. Fortunately it had a good loudspeaker system, and those in the halls could hear. As tried and true Mormons got offended (after the first hour) and left, others slid into their seats, so the seats were always full during the two hours we were there, with people still seated on the floor of the carpeted aisles.

I introduced Sonia by saying I had always believed in women's rights, giving something of my own Mormon background and of my kids growing up in the First Ward where Sonia grew up. In the early 1970s the women's movement came to USU. I had asked the counseling and testing service why they had no women on the staff, and they said, "Women like to be counseled by men." (Laughter.) Then I said Marilynne Glatfelter was the first woman to join their staff. Marilynne, bless her heart, made trips from down in front where we were, up the aisle into the hall, to get a paper cup of drinking water for Sonia. It was terribly hot in the auditorium. I also introduced Pat Gardner, who initiated women in literature classes and had succeeded me as chair of the Women's Studies Committee. Then I said that we three women faculty took the responsibility for this public meeting, and as women who believe in women's rights we wanted the audience to hear from another woman who believed in women's rights.

The audience was obviously split. The anti-Sonia forces tried to bait her during the question period, but she was too skilled for them. The beginning question asked for the wording of the ERA, and Sonia who, I had discovered, carried it on a card in her purse was going to go over and get her purse, but I rose to my feet, took the microphone and quoted it slowly and effectively from memory. (Applause). A good thing I did, because she would have broken the spell she had cast if she went as far as her chair and purse. Sonia was absolutely the best speaker I had heard in my life. Three male political scientists returned to their department after hearing her, still spellbound. (So maybe the trip to chair and purse would have been all right).

The verbal opposition was mostly male. The pro-Sonia was mostly female hand clapping. There were some anti-Sonia hecklers who whispered and made remarks but were promptly shut up by those who said, "Be quiet, we want to hear what she has to say." After the first hour I saw a number of older people leave, obviously offended.

Sonia told about the Virginia Mormons defeating ratification of the ERA and simultaneously defeating four pieces of state legislation women had worked hard for. One was a bill that gave a woman who had never worked property rights on her husband's death. Another was police power to pursue fathers who had abandoned their families and were not paying child support. These bills went down the drain.[35]

The best pictures of Sonia appeared on the front page of the Logan High School newspaper, *The Grizzly*.[36] Sonia had graduated from Logan High and was invited to speak there. The pictures and the news story reported her visit respectfully.

A lot of things happened in the next few years, but to make a long story short, Sonia tried to get on the ballot of the Citizen's Party in Utah for possible election as president of the United States. I signed her petition when Carol Clay brought it around. Sonia needed only three hundred names, most of them from Utah, Salt Lake, and Weber counties.

The county clerks in Utah and Weber counties did not verify the signatures and take the petitions to the Capitol, a fact discovered too late. In our county, the clerk promptly phoned his friends to tell them who had signed the petition. Ida Harris, Sonia's mother, was incensed because this was a breach of confidence that could cause bishops to call people on the carpet for signing the petition. Carol Clay phoned the county clerk and spoke harshly enough that he phoned back his friends to apologize.[37]

The Equal Rights Amendment died, unratified by the needed three states, in June 1982.[38]

My Mormon Connection

In spite of being a fifth generation Mormon, I left the LDS Church in 1989. Barrie had been excommunicated a few years earlier. She suspects it was because of the audacity of her book *Rethinking the Family: Some Feminist Questions.*[39] My other daughters, my sons, and I requested to have our names removed from the membership rolls. This was done by our local bishops. In the 1990s the church excommunicated and disfellowshipped a number of liberal intellectuals and feminists, and that's precisely what we are.[40] Barrie says we are "ethnic Mormons" because we have a warm appreciation of our Mormon heritage, but we strongly disagree with certain aspects of Mormon theology, and we require more freedom of thought than today's LDS authorities permit.

Without trauma I moved from the Mormon Church and joined the First Presbyterian Church of Logan because of their long history of working for good causes, because they encourage freedom of thought and expression, and because I have always had close friends there. I find it possible to be both an "ethnic Mormon" and a Presbyterian. My friends in the First and Fifth Wards are still my friends, especially those who were rearing their children when Wynne and I were rearing ours.

The continuing tie between the Mormon church and the Republican party is troubling. Thad Box, who is retired from USU, writes a column for the local *Herald Journal.* After writing a column on the tie between church and political party, he was surprised that he received no negative comment. The explanation seems to be that Mormons are so used to sustaining church authorities that they carry this habit over into their politics.[41]

11 The University, Women, and History

Women and International Development (WID)

It seemed to me that it snowed or rained every Monday of March and April 1980, as I made my way across campus to late afternoon meetings to plan a workshop on women and international development. This workshop was the response of the College of Family Life to the challenge of Title XII of the Foreign Assistance Act administered by the United States Agency for International Development (U.S. AID) The purpose of Title XII was to strengthen the university's ability to place people in foreign assistance assignments.

The Percy amendment to the Foreign Assistance Act urged projects which "tend to integrate women into the national economies of foreign countries, thus improving their status and assisting the total development effort." To date these had been empty words, but we hoped to give them some meaning. We titled our workshop, "The Work of Rural Women across the World," and held it May 1–3. It drew 120 men and women.[1] International women on our campus from Ethiopia, Zambia, India, and Mexico described rural conditions in their home countries, and we heard from our own husband-wife teams who had worked overseas.[2]

The College of Family Life did not have overseas projects as some colleges did, but we created a Women and International Development (WID) program that sponsored a cross-campus meeting every three weeks to hear speakers with experience in developing countries. We urged those with projects—irrigation engineers, range management specialists, animal husbandry specialists, and the agricultural education people—to pay particular attention to indigenous women's needs in countries where they were working. And we urged them to put women on their teams. This was easier said than done.

In early 1981, I became WID coordinator, a newly invented and unpaid position. Our meetings with invited speakers had as many as twenty-five present, including two deans. I also attended an orientation on Somalia for people from Utah State University and Colorado

State University, who were planning to go to Somalia for U.S. AID. The team included eleven male agricultural engineers and agricultural extensionists and their wives.[3] No woman was assigned to the Somalia team although I urged appointment of Flora Bardwell, extension nutritionist. I was told that the Ministry of Agriculture in Somalia refused to extend its scope to nutrition.

However, another project and very large one was the Second Phase of Water Management Synthesis, which advised U.S. AID projects worldwide on water resources and irrigation. Jack Keller of irrigation engineering, with anthropologist Jon Moris, included a strong WID component in it.[4]

Increasingly our WID turned its attention to needs of international women on our campus. The College of Family Life created a two-year applied science associate degree called Food and Family in International Development. The idea began when Afton Tew, a counselor in the international student office (much later she became director), stopped me one day to say there were international wives marooned in their apartments, who wanted to be in classes earning degrees. A degree carried real prestige in their home countries, but they couldn't afford the tuition and books. They often knew less English than their husbands, and the care of their small children meant they couldn't take a heavy class load. A two-year degree might be a partial solution.

With help of Title XII money we brought Nancy O'Rourke on board in a part-time position to work on this curriculum project, which was guided by a remarkable blue ribbon committee from across campus. Dean Joan McFadden of Family Life suggested that, during the slow process of getting the degree approved, we should go ahead and offer classes. During winter quarter 1983, there were special sections of two courses: Nutrition for People, and Child Guidance.

During spring 1983 the Agricultural Education Department offered Food Production, and Molly Longstreth and I taught a new course, Family Resource Management. Eleven international wives were in our class, from Nigeria, Cyprus, Iran, New Zealand, Japan, Korea, Mexico, Bolivia, and Brazil. Child care was provided, but one student brought her baby girl with large brown eyes and hair in tiny corn rows, and if she became fussy the mother simply nursed her, and then the baby napped.

Half of our students already had degrees from institutions in their home countries. One was a pharmacist and one had a degree in civil engineering. Several who studied mainly physical sciences before coming to USU became interested in social science, and one decided to make teaching home management her career. One student was an artist, with deep psychological understanding of people. Another student had operated her own day care center in her home country before coming here and would return to it. The center was her dowry, given to her by her mother when she married.[5]

By the end of summer the Board of Regents had approved our degree and further courses were designed as needed. I asked to step down as WID coordinator. Nancy O'Rourke succeeded me and continued to supervise the associate degree program. Her codirector was Maxine Stutler with ten years' experience in Latin America.[6]

Each year at USU, I continued to teach the introductory women's studies course and the graduate course "Family and Economic Change," which by now was filled with wonderful WID materials. Both courses continued to offer credit in two departments—Sociology, and Home Economics and Consumer Education (HECE). Our associate degree program was doing well. In December 1984 a full page *Salt Lake Tribune* article described the program, with pictures of Nigerian women and their children, and a picture of the codirectors.[7]

In January 1985 I was again teaching the international wives' course, "Family Resource Management," this time with Jean Lown because Molly Longstreth had taken a position at the University of Arizona. The husbands of our students were studying for doctorates in range management, agricultural education, irrigation engineering, sociology, and demography. The Departments of Irrigation Engineering and Range Management paid for tuition and books for their graduate students' wives. Jack Keller wrote in *Staff News,* "If spouses can study while here in the United States along with their husbands, it will increase their abilities at home. The education these women receive enhances the degrees earned by their husbands."[8]

International agricultural economists were meeting in Spain in early fall 1985 and I decided to go with Gertrude Gronbech, whom I had known for years—we had been graduate students together at Iowa State. She worked for the Department of Agriculture in Washington D.C. and attended these international meetings, which occurred every three years. I wanted to find out if women's work in agriculture was recognized. Not much, it turned out. The one exception was a workshop led by Irene Tinker on women's work in developing countries, from which I learned a great deal.[9]

At USU, funds for WID and our associate applied-science degree in Food and Family in International Development were drying up, and

HECE was hard pressed to continue help. Title XII funding from U.S. AID would cease July 1, 1986.

By September 1985 higher education and the public schools of Utah were in deep trouble because state taxes had not brought in expected revenue. The governor would not call a special session of the legislature because it was an election year. He ordered a new 3 percent cut. Jane McCullough, head of HECE, had already eliminated two undergraduate majors, and if our associate degree were eliminated, the department could manage. There simply were no matching funds to support our associate degree, and U.S. AID did not consider education of wives of international students to be important.

Six international women completed the associate degree, and then it vanished. Sixteen had enrolled altogether, but fortunately some who began the program were able to work toward a bachelor of science degree instead.[10] The Sociology Department took over the WID program and the WID library, and sociologist Pam Riley, with extensive international experience, began teaching a well-attended course on women and international development. So our early efforts were not in vain.

Historical Papers and a Promotion

I got to wondering why so little had been written about the history of women in land grant colleges, so I wrote this paragraph:

> Land grant colleges began in a variety of settings. Michigan's began very early, in a forest. The Kansas college was four stone buildings and a president's house set in a prairie with buffalo bones bleaching in the sun. Utah's college was placed on sagebrush benchland with a canyon behind it, the source of stiff morning winds and irrigation water.[11]

I put this into a family letter and said it was the beginning of a paper about women and home economics in the history of land grant colleges that I would present at the women's research conference to be held at the University of Utah in October.

Earlier that year (1984), as I contemplated turning seventy years old, I decided I'd better see if I could move from lecturer to professor emeritus because I'd heard of cases on other campuses where women who had been lecturers for twenty years were summarily fired and disappeared forever. I thought I was worth a higher status than lecturer and wrote a letter to the two department heads for whom I was teaching.[12]

Little action occurred until October, the month I presented my paper at the University of Utah conference. Dean Joan McFadden had left USU to become executive director of the American Home Economics Association. She would be there for five years and then return to USU. Bonita Wyse was by then dean of the College of Family Life. She appointed a promotion advisory committee for me, with Jon Moris of anthropology as chair. The others were Don Dwyer, head of range science; Larzette Hale, head of accounting; Eastman Hatch, professor of physics; and William Stinner, professor of sociology.

Dean Wyse told me to gather up all my materials for consideration, and in due course the committee recommended full professor status. My age made it professor emeritus. I came under the paragraph on "exceptional cases" in "Guidelines for Tenure and Promotion." The committee's letter of recommendation included a sentence about my "developing two new courses, one on sex roles and the other on women in development at a time when they were not yet fashionable and when there was no precedent to follow."[13]

In the meantime I pursued the matter of women and land grant colleges, showing how often women were invisible. A month after giving my paper at the University of Utah, I repeated it for the Logan branch of the American Association of University Women at a public meeting held in the Logan City offices. A very good crowd attended. There was a lot of back and forth discussion as I proceeded because so many of the women had had matching experiences. It was an exciting meeting.

Sarah Ann Skanchy, who was on the city council and not a faculty wife, said that military wives faced a similar situation. And Nancy Williams, younger than my generation, said she was at Los Alamos, and there were wives with masters degrees and higher and absolutely no employment available to them, and consequently there was a lot of alcohol abuse.[14]

For the *Seventy-second Faculty Honor Lecture*, which I was invited to give, I elaborated on my paper on women in land grant colleges. The first woman to give the lecture had been Almeda Perry Brown, research associate professor in home economics, who gave the third lecture in 1944, on the nutritional status of some Utah population groups. Fifteen years later another nutrition scientist, Ethelwyn Wilcox, gave the twentieth lecture on good nutrition for the family. Ethelwyn was the graduate student at Iowa State who loaned me her typewriter when the dorm fire destroyed mine. Another fifteen years later, in 1974, the third woman to give the lecture was Veneta Nielsen, a poet in the English Department. I would be the fourth woman, eleven years after Veneta.

The honor lecture was always printed before the event so it could be given out the evening of the lecture. It was always printed in a six by nine inch size with a paper cover, often in light blue, although mine was light green. The cover listed me as Professor Alison Comish Thorne. Most lectures didn't highlight rank on the cover, but this was the voice of women faculty telling the world that another woman had made it. In 1985 there were six women full professors at USU, not counting retired ones. In 1972, when the women's movement began on campus, there were also six. Not much progress, but we did have women in the pipeline.

The title of my lecture was "Visible and Invisible Women in Land-Grant Colleges, 1890–1940." Linda Speth, director of the Utah State University Press, edited my manuscript with great care and sensitivity, and I presented it October 8, 1985, in the Student Union auditorium.

My children came home ahead of time for it. We had lots of visiting and merriment and good meals, especially when Lance did the cooking. We spent Sunday at the cabin, a gorgeous day with autumn colors at their best.

On Tuesday I taught my Sex Roles class of fifty students and introduced Sandra and Carolee (Kip's wife), who were sitting back in a corner as spectators, while Barrie and Avril sat up front because they were to describe their research. Kip and Lance wanted to come but there just were not enough chairs. Barrie, who was on the faculty of Michigan State University, told about her work with school age children, and then told about Carol Gilligan's analysis of the way men tend to think, and the way women tend to think. Then Avril, who was on the faculty of Wellesley College, told about her research with introverts and extraverts, and that she had asked faculty why it matters whether people are one or the other.[15]

At the lecture that evening the family sat on the second row. I was out in the foyer greeting people, many of whom were retired faculty members and their wives. Younger faculty were there in overwhelming numbers and there were students. Jerrilyn Black of the American Association of University Women handed me a bouquet of pink and white carnations. All the board of Planned Parenthood were present. This was the night of their monthly meeting but they postponed it so they could come. The auditorium was filled. President Stanley Cazier and Shirley Cazier were there, the provost, vice-provost, assorted

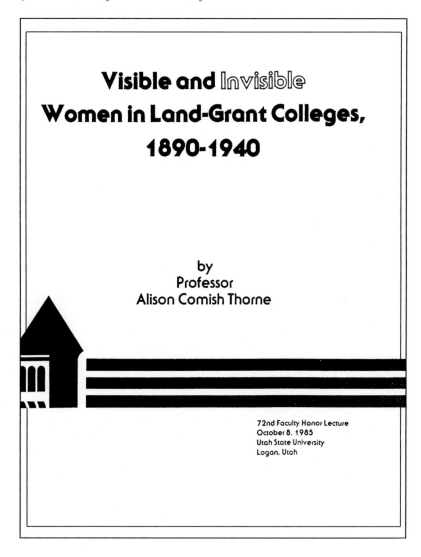

Visible and Invisible Women in Land-Grant Colleges, 1890-1940

by
Professor
Alison Comish Thorne

72nd Faculty Honor Lecture
October 8, 1985
Utah State University
Logan, Utah

deans, and the two men who had won the Wynne Thorne Research Awards at commencement.

Jane McCullough introduced me, and then I had the platform to myself. I stood behind an oak podium. It was all very informal. I spoke the lecture, reading only what was vital, ad libbed considerably, and from time to time the audience broke out into laughter. I invited questions at the conclusion and there were quite a few, some being not questions but comments, as when William Sigler of the College of

Natural Resources said he and his family survived six years in Ames, Iowa by making good use of the free buttermilk spigot.

Historical writing was becoming my thing because I had discovered how many unread sources there were. Faculty Women's League asked me to speak on the history of the league in commemoration of its seventy-fifth birthday. In preparing my paper I read all of the league's past minutes—fascinating stuff. Allie Burgoyne had given a historical paper, "Our University as I Know It," on the occasion of Faculty League's fiftieth anniversary in 1958. I found a copy of her paper in Wynne's files and made good use of it in both my Honor Lecture and my paper for the league. Ann Buttars of University Archives promptly photocopied Allie's paper for their collection.

The league paper became a long one, and when I finally presented it, on March 7, 1986, I could give only excerpts. It was heralded as part of Women's History Month. I considered it a unique paper because I concluded with thumbnail sketches of five women active in Faculty Women's League and in university affairs: Allie Burgoyne, Edith Bowen, Ethelyn Greaves, Almeda Perry Brown, and Jennie Israelsen.[16]

Commencements

When we were young, my sister Elaine and I sometimes attended commencement with our mother, walking across the Oregon State campus— usually it was sunny and warm—so we could watch our father march in cap and gown, and sense the excitement of crowds of people. So when I had my own youngsters I repeated the ritual, I suppose to imbue them with pride in the academic. I knew I was entitled to wear a doctoral gown and was a little envious of the marching faculty as I herded my young fry along the roadway between Old Main and the Field House.

Later I stopped taking them to campus, and myself sat with the wives of officials because Wynne was in administration. The Field House got very crowded and the ceremony got very long when Franklin S. Harris was president because he insisted that every graduate had the right to walk across the stand. Sometimes it got fearfully hot in the top of the balcony where many young mothers with babies sat, and I worried about them.

After the Spectrum, with its basketball floor and vast seating, was built, there was plenty of room for everyone. I especially remember the 1964 commencement because Juanita Brooks received an honorary doctorate. I sat beside Will Brooks in the reserved section, enjoying his

Pete Schropp/Herald Journal
Alison Thorne has long been active in the women's movement.

March 16, 1986, on the steps of the original west
entrance to the south wing of Old Main.

presence because he was one of the warmest and friendliest men I had
ever known. When the degree was conferred on Juanita—she looked
so small and so far away from us—I turned to Will and said, "We are
so proud of Juanita." He squeezed my arm and looked into my eyes
with those big brown eyes of his and said, *"Oh, we are proud of her!"*[17]

After Wynne's collapse on the stand at the 1971 commencement, he
refused to march again or sit on the stand, but made an exception in
1975 when he received an honorary doctorate. Wynne was often away
on international assignments at commencement time, so sometimes I
marched, wearing the Iowa State University hood that he bought when
he took his degree there. We never owned a gown. We rented.

After Wynne's death and the creation of the annual D. Wynne Thorne
Research Award, I tried never to miss commencements, even going in
1982 though I disapproved of the choice of the commencement speaker,

former USU student Paula Hawkins who was a United States senator from Florida. She was against the Equal Rights Amendment (ERA) and her talk was mostly about "see what a great woman I am, and anybody can do it in America," with quotations from even Herbert Hoover. She gave no consideration to current unemployment. Jane McCullough observed that Hawkins's talk was bound together with cliches.

Early on as commencement was planned, Dean Joan McFadden refused to help hood Hawkins because she had accomplished nothing of distinction to warrant such an academic honor. Joan told this to J. R. Allred, who was chair of the commencement ceremonies, and he was nonplussed. So Dean Lye of Humanities, Arts, and Social Sciences (HASS) did it in her place. A young woman receiving a master's degree in range management had taped ERA in white on the top of her cap.[18] My friends and I hoped that Paula Hawkins got a good look at that ERA as the young woman walked back to her place, diploma in hand.

In great contrast, we heartily approved when Esther Peterson spoke at the 1985 commencement and received an honorary doctorate. I wrote the citation, detailing her work in the labor, women's, and consumer movements. She had served under Presidents Kennedy, Johnson, and Carter and was then working for the United Nations on international guidelines for consumer protection. I described that commencement in a letter to Duncan Brite, retired from the history faculty and living in California. I thanked him for sending me materials for the citation, and then, because I knew he missed USU and wanted details, I wrote:

> Esther Peterson gave an excellent talk, and the audience
> responded at particular points with applause; afterwards she got a
> standing ovation! The only time any of us can recall that a com-
> mencement speaker received a standing ovation. She really took
> the Reagan administration to task. Had a nice sense of humor, and
> knew when to emphasize her LDS upbringing.

> Nancy O'Rourke and I had sent her the brochure for our associate
> degree in food and family in international development, and she
> had expressed an interest in meeting with our international wives
> who are students in the program. So we had lunch the day before
> commencement, as soon as she arrived on campus . . . Esther
> Peterson will be going to Nairobi in July to the international
> women's meetings, end of the International Women's Year Decade
> of the United Nations.

In her talk Peterson called herself "an old radical," a term I especially liked because I would like to be called that. Five years later, on her eighty-fifth birthday, Peterson was honored with a celebration attended by nearly one thousand people in a large and crowded hotel dining room in Salt Lake City. I was there and it was a delight for me to talk with her about the standing ovation she received at USU. She remembered.[19]

In the history of women honored at USU commencements, it is important to name May Swenson, the distinguished poet who grew up in Logan on Fifth North, in the shadow of Old Main. Hers was an excellent talk, given in 1987, and the women faculty were there in force to see the awarding of her honorary doctorate. Today she lies buried in the Logan cemetery across from the Spectrum where she received the degree, under the sky and trees she knew when young.[20]

I will close this description of commencements by telling of Tom Emery, the brilliant biochemist chosen in 1986 to receive the D. Wynne Thorne Research Award. This is our exchange of letters.

May 16, 1986

Dear Alison:

I was really honored to be named the recipient of the Wynne Thorne research award this year. As part of the award, President Cazier invited me to a commencement breakfast and to be on the platform at commencement. Of course, I was intending to accept when, upon reading the newspaper last night, I found that to do so would put me in a very hypocritical position. Several years ago I complained vigorously to President Cazier about Utah State University awarding honorary degrees to church authorities, but this year it has seen fit to award a degree to Gordon B. Hinckley, whose only claim to fame appears from the newspaper article to be as an LDS church official. I told President Cazier before that I would not attend USU commencement exercises so long as that policy was in effect, so my conscience will not allow me to sit on the platform with Mr. Hinckley. I sincerely hope that you can appreciate my position on this matter, whether or not you personally agree with it. I have written President Cazier explaining my position and the reason why I will not be attending commencement exercises this year, or any year until there is a change in university policy on this matter.

Sincerely,
(signed) Tom
Thomas Emery
Professor of Biochemistry

May 18, 1986

Dear Tom,

Congratulations on being the recipient of the D. Wynne Thorne Research Award. Bartell Jensen always phones me after the decision is made—not for my approval exactly, more as a point of information. But I do always give my approval, and particularly so in your case because I understand that you do excellent research.

I appreciate your objection to USU giving honorary doctorates to LDS Church officials simply because they are Church officials. If Wynne were here he would agree with you . . .

Wynne fought Church domination at Utah State Agricultural College in the early 1950s—that appalling situation of Governor Bracken Lee and the LDS official on the Board of Trustees who between them, with help from certain others, came close to destroying the College.

At a later date, when Juanita Brooks was to receive an honorary doctorate, a Church official was also receiving one. Because she had written *Mountain Meadows Massacre*, she was under a Church ban and could not speak at sacrament meetings or teach. Nor could her husband, Will. Wynne had to be out of town that Commencement, but I would be there as Wynne's wife, sitting with families of dignitaries. Wynne told me to make sure Juanita was not brought face-to-face with that Church official. I sat with Will and their son through the exercises, and at the luncheon afterwards, steered them to a table a safe distance from the Church people. There was no confrontation.

I am taking the liberty of sending a copy of your letter and of my reply to each of the children. They are all rebels, and will see how important it is to you to stand by your principles, and will recognize that they too have a legacy of this nature.

Sincerely,
(signed) Alison

On May 21st I received a brief handwritten note from Tom: "Thank you very much for your letter. I really appreciate your support!"

That year I did not attend general commencement but went to College of Science ceremonies afterwards. No top LDS authorities were there when Tom Emery received the D. Wynne Thorne Research Award.[21]

The USU Centennial

In some ways my view of the University's centennial is not that of the top officials because I am neither male nor a traditional Mormon. I was, however, a member of the Centennial Cornerstone Committee, and when the cornerstone of Old Main was opened and its contents displayed, I began to wonder what sort of ceremony graced the original laying of the stone.

Although the Territorial Legislature acted in 1888 to found the Agricultural College of Utah, the cornerstone was not laid until July 27, 1889. It seems to have been a quick affair. "The arrangements were hurriedly made in order to have the stone laid while members of the Board were in the city. There were present at the ceremonies, however, a large number of leading citizens of Logan. The Fireman's Brass Band furnished suitable music." Reverend Mr. Green offered prayer and Reverand Mr. Steeves, James A. Leishman, and the territorial governor spoke.[22] It appears to me that Mormons did not dominate the program. Governor Thomas, a federal appointee, was certainly not Mormon. No woman was on the program.

Among curious items in the small oblong tin box of the 1889 cornerstone is a voting registration slip indicating that bigamous and polygamous men could not vote. There is a pamphlet letter from Aaron DeWitt of Logan to his sister in England explaining the reasons why he left the LDS church with its "beastly, black hearted, bloody priesthood."[23] Apparently as counterbalance, there is a Deseret Sunday School Union leaflet on "Jesus as a Boy." There are business and trade items, coins, script, etc. Somebody put in horehound candy which stained some items brown.

A year later when the south wing of Old Main was ready to be occupied, and one week after its doors opened, a proper dedicatory ceremony was held in the auditorium on September 4, 1890. Territorial Governor Arthur Thomas planned it and among the speakers he invited Mrs. Sarah Walker Eddy, a Methodist of Salt Lake City, to speak on women and higher education. Governor Thomas was Methodist. Eddy spoke of the importance of women in the home, and went on to say that "every girl ought thoroughly to fit herself for some definite calling aside from the home." Her oratory brought much applause and the *Logan Journal* called it the most noted effort of the day. The governor commended her for her talk and offered her a job at the new college. She became professor of history.[24] The non-Mormon governor apparently had considerable power in designing the ceremony and appointing faculty.

Fifty years later, in 1938, the semi-centennial of Utah State Agricultural College was celebrated during President E. G. Peterson's administration. (Wynne and I moved to Logan a year later.) It began the morning of March 8 with a general assembly in Old Main auditorium. Prayers and all the talks were by men, predominantly Mormon. No woman spoke, but Miss Thelma Fogelberg played a piano solo, having been invited to do so because her mother, Vendla Bernston, was the first student to enroll at the A.C. Governor Henry H. Blood and former presidents of the college were among those who spoke. Chief exception to almost complete Mormon control of the program was Frederick P. Champ, president of the Board of Trustees, an Episcopalian, and a powerful figure in the business community. Following the general assembly, the cornerstone with its tin box was opened at noon.[25]

In June 1938 at commencement time there was a four day celebration of the semi-centennial with considerable attention to the topics of home and of family relations. Elder Stephen L. Richards of the LDS church spoke. Non-Mormon speakers from off campus included Dr. Paul Popenoe, then of considerable fame in the field of family relations. No woman speaker was on the main program even though home and family relations were major topics. One evening there was a musical program. The final day, June 7, was commencement with an address by Robert G. Sproul, president of the University of California. The cornerstone was closed and resealed at noon.

At the bottom of the printed program for the four days, almost as an afterthought and in small type, is this sentence: "Anne Carroll Moore of the New York Public Library Will Conduct a Clinic on Literature for Children on Monday and Tuesday in the Children's Room, Library."[26]

Even less visible than Anne Carroll Moore was Abby L. Marlatt, first professor of domestic economy at the A.C., who came from Kansas Agricultural College in 1890 with a master's degree in chemistry, and who left the A.C. in 1894. She received an honorary doctoral degree from Utah State Agricultural College in 1938. I learned this not from histories written on our campus, but from her biography in *Notable American Women*. By 1938 Marlatt had been director of home economics at the University of Wisconsin for thirty years. No one seems to know whether Marlatt actually made the trip to Logan to receive the honors.[27] When the cornerstone was closed and resealed at noon on June 7, 1938, it contained a new copper box measuring roughly twelve inches each way, to hold the original tin box with its contents, plus the many items added in 1938, including the yearbook of Faculty Women's League and the program of a concert that league sponsored. However, these two items are missing in the 1938 typed list of contents (invisible women again), even though these two items were, and still are, in the copper box.

Whereas the semi-centennial lasted three months, the hundred year celebration began a year early and lasted through 1988. The corner-stone was opened March 9, 1987, with a program immediately following in Old Main auditorium. Meanwhile contents of the box were put on display in Champ Hall by Jeff Simmonds, USU archivist and an Episcopalian. Because Mormons dominated the centennial, just as they dominated the semi-centennial, I am impelled to give Simmonds' religious affiliation.

As people gathered for the program in the auditorium it was a warm reunion of the LDS priesthood—joyful greetings male to male, the warm clasping of hands and touching of shoulders. I felt like an outsider and wondered why the university seemed owned lock, stock and barrel by Mormon men. But maybe I was just in the wrong corner of the auditorium. George Ellsworth, historian and chairman of the Cornerstone Committee, gave an excellent talk, the music was fine, and the historical slides interesting. People in the audience who had attended the 1938 celebration were asked to stand, and there were quite a few. I found this to be heart warming.

In April there was a centennial recognition dinner and a centerpiece opening conference, but women had scant share of the limelight. There were only three women out of thirty centennial recognition recipients, and only two women out of the twelve who read citations. On the first day of the centerpiece meetings the only mention of a woman was when an engineer spoke of Charlotte Kyle teaching English to engineering students.

Fortunately on the second day, Leonard Arrington in his plenary address gave considerable attention to Almeda Perry Brown and the field of nutrition, and to Mignon Barker (Richmond), the first Black woman to graduate from Utah State.

As for the workshops, there were twenty-two moderators, none of whom was a woman. Four women in the twenty-two sessions were recorders. I could not attend on the last day but phoned Maxine Stutler, who went. The workshops were on matters of extension and on international programs. Maxine and Marilyn Noyes sat through these. When John Neuhold later summarized the entire conference, he said the grass roots are women, who have no say in anything. I turned to Maxine and asked if she had said that, and she said yes.

Dean Peterson had certainly done his homework in more ways than one. He gave an excellent paper, the final presentation of the conference, and among the many subjects he touched on was the family. He said he had learned from Dean Bonita Wyse about single-headed families, substance abuse, the elderly, poverty, pay inequity, consumer problems, and management of resources. But this was only two paragraphs.[28]

That was the opening conference. One year later at the closing conference more women were involved than earlier although none played a major part. A fine observation, in my view, was Marilynne Glatfelter's commendation of the presence of older women students at the university.[29]

I really shouldn't complain about the treatment of women at the centennial because from the beginning I was a member of the Cornerstone Committee. I had seen the contents of the early tin box and the contents of the copper box of 1938. At 5 P.M. on March 7, three members of the Cornerstone Committee including me, George Ellsworth, and Richard Lamb, plus a handful of university officials, gathered to place centennial items in the capacious copper box of 1938.

Just before we began, I noticed that an issue of the USU alumni publication, *Outlook,* was slated to go in, and inside was a page interview of Karen Morse with her picture and remarks about the necessity of training more women scientists and engineers, so I wrote across the bottom "On Feb. 26, 1988, Karen Morse became the new dean of science."[30]

I also made sure that the Faculty Women's League yearbook was put into the box along with two programs of the Women's Center and material about women's athletics. Lots of other stuff went in of course, and then the small oblong tin box of 1889 with its hundred year old contents, and on top of everything the two USU flags that orbited the earth with Mary Cleave and Don Lind, astronauts who are USU alumni. Leona Duke, assistant to William Lye, vice president for public relations, packed the box, and I wrote down each item just before it went in. Then I rushed home to type what turned out to be a two and one-half page list which George Ellsworth showed the governor next day and which went into the box.

On the great day of March 8, a huge cake was cut and served with free ice cream in the Student Center. Students had filled two thousand blue and white balloons with 100th birthday on them, and these were tied all over the campus. The official ceremony was in The Fine Arts

Center's Kent Concert Hall, with an overture played by the USU Symphony, written by Dean Madsen of our faculty, and the governor spoke, as well as President Cazier. Then I walked across campus with friends to the cornerstone closing at Old Main. It was a day of surprising beauty with sunshine, blue sky, and snow on the mountains.

The Faculty Women's League yearbook that went into the box listed 296 members. Frances Richardson, league president, and her officers had sent out notice that those who paid their dues would have their names in the yearbook and therefore in the cornerstone. The yearbook also contained a brief history of league, written by Gwen Haws, faculty wife and USU Editor. At the end of the yearbook was a list of former league presidents, listed by their husbands' names. Looking it over I realized I had known all but one of them because the early ones were still living when I arrived in Logan.

Fifty years from now when the cornerstone is opened and posterity sees those 296 names, it may appear that Faculty Women's League was wonderfully successful. Well it wasn't, because only a handful of women were attending its meetings and it soon went out of existence. Other interests, including paid employment, claim women's time today, and it's a rare woman who wants to be known solely through her husband's position at the university.[31]

Besides the league yearbook, into the copper box went two items from Janet Osborne, director of the Women's Center. One was the program of the meeting, which honored community women of achievement who are over sixty-five. The other was the Women's Center program for National Women's History Month, March 1–31, 1988. The month began with a keynote talk by Karen Shepherd, founding editor of *Network,* "a monthly publication for progressive Utah women" published in Salt Lake City. Just reading my notes on her talk makes me want to redouble my efforts to make women visible. Karen Shepherd said, "The absence of women in history is as great a mystery as where the Mayans went . . . We must not let the curtain of forgetting fall again. One generation can lose it." Karen Shepherd, a Democrat, later was elected state senator, and in 1992 was elected to the United States House of Representatives, a great victory for Democrats of Utah and for women. However, she served only one term.[32]

The Women's Center sponsored various other programs during March, with Sara Weddington speaking at Convocation on the final day. Weddington was chief advisor to President Jimmy Carter on women and minority concerns and was the attorney who won the landmark United States Supreme Court case, *Roe versus Wade*, which legalized abortion.

I, too, gave a centennial lecture. It was on March 4 and I gave it to an overflow audience in a classroom in Old Main, after first touching for good luck the ancient podium that my father debated from in 1910, which survived the Old Main fire of 1983 and now stands in the Sociology Department.

The invitation to give this lecture came from my departments, HECE and Sociology, and from the Women and Gender Research Institute (WGRI). At Utah State University, WGRI is the single most important women's invention of the 1980s. It encourages women to do research and promotes research on gender-related issues. Such encouragement is needed because of "the still small number of women in academic positions at universities nation-wide, women's academic isolation, and the need to ensure that both men and women are integrated into and can maximally contribute to academe."[33]

I titled my lecture, "Family and Community Studies from a Feminist Perspective." I based it on early Utah Agricultural Experiment Station bulletins and some university extension records, and particularly highlighted the research and activism of Almeda Perry Brown, home economist and nutrition scientist, and of Carmen Fredrickson, sociologist. As for the "feminist perspective," I asked whether women were mentioned and whether they and what they did was considered important. The front cover of my published lecture carries the picture that Almeda Perry Brown placed on the front of her 1936 Agricultural Experiment Station bulletin—two girls standing back to back in cotton dresses, cotton stockings, and tennis shoes.

> Brown's fourth bulletin concerned the weight-height-age relationships of rural and urban school children. She found that urban children weighed more and were taller than rural children. The rural girls were lowest in weight for their height. Brown suggested the causes were environmental and not genetic . . . She found that essential vitamins were absent from rural children's winter diets, a matter of much concern.[34]

Brown's bulletins were published in the 1930s and reflected the poverty of the Depression. She also knew the rural poverty of the 1920s when she worked for the Extension Service in Cache and Box Elder counties. I judged Brown to be a feminist because she placed a picture of two girls on the cover of her bulletin, when she might have shown boys or a mixed group. As Extension agent she was seeking to support her own children, and she was active in the Business and Professional Women's Club (BPW), which favored the Equal Rights Amendment. When invited to be listed in *American Men of Science* she declined because it had not been renamed *American Men and Women of Science*.

Sociologist Carmen Fredrickson, coming later than Brown, was another advocate of social justice and women's equality at USU. These concerns are evident in the Experiment Station bulletins that she authored and co-authored. Like me, she belonged to the local Women's Legislative Council and encouraged its initiation of the "war on poverty" in the 1960s, and she and I worked together on the Governor's Committee on the Status of Women. Fredrickson began a course on women twenty years before the women's movement came to campus.

In summary, there were several women's issues at Utah State University in the 1980s and into the 1990s. The Women and International Development program (WID) originated in the Home Economics and Consumer Science Department of the College of Family Life, and in 1985 was transferred to Pam Riley and the Department of Sociology.

WGRI (The Women and Gender Research Institute), a campuswide activity, was created to encourage and provide funding for women doing research and for men and women researching gender issues.

Increasing interest in the place of women in the history of land grant institutions, particularly our own, resulted in a flurry of papers. Preceding the USU Centennial of 1987–88, I gave a Faculty Honor Lecture on "Visible and Invisible Women in Land-Grant Colleges, 1890–1940." I also wrote the history of Faculty Women's League for league's seventy-fifth birthday, and gave a centennial lecture on "Family and Community Studies from a Feminist Perspective," based on Utah Agricultural Experiment Station bulletins.

A quick survey of the founding ceremony of our institution, and the fifty-year celebration of 1938, and finally, the centennial, reveals that women played a very small part. Commencements occasionally included women who received honorary doctorates and were commencement speakers.

12 Gathering Up Loose Ends

As a woman, I believe that "gathering up loose ends" says something about knitting, or perhaps weaving. It is an intuitive feeling about finishing up, and I use it here to summarize diverse but important matters.

The National Government and Concern
for Social Justice

Utah Agricultural College had its origin in 1888 when the federal Hatch Act offered $15,000 for an experiment station, and the Utah Legislature voted to accept it and build an agricultural college as well. Land grant colleges were an invention for social justice, giving farm families and working people access to higher education. These institutions were designed to level the playing field. Over the years, federal funding played a varied role in university, state, and community affairs.

The history of federal action for social justice in the twentieth century shows some high points, beginning with the Progressive movement that brought anti-trust legislation, improved labor conditions, and introduced the first income tax, widows' pensions, prenatal clinics, the Pure Food and Drug Act, and dozens of other reforms. Jane Addams and Sophonisba Breckinridge in Chicago were only two of many women who were leaders in the Progressive movement. I have already described the women's club movement, and women's work through rural extension programs. Although women in the Progressive movement could not vote, they set the terms of political debate. Their goals, moreover, were not modest: They hoped to create a just society that protects the weak, rewards the inventive and restrains greed.

The next decade of intensified federal concern began in the 1930s with Franklin D. Roosevelt's New Deal programs. The Wagner Labor Relations Act guaranteed the right of workers to join unions and bargain collectively. The Social Security Act of 1935 brought security to the elderly and programs for the poor. Margaret Reid's rural housing survey in Iowa had Works Projects Administration (WPA) funding and became background for the Rural Electrification Act. The Civilian

Conservation Corps brought young men to the West to terrace mountain slopes, preventing soil erosion and mud slides. In Logan Canyon today there are still foot bridges and picnic areas built by the Corps.

Juanita Brooks had WPA funding to collect pioneer diaries in southern Utah, which started her on a distinguished career of writing history. At our university, WPA money built the Commons (Family Life) Building where, thirty years later, I was assigned office space. I had an office in that building during my twenty-two years of teaching.

Federal action of the 1930s and 1940s boosted succeeding years when there were still public works projects, veterans' benefits, student loans, and housing subsidies. President Harry Truman could report in 1953 that eight million veterans had been to college thanks to the GI Bill.[1] Our campus was bulging. The 1950s also saw high rates of unionization and heavy corporate investment in manufacturing, which led to a steady rise in real wages.

The next decade of intensified federal concern became the 1960s, when President John F. Kennedy was the inspiration behind Lyndon Johnson's Great Society (War on Poverty) programs. The Economic Opportunity Act of 1964 made possible Project Head Start, Community Action efforts, college work study, and other programs. Most continue today. As a school board member I saw Title I of the Elementary, Secondary Education Act of 1965 benefit children from low income families. It still continues.

The Equal Pay Act of 1963 came in handy when, ten years later, our campus feminists helped women custodians get pay equal to that of men. Women made good use of Title VII of the Civil Rights Act of 1964, which prohibited discrimination against women in employment, and I benefited because it outlawed anti-nepotism rulings. Medicare, a vital program for millions, became law on July 30, 1965. Medicaid also came into being. When the 1960s closed, the health and nutrition of poor children was at its high point, and child poverty had reached it lowest level in United States history.

The 1970s saw growth of the anti-Vietnam War movement, the environmental movement, and the women's movement. But the next decade, the 1980s, proved economically to be another kettle of fish. Early in that decade, Dean Phyllis Snow asked me to create a course dealing with how the economy affects families. So I did, calling the new course, "Family and Economic Change." The oil crisis had created unbelievable inflation, yet the economy was in the doldrums, resulting in stagflation. I taught about stagflation, and I wanted to include information on the distribution of family incomes, but I couldn't find much. So I went to see Ross Peterson of our History Department, a compassionate man who, for several years, chaired our county Democratic party, a discouraging task in such a heavily Republican state. Ross didn't know any recent books on income distribution, so I did the best I could, suspecting, but not being sure, that the gap was widening between rich and poor. Not until the end of the Reagan-Bush years did the country wake up to the fact that indeed the gap had widened, and the middle class was in decline. The Reagan-Bush administrations skillfully concealed the statistics, and by 1996 this was the kind of economic situation we were in:[2]

> During the twenty years since 1974, four-fifths of American households had declining incomes, while the top one percent of households received 17 percent of total income and owned 42 percent of the wealth.
>
> Real wages of supervisory employees declined.
>
> The minimum wage is at its lowest purchasing power in 40 years. It is impossible for a person with a family, working full time, year round at this wage to keep out of poverty.
>
> Congress seeks to cut back Legal Service lawyers who help low income people. The rules remain stacked in favor of the rich and powerful.
>
> Corporations are raking in profits from productivity growth instead of raising wages. When they downsize, employees lose their jobs but stockholders gain.
>
> The income ratio of chief executives to the average worker in major corporations grew from 40 to 1 in the 1970s to 187 to 1 in 1995. Chief executives are pocketing huge bonuses and stock options because they have abandoned their employees and communities.

This picture continues today. The worship of a free market system, heightened by the global economy, forgets the need for rules of fairness to protect the less fortunate and to keep communities alive. Instead of facing economic realities, too many in Congress and state governments spend their time on subjects such as abortion, gay issues, illegal immigration, and the decline of "family values." Not that I have anything against family values. I searched for values for too many years to let them become the monopoly of the radical right today.

However, a ray of hope lies in the fact that the First Amendment contains the means of a cooperative discourse between right and left. Such discussion is encouraged by the Freedom Forum First Amendment Center at Vanderbilt University in Nashville, Tennessee.[3] Sponsored by twenty-one diverse national organizations, including such opposites as the Christian Coalition and People for the American Way, the center shows how a debate can occur that forges public policies to serve the common good, particularly in public education.

But the economy continues to be of deep concern. Here and across the world it is devastating for women, a fact highlighted at the United Nations Fourth World Conference on Women, held in Beijing in 1995. In an attempt to focus world attention on women's needs, which include the needs of their families, Hillary Clinton addressed the conference and emphasized that "women's rights are human rights."

There is a backlash against Hillary Clinton, and a continuing backlash against second wave feminism. The historian Ruth Rosen has written, "The political backlash against feminism is brutal . . . [L]et us remember that these gender skirmishes, while they leave terrible scars, also publicize great injustices and help redraw the national agenda."[4]

I fervently hope that the national agenda gets redrawn, but government can't do everything. There are other yeasts in the ferment of public activity and community life, yeasts that work to improve economic and social well-being. Feminism is one of them.

Second Wave Feminism and Family Work

In the history of land grant institutions, home economics was assumed to be a field for women. Indeed, this new field was invented by Ellen H. Richards at the turn of the century to give academic employment to women, well educated in the sciences, who could not find academic positions because of discrimination. A major focus of home economics has been the work that women do for their families. Some second wave feminists disdained women's work at home, but later changed their minds. Alice Rossi is a good example. Still later, Carol Gilligan strengthened the idea of "care."[5]

Although I have strongly criticized perfectionist standards in the home, I have always considered household and family work to be important in spite of being devalued by society. In teaching the introductory women's studies course, I included early domestic writers Catharine Beecher, Ellen H. Richards, and Marion Harland, followed by class discussion of current studies of time devoted to household and family work. This course gave credit in both home economics and sociology. I strongly agree with today's feminist agenda, which includes the ideas that men should share domestic work, and that child care by other than parents should be available.

Action against family violence is also central to the feminist agenda. Every year on our campus each college has a week that highlights a topic of concern. Under Dean Bonita Wyse's guidance, the College of Family Life explored the problem of family violence in February 1985 and invited Barrie to give a convocation lecture on this subject. I went to the Salt Lake airport to pick Barrie up.

In her lecture Barrie indicated that, without the women's movement, problems of violence and abuse would not have come into public focus. By then in our valley we had Citizens Against Physical and Sexual Abuse (CAPSA), but it lacked an adequate safe house. The first step toward one had been taken when Jenny Box took an abused mother and her children into her home.

Part of the conference featured a panel composed of Kathy Sheehan, director of CAPSA; Roberta Hardy, Child and Family Support Center; Dr. Marilynne Glatfelter, psychologist; Cheryl Hansen, deputy sheriff of Cache County, Dr. Bartell Cardon, director of Bear River Mental Health Services; and Dr. Kim Openshaw, marriage and family therapist. The workshop was organized by Jean Edmonson, of the Home Economics extension, who was active in going out across the state with a message against domestic violence.[6]

The immediate result of that conference was a community fund drive for a safe house for battered women. The drive had the whole hearted support of the LDS church and people of many faiths participated. A key mover was Ann Jurinak, who is Catholic, as is Dean Wyse. In this case, Mormons joined those of other faiths in encouraging community action for a good cause.[7]

Regardless of accusations that home economics is a conservative field, I have witnessed much pragmatic feminism among home economists at USU including a survey of teen age sexual behavior, a project on treating child abuse, a study of how women can start small businesses in rural areas, and the training of low income women to be nutrition aides. An extension specialist works with Vietnamese refugees. In the public schools boys as well as girls take home economics. USU trains parent educators for high schools and alternative school programs.

The label "home economics" has had a precarious existence in the last half century. Some colleges and universities renamed their schools of home economics early on. At USU the College of Family Life was established in 1959, and the Department of Home Economics was subsumed within it. For years Cornell and Michigan State have had colleges of "Human Ecology." In 1987 Iowa State University changed its 116–year-old College of Home Economics to the College of Family and Consumer Sciences. Recently USU's Department of Home Economics was renamed the Department of Human Environments, retaining the initials HE. Nationally, the American Home Economics Association has become the American Association for Family and Consumer Sciences. These new titles were intended to free curricula from the historical assumption of female monopoly and to encourage a broadened scope.[8]

The Challenge of Feminist Economics

I met feminist economists at the annual meetings of the Allied Social Science Associations in Boston, in January 1994, when snow storms blanketed the city. Janet Shackleford, president of the International Association of Feminist Economics, had invited me to give a paper on women mentoring women economists in the 1930s, in the session on recovering lost contributions of early women economists. So I wrote about my experiences with Elizabeth Hoyt, Margaret Reid, and Hazel Kyrk. When I sat down after giving my paper, Mary Ann Dimand leaned over and said, "I want to publish your paper in a book I'm working on." Startled, I gathered my wits together and said, "Fine!" It became chapter four in *Women of Value: Feminist Essays in the History of Women in Economics.*[9]

Feminist economists have joined feminists in other disciplines to question the very borders of disciplines and to undertake research that crosses them. The philosopher, Sandra Harding, wrote in the first issue of the new journal *Feminist Economics*:

> Feminist work in economics and other social sciences, as well as in
> biology, and the humanities, has made its greatest contributions to
> growth of knowledge when it has been able to step outside the
> preoccupations of the disciplines, and from the perspective of one
> or another of the diverse political discourses constructed from the
> perspective of women's lives and interests, take a fresh look at
> nature, social relations and ways the dominant discourses have
> represented them.[10]

Feminists are looking at poverty, inequality, and unemployment, and they are bringing feminist issues into introductory economics courses. They are looking at economic reform and the status of women in other countries, as evident at the Beijing Conference of Women in 1995.

In particular, feminist economists have challenged neoclassical economics, the economic theory that dominated the twentieth century. Neoclassical economics spoke of economic man, a rational being, and his relationship to production. This theory placed great emphasis on the market system and assumed that competition is the key to production. Economics was considered value-neutral because it concerned itself with means, not ends. In contrast, feminist economists ask where individuals and families get goods and services for their daily living. Provisioning is the emphasis, and it doesn't all come from the market system. Care giving within the family is an important part of provisioning—so are governmental services—and not all of these go through the market system.[11]

To return to my own beginnings, I first learned of consumption economics when my father wrote his book, *The Standard of Living,* in 1923. I completed graduate work in this field in 1938, and in the years that followed, Wynne Thorne and I lived consumption economics, seeking to make wise choices among goods and services. In 1965 I began teaching at USU and my courses held a generous component of consumption. With the creation of feminist economics and its term, provisioning, I came full circle when an issue of the new journal, *Feminist Economics,* honored my professor, Margaret Reid, for her contributions to the field, contributions that remain valid today.[12]

In the tradition of my professor, Elizabeth Hoyt, who fifty years ago began sending books to African libraries, I recently sent twenty-seven years of *Signs: A Journal of Women in Culture and Society* to the Tanzania Gender Networking Programme in Dar es Salaam, a project which is creating a Gender Research Centre. Things do come full circle.

Commencement of 2000

Kip Thorne and I received honorary doctorates at this commencement, and he was commencement speaker. It was not Kip's first honorary doctorate. He has probed the extremes of gravity including black holes, neutron stars, and other exotic deep-space objects, and has "led the way in converting Albert Einstein's General Theory of Relativity from a purely theoretical science into an astrophysical and observational one."[13] At Caltech, where Kip is Feynman Professor of Astrophysics, he has trained forty Ph.D.s, who in turn have trained others. In preparing his commencement talk for USU, Kip asked me to send him what I knew about the commencement of 1900. So I told him that Old Main did not yet have its tower, only the south and north wings. My Aunt Hattie Comish was a student in the two-year domestic science program in 1900 (my father would graduate in 1911), and Aunt Hattie had told me that as a student she used to walk up Old Main hill. There was often mud. "It was three steps forward and slide back two." Sometimes the administration put straw on the path to ease the way. Then Kip compared the very real problems the class of 1900 faced with those that the class of 2000 will face.

I especially appreciated the fact that in the printed program, opposite the page with my picture and citation, is the picture and citation of sociologist Richard Krannich, who received the D. Wynne Thorne Research Award. So three Thornes of our family were recognized at commencement May 6, 2000.

As I stood at the podium waiting to be hooded, I looked over at Kip and winked. After the hood was in place, he got to his feet, grasped me around the waist and kissed me with such vigor that my cap began sliding off the back of my head, to considerable applause.

This honorary degree came to me for long time work for social justice, and especially for work on women's issues. This land-grant institution offered me opportunity, although it was a long time coming. And I did not earn this degree by myself. Many, many others worked with me in the struggle for equal rights in the twentieth century.

Appendix: The Life and Career of Wynne Thorne

Wynne appears in every section of this book except the first, which deals with my early life before I met him. To fill out the story of his life and career I have written this appendix.

David Wynne Thorne was born December 19, 1908, in Perry, Utah, then called Three Mile Creek. His parents were Milton Jefferson Thorne and Elmerta Eugenia Nelson. Wynne inherited his father's sandy red hair and tendency to freckle, and from his mother, it is said, he inherited his happy disposition and his Danish looks. He and his older sisters, Rhea and Lora, were born at eighteen month intervals. When Wynne was four and one-half years old their mother died giving birth to a son, Leland.

Milton's sister, Addie Nelson, took the baby into her family for that first year, while Milton's mother, Rebecca Thorne, cared for the three older children. Milton then married Ida Vilate Young, librarian of Brigham City's library. In choosing to marry Milton and take on his four children, Ida gave up a promising career. She had planned to go to Madison, Wisconsin, that year to further her education, yet she never regretted the choice of marrying.

Ida asked Elmerta's children to call her Aunt Ida because she thought the title "mother" should be reserved for their biological mother. Her daughters-in-law called her Aunt Ida too. I think this custom derived from the fact that in polygamous families—and both Ida and Milton grew up in polygamous contexts—plural wives were called aunts. Later Ida wished she had taught the four older children to speak of her as their "other mother," but she did not know of such a title at the time. Ida gave birth to Dee, June, and Marlowe, and, from my observation, I know all the children considered themselves full brothers and sisters.

Ida kept a day-to-day diary and sometimes a journal. She wrote that they used fifty pounds of flour every nine days, baking eight loaves of bread and a pan of biscuits every other day. Her yeast came from Aunt

Rose Young who got it from the Agricultural College, and Ida kept it alive for twenty-eight years by adding sugar and cooked potato water. Everyone worked. It was subsistence farming, and the boys milked cows and thinned sugar beets. Dust from the fields infiltrated Wynne's lungs and made him barrel chested.

Milton, a civic minded man, was elected mayor of Perry in 1929 and again in 1933. Running on the Democratic ticket, he was elected to the Utah State Legislature in 1939 and 1941, where he served with distinction on three committees: irrigation, appropriations, and education. I recall the appreciation of Utah State Agricultural College officials for his support of their appropriations requests.

When Wynne graduated from Box Elder high school, completing the four years in three, one of his teachers said he was the brightest student ever to graduate. Wynne next attended Weber Junior College in Ogden for two years. Ida wrote, "He, with his father's help, bought a used bus mounted on a Reo Speed Wagon chassis. He was able to get a busload of passengers from Brigham City and vicinity to go to Weber each day, which helped to pay his college costs."[1]

There was a lot of engine trouble, which meant weary evenings putting the bus in shape to drive the next day. Some of Wynne's classmates called him "the truck driver" when they wrote in his Weber yearbook, *The Acorn.* "Dear Turk, I feel very fine that I am able to write at all after hitting the pigs, turkey, car etc." Wynne's nickname was Turk for turkey red, referring to his sandy red hair. And as Wynne told it to me, he did hit a pig in Willard, but it got to its feet and ran off. That's the only thing he hit.

Wynne disliked being called Turk and that's why, when his first son was born with much brighter red hair than his own, he insisted on a short interesting name that people would use without resorting to a nickname. That's why Kip is named Kip.

After Weber Junior College, Wynne served an LDS mission in England. He, along with other missionaries, sailed on the *Leviathan* on February 6, 1929. The next December his brother Dee died on Wynne's birthday, the nineteenth. Dee underwent an ordinary hernia operation but developed an unexpected and lethal blood clot. The family did not cable the tragic news because it was Wynne's birthday and Christmas was so near. Instead, they wrote letters and sent carbon copies of the talks given at the funeral, knowing they would arrive after Christmas. Wynne walked London streets all night long after he got the letters, trying to realize that his brother was gone.

After completing his mission, Wynne came home in February 1931, worked on the family farm all spring and summer, and in the fall enrolled at Utah State Agricultural College, earning his way by working in the chemistry laboratory for C. T. Hirst, who held an agricultural experiment station appointment and, therefore, had research funding. Wynne did well in his classes and especially appreciated Sherwin Maeser, head of Chemistry, who not only was a fine teacher but invited his best students to his home to play chess.

A quick glance at his graduation picture in the yearbook, *The Buzzer*, shows that Wynne belonged to Phi Kappa Phi and Blue Key, and was "Barb pres." There's no picture of the Barbarians (or Independents) although there are pictures of Panhellenic councils and members of fraternities and sororities. Yet the Barbs, while Wynne was president, took the student body office elections away from the Greeks, who until then had dominated.[2]

Toward the end of Wynne's senior year, Dr. Rudger Walker, an Idaho native who was on the Iowa State College faculty, visited the A.C. campus looking for graduate students. Although Wynne was a chemistry major, Walker suggested a fellowship in soils at Iowa State, and Wynne took it, a first step in his future career as an agricultural scientist. Wynne's appointment was a research fellowship in soil bacteriology with a fifty dollar per month stipend. He joined an ongoing project on nitrogen fixation. Specifically, it was a study of how the soil bacteria, rhyzobium, grow and respire in the juices of leguminous plants. Wynne's graduate research produced seven technical papers coauthored with R. H. Walker, and two co-authored with the head of the Soils Department, P. E. Brown.

As the time for Wynne's dissertation defense approached, he was uneasy because the graduate dean, R. E. Buchanan, was himself a distinguished microbiologist and could ask tough questions. Wynne, who was on good terms with everybody, learned from the dean's secretary, Ruth Confare, that if one gave her a box of candy she would keep the dean away from the defense. So Wynne gave her the candy. Imagine his astonishment the next day, after his successful defense without presence of the dean, when he happened to meet Dean Buchanan on campus. He said, "Thanks for the candy. Ruth Confare shared it with me." Wynne took his Ph.D. in June 1936. He had acquired his master's in one year, and his doctorate in two more years, something of a record.[3]

The Depression continued and job prospects were miserable. However, Walker left Iowa State for a position with the Forest Service at the Intermountain Forest and Range Experiment Station in Ogden, a position he would hold from 1936–38. To replace him, Iowa State offered Wynne a position as assistant professor of Agronomy, which combined teaching and research. Wynne accepted but realized that to remain more than one year would be a dead end, so he kept seeking a position elsewhere.

Wisconsin and Texas

Wynne accepted a summer position at the University of Wisconsin in the Department of Bacteriology and Biochemistry, working on rhyzobium with R. H. Burris in the microbiology lab. When I completed my summer teaching at Iowa State, Wynne and I were married on August 3, 1937, and set up housekeeping in an apartment in Madison.

In the middle of August, Wynne received an offer of an associate professorship from Ide P. Trotter, head of Agronomy at Texas A & M. He accepted with alacrity, and in September we moved to College Station to live among Texas Aggies. Wynne's teaching load was the heaviest in the department and there was no research appointment in the agricultural experiment station, but he snatched time to study the nature of surrounding soils. It was a nine-month appointment, and summer 1938 found us once again in Madison, with Wynne working on rhyzobium with Burris and also with Perry Wilson. Then we returned to College Station for a second academic year.

Wynne was working very hard and suffering from hay fever. We sometimes wished we were elsewhere. In the meantime Rudger Walker had left the Forest Service in Ogden to become dean of Agriculture and director of the agricultural experiment station at Utah State Agricultural College. He offered Wynne a position as associate professor of Agronomy, which included a half-time appointment in the experiment station. Wynne accepted.

Teaching and Research at Utah State Agricultural College

Wynne enjoyed his work at the Agricultural College, and often said, "I'd do this even if they didn't pay me." His course on irrigated soils resulted in a textbook, and while working on it he became head of the Agronomy Department, a position he would hold for eight years (1947–55). *Irrigated Soils, Their Fertility and Management,* co-authored with Howard B. Peterson, was published in 1948, followed by a revised edition in 1954. It became internationally known and was translated into Spanish, Russian, and Hebrew.

From 1940–60 Wynne did research on soil fertility, plant nutrition, and chemistry of minor elements, and of saline and alkaline soils. He studied iron, phosphorus, manganese, zinc, calcium and sodium. He published research on fruit trees and shrubs, management of irrigated pastures, and the quality of irrigation water. Some years after his death, international meetings held at USU on the subject of iron in plants paid tribute to Wynne and his graduate students for this early research.[4]

Wynne believed that his students should have as good a start as possible toward professional careers. The list of his co-authored articles brings back to me these students' names and I can see each of them clearly in my mind's eye: Arthur Wallace, Parker Pratt, Larry Burtch, Willard Lindsay, Lynn K. Porter, Jerry Jurinak, Gene Miller, and R. L. Smith. Charl Brown was another one. And I also remember Louay Kadry from Iraq who subsequently had a long career with the United Nations Food and Agriculture Organization in Rome.

At USAC Wynne gave the Tenth Annual Faculty Research Lecture in 1951, taking his title, "The Desert Shall Blossom as the Rose," from Isaiah. An introductory section on the Tigris-Euphrates basin told of the early great canals and how they ultimately salted up. Seven years after giving this lecture, he saw from a helicopter the borders of the ancient Narwan canal.

The faculty association had initiated annual Faculty Research Lectures in 1942, and over the years Wynne and I attended nearly all of them. Willard Gardner presented the first one, entitled, "The Scientist's Concept of the Physical World." Gardner's list of publications, appended at the end of his lecture, gives a glimpse of the evolution of soil physics, a field which he founded. Wynne told me that Gardner was so famous as founder of soil physics that his picture hung on the walls of the Rothamsted Experiment Station in England.

It is interesting to note that, in 1950, Willard Gardner's son, Walter Hale Gardner, received one of the first two Ph.D.s to be granted at Utah State. Walter Gardner took his degree in soil physics, and Wynne signed his dissertation as major professor, with Willard Gardner signing as thesis director. The thesis was only thirty-one pages long and full of mathematical symbols.[5] I recall Walt bringing it to our house for Wynne to read, and afterwards I asked Wynne if he understood it. "No," said Wynne in all honesty. "Only Walt and his father understand it. His father typed it, because his typewriter has proper symbols, and Willard Gardner in his early years was a court reporter. That's how he learned to type."

A candid recital of events of the early 1950s must include the fact that it was a time of troubles for USAC. Governor J. Bracken Lee and the Board of Trustees overstepped their legal responsibilities and reached down into administrative and faculty affairs. Wynne chaired the Faculty Association Committee on Faculty Relations and in this capacity battled the board and Governor Lee. The governor was responsible for dismissing President Louis Madsen in 1953. But Madsen's was not the only abrupt dismissal. In 1950 the board had cut short the tenure of his predecessor, President Franklin S. Harris.

After Madsen, the next president was Henry Aldous Dixon, former president of Weber Junior College. Dixon was well aware of the uneasy relationship of USAC to the governor and trustees. In the summer of 1953, when Dixon arrived on campus as president, he said to Wynne, "Stay away from me. I find you too controversial." Stunned, Wynne did stay away by leaving for a sabbatical year in Knoxville as chief of the Soils and Fertilizer Division of the Tennessee Valley Authority.

Administration of University Research

We came home from Tennessee in the fall of 1954. In November after a brief political campaign, President Aldous Dixon was elected to Congress to replace Douglas R. Stringfellow, a World War II veteran who had been giving dramatic accounts of his heroic war experiences, and then confessed on television that they were untrue. With the departure of Dixon, Utah State had lost three presidents in four years. After insisting on certain concessions from the Board of Trustees, Daryl Chase became president in December 1954, a position he would hold for nearly fourteen years. Under him the college's name became Utah State University in 1957.

Upon recommendation of Dean Walker, President Chase immediately proposed that Wynne Thorne be appointed director of the Utah Agricultural Experiment Station and of University Research. Board of Trustee membership had changed and the appointment was approved, along with creation of a Division of University Research and approval of Wynne's strategy to broaden the scope of research possibilities across campus for faculty who lacked access to experiment station funding. Nine month faculty could now apply for research money for

VENEZUELAN visitors, Pausolina Martinez and Dr. Pedro Rincon Gutierra, and Dr. Vaughn Hansen, director of USU engineering experiment station, examine a newly-published Spanish translation of a soils resource book authored by Dr. D. W. Thorne, right.

Herald Journal September 22, 1963.

the summer months, available from USU's uniform school fund allotment. This was state income from mineral leases on state and federal lands, an income that was growing rapidly because of oil and gas development and uranium exploration.

Wynne defined research as any scholarly activity and said that research supported by uniform school funds could include any creative activities such as art, music composition, or writing as well as traditional research in biological, physical, and social sciences. On his suggestion, a university research council representing all colleges was created to recommend awards of research money.

The agricultural experiment station continued to have the largest research appropriation of any unit at USU, amounting at this time to almost two million dollars a year. Wynne administered the station along with seeking out other sources of funding. He took on regional and national assignments, among them serving as director of the Western

Dr. Daryl Chase, second from left, president of Utah State University, with vice presidents, Dr. D. W. Thorne, research; Dee A. Broadbent, business, and Dr. Milton R. Merrill, academic affairs.

Summer School 1967.

Agricultural Experiment Station Directors. Earlier he served as president of the Soil Science Society of America (1955–56), having previously been president of the Western Society of Soil Science. Other aspects of his career can be glimpsed from his list of publications.[6]

Wynne initiated annual Experiment Station Day which included an evening banquet. In an unusual paper read at the banquet on February 20, 1960, he summarized an interdisciplinary research project on arid lands research at USU:

> This highly successful research program began with reports of W. P. Thomas that our income from grazing lands in the state was frightfully low. O. W. Israelsen calculated that water falling on these lands was being largely wasted and only about 1 percent was reaching our streams . . . Four of our geneticists and plant breeders tackled the problem: Sid Boyle, Douglas Dewey, Marion Pedersen and DeVere McAllister . . .

> The resulting plant was given the name of cactile grass but soon became known as cackle grass. It had small tufts of grass blades where the spines of the barrel cactus usually appear. But most important of all, had a luxuriant growth of grass and legume on the top, which during dry weather derived water from the barrel of the cactus part. Unfortunately the bulk of the forage on top of the barrel was about 10 feet high . . .

Fortunately cackle grass is winter hardy and easy to establish under our Utah conditions. (Wayne) Cook, (D. L.) Goodwin and (Larry) Stoddart established several plots of about 10,000 acres each for detailed and controlled observations and these are spreading rapidly crowding out sage and rabbit brush . . . But since livestock could not reach the feed, some of our cattlemen started to doubt the value of this new forage . . .

A group headed by Jim Bennett together with Doyle Matthews, Gene Starkey and Dave Carson tackled the problem with typical USU ingenuity and imagination . . . It was decided to cross the giraffe with our Rambouilet sheep . . . An animal named "Gireep" resulted which resembled somewhat the sheep but had a neck long enough to feed on even the tallest cackle grass . . . The gireeps proved hardy and prolific. The meat was good with a slightly banana-like flavor, no doubt due to the tropical ancestry. . . .

There was just one flaw. The fleece proved to be a curious material different from both hair and wool, and therefore, given the name of Hool. Now our chemists and textile specialists entered the picture.

Florence Gilmore and Elmer Olsen . . . went to work on the problem . . . Miss Gilmore had the brilliant idea—it could be used to make women's hats. The fad caught on and millions of hats were produced. Our cattlemen became wealthy. But women are fickle and fads changed. Just as disaster seemed imminent Elmer Olsen discovered that the product burned with terrific ferocity and he conceived that it would make an excellent rocket fuel. Soon rockets will be driven by Hool from USU produced gireeps.

This report, with illustrations by an unknown artist, appeared in the Christmas issue of the 1960 *Agronomy Newsletter* under the title of "Wow! Gireeps and Hool." In a more serious vein, a year later Wynne presided over a symposium held in Denver on "Land and Water Use" which became a book by that title.[7]

Every early November Wynne was in Washington D.C. for meetings of the Experiment Station Directors' Section of the National Association of State Universities and Land Grant Colleges. He served on the Committee of Nine of the directors' section, and in 1961–62 was section chairman, which meant being chairman of all state directors.

In 1965 Wynne became USU's first vice president for research, and in real life as in the "gireep" fantasy, he strongly encouraged cooperation across disciplines. The Ecology Center, the Desert Biome, various

Gireeps and Hool

research-based institutes, and the Environment and Man program came into being. Wynne served seven years as vice president and then, for his final two years at the university, because of health problems, he chose to step down and serve only as director of the agricultural experiment station.[8]

Wynne's final nine years at the university continued his strenuous pace. They were years in which he insisted that undergraduate as well as graduate students should have opportunity to do research, a belief spelled out in 1969 in a rather famous paper.[9]

When he retired in 1974, at age sixty-five, the research momentum he started in 1955 had culminated in 1972–73 in 1,636 publications by faculty, including seventy-five books. The research expenditures in fiscal year 1973–74 amounted to well over eleven million dollars.[10] At commencement in 1975, the university recognized his work by awarding him the Honorary Doctorate of Science.

At the time of Wynne's retirement Eastman Hatch, of the USU physics faculty, wrote to him:

> When I came to this university five and one-half years ago, it soon became apparent to me that there was a human dynamo over in Old Main who was responsible for the fact that while the total grant picture at most universities (including the one I came from) was becoming very bleak, Utah State University's funding for research was increasing every year. Of course the faculty had a great deal to do with this—but so did you. The policies provided by you and the Research Council under your direction created the atmosphere and the incentives which enabled this unusual record. . . .
>
> Utah State is one of the most successful universities in getting interdisciplinary programs off the ground and running. Your policies and active cooperation have been a large factor in this achievement. Your mark will remain on this university for years to come.[11]

Consulting Experience

Over the years Wynne had a lot of irons in the fire. One of them was consulting. The earliest (1958) was his trip to Iraq to advise the government on soil and water problems, followed by a visit to the USSR as part of a soil and water team.

Later he was hired by the engineering firm, Charles T. Main, to be a consultant on the California Water Plan, that vast project bringing water south from northern California. During the middle of July 1960, he toured the twenty-six California counties that would be affected, and returned to spend days at our Logan Canyon cabin, writing the report and verifying locations on a large map of California suspended from the cabin's balcony. Barrie typed the report for him.[12] In November Wynne was offered the position of director of the New Jersey Agricultural Experiment Station, but declined, saying his interest lay in arid lands.[13]

Wynne consulted for the Shell Oil Company Experiment Station in Venezuela in 1961. Later he went to Ecuador for Charles T. Main to evaluate development in the Guyas River Basin. He went to Bolivia for the United States Agency for International Development. He went to India for Parsons Engineering. The National Academy of Sciences published the East Pakistan report he wrote for the World Bank.

Teaching and research were no longer part of his work, and I asked him why he did administration and consulting. He said because he knew he could do it better than anyone else around, and he hoped his international work would benefit world food production and starving people.

In early 1973 Wynne had heart surgery, a triple bypass at the LDS Hospital in Salt Lake City. Avril and Lance, students at the University of Utah, lived in a house on the Avenues, so I stayed with them. Every morning in the chill air I wiped smoggy film off my windshield and drove to the hospital to see Wynne. Later he spoke lightly of his surgery in his talk to Logan Rotary. Among his papers are these typed sheets:

> I was asked to tell you what I have been doing in the past year—other than attending Rotary. First I had a new heart plumbing job. The old corroded pipes were replaced with new ones—fresh from my own leg. I feel wonderful and hope the same for each of you.
>
> I have been to India twice, once last July and second in early January. I completed two short missions for the UNDP, one covering 10 countries in the Middle East and North Africa to examine their cereal variety testing and breeding programs and one in Ethiopia to review their agricultural research activities . . . I am concerned and I hope you, too, are concerned about the future well-being of all peoples in the world. I have travelled more than most—spending at least modest periods in 25 different countries. I have found the same basic human values in people of every nation, the same strengths and similar weaknesses . . .
>
> In developing countries there is no social security. Children are the primary old age insurance. These countries are increasing population by 2.5% per year or more. This means doubling of population in less than 25 years . . . How can this be managed, where will the food come from? The U.S. and many other countries have been providing technical assistance to help in food production for 25 years or more, yet these countries are still on the verge of famine.

Wynne observed that most national unilateral assistance programs are short lived. He saw more hope in international research centers. The first two such centers, supported by Rockefeller Foundation and Ford Foundation, involved research on corn and wheat in Mexico, and on rice in the Philippines. Additional centers were created with funding from the Ford, Rockefeller, and Kellogg Foundations, from the United Nations Development Programme, and from twenty-five nations.

Wynne represented those twenty-five nations on the board of governors of the International Center for Research in the Semi-Arid Tropics (ICRISAT). Until his death in 1979 he went to India two and three times a year for meetings.

Every three years board members' wives got a free trip to Hyderabad. I chose to go along for the January 1975 meetings and left the United States in early December 1974 with friends Ione Bennion and Alta Crockett. We saw Hawaii, Samoa, and New Zealand. Wynne caught up with us in Sidney, Australia. We were in Adelaide, Australia, for Christmas with Carolyn Steel, and at the International Rice Research Institute in the Philippines for New Year's. We reached Hyderabad in time for Wynne's board meetings, and attended the dedication of the new ICRISAT campus by Indira Ghandi. We traveled north to visit Marathwada Agricultural University in Parbahni, at the invitation of Vice-Chancellor (President) D. K. Salunkhe. Born in India, Salunkhe was a longtime USU faculty member and had taken a three-year leave to work with Marathwada University. He and his faculty were most kind to us, and besides visiting the campus, we were taken to see the famous Ajunta and Ellora caves. The next year, Wynne was again at Marathwada Agricultural University, this time to receive an honorary doctorate on January 17, 1976, a degree of which he was very proud.

Continuing the saga of our round-the-world trip: Wynne was with us when we went to Teheran, before the fall of the shah. Then we all four went on to Rome where Wynne learned from UNDP that he was to go to Libya because their government wanted to know what to do about the water they had struck in the desert while drilling for oil. We three women went on to Spain and home. In early March, Wynne returned to Logan with amazing tales of Libya.

In July 1976 I made a quick trip with Wynne to London, where four candidates for ICRISAT director were interviewed. They came from across the world. During the day while the selection committee interviewed, I went out to see the sights of London in spite of the very hot and dry weather, and on July 4 saw England celebrate the independence of the United States with considerable fanfare. Each evening I had dinner with the committee and the candidate and wife just interviewed. The choice was New Zealander Leslie Swindale, director of the Agricultural Experiment Station in Hawaii. His wife Delle, a New Yorker, had her Ph.D. from Cornell in ecology.[14] They were very bright and friendly people and during their years at the Institute made great contributions.

Retirement and Continuing Professional Work

Wynne retired the summer of 1974. Determined not to breathe down the necks of those who replaced him at USU, Wynne suggested in the fall that we drive across Canada to Orono, Maine, where he had been invited to evaluate the agricultural experiment station of the University of Maine. We stayed two weeks, saw the New England autumn colors, and then drove slowly home cross country, stopping to visit Marlowe and Merle Thorne at the University of Illinois, Urbana, where Marlowe was head of Agronomy. Soon after our return, we started the round-the-world trip described above. Wynne got home from Libya in early March. On March 21, 1975, annual Experiment Station Day occurred, but this time it was informally known as Wynne Thorne Day.

More than three hundred people attended. We were particularly happy to see the Burnell Wests, with whom Wynne stayed in Iraq. There were many friends, former graduate students, and relatives. Wynne gave a major address on progress and direction for the future, and Willis L. Peterson, an economist at Minnesota, spoke.

Among the distinguished visitors, most of whom spoke, were Thomas J. Army, vice president of Great Western Sugar, from Denver; Mark Buchanan, director-at-large of the Western Region Agricultural Experiment Stations; J. B. Kendrick, vice president for research of the University of California, Berkeley; Roy L. Lovvern, administrator of the Cooperative State Research Service, Washington D.C., who was responsible for Wynne's assignments to review experiment stations; and Rex Thomas, regional administrator, Agricultural Research Service, Berkeley.

The dinner was humorous from beginning to end as our faculty and wives brought out old stories. But the greatest surprise was when Al Southard and LeMoyne Wilson presented Wynne with the Utah Agricultural Experiment Station Bulletin, *Soils of Utah,* which had been years in completion. It had taken a long time to get all the soils of the state mapped. This was the only published version, the rest being still in press. Al had really sat on the printers to get this one done in time for the dinner.[15]

Life went on. Besides evaluating the Maine Agricultural Experiment Station Wynne evaluated the stations of Rhode Island and of Maryland. I was with him on his two-week visit to the University of Maryland during a very cold winter, at the time of President Jimmy Carter's inaugural, which we watched on television in our motel room. It was just too cold to go over to Washington, D.C.

Wynne also worked for the Board of Agricultural and Renewable Resources, which functioned under the National Research Council. This appointment began before his retirement when he was editor for the Committee of Fifteen, which wrote *Our Daily Bread: A Report to the Nation on Its Food Supply* (1973).

Because I kept gathering material on measures of quality of life, Wynne asked me to write a paper with him for a symposium of agricultural and forestry scientists to be held at the annual AAAS meetings in Denver in late February 1977. We entitled our paper "Land Resources and Quality of Life." The symposium papers became the book, *Renewable Resource Management for Forestry and Agriculture.*[16]

At the same time, Wynne and Marlowe were writing their book *Soil, Water, and Crop Production,* designed to help advisers working with farmers, public leaders, and others seeking to improve crop practices. Wynne and Marlowe wrote twelve chapters and invited authors wrote seven.[17]

Toward the end of 1978, Wynne came home ill from a brief consulting trip to Syria. Surgery to reactivate a failed kidney did not help, and not until two and a half weeks before his death was he diagnosed as having cancer of the liver, which had spread from colon cancer. He died on February 15, 1979.

"He died with his boots on," his colleagues said. I know he would have wanted it that way, but I also know that he desperately wanted more time.

Five years later Rulon Albrechtsen asked permission to name a new hard-red spring wheat for him. He said that one can't very well name a wheat "Thorne" but the name "Wynne" would do very nicely. That's what the new wheat became.[18] It is in interesting company because earlier hard-red spring wheats had been named Fremont, Borah, and Powell.

Perhaps the most lasting recognition of Wynne's contributions to Utah State University is the D. Wynne Thorne Research Award given every commencement. When Kip and I received honorary doctorates at USU on May 6, 2000, in the printed program opposite the page with my picture and citation was the D. Wynne Thorne Research Award recipient, Richard Krannich, sociologist. I like to believe that Wynne was there in spirit, especially because Kip was commencement speaker.

Postscript: What Became of the Children?

Kip S. Thorne is Richard Feynman Professor of Theoretical Physics at the California Institute of Technology. He married Linda Peterson and they had two children, Kares and Bret. Kip later married Carolee Winstein.

Barrie Thorne is Professor of Sociology and Women's Studies at the University of California, Berkeley. She married Peter Lyman and they have two children, Abby and Andrew.

Sandra Thorne-Brown is an urban forester in Pocatello, Idaho. During the time her husband, Robert Brown, was a graduate student at the University of Washington, Seattle, and at the University of Tennessee, Knoxville, Sandra taught in elementary schools.

Avril Thorne is Associate Professor of Psychology at the University of California, Santa Cruz. She married Joe Christy and they have a daughter, Emma.

Lance G. Thorne creates and builds beautiful furniture. He lives in Takilma, Oregon and is a strong environmentalist.

Acknowledgments

This book would never have materialized without the confidence of my late husband, Wynne Thorne, who, I believe, is looking down on his family, astonished that the dishes finally got out of the sink. Our five children, Kip, Barrie, Sandra, Avril, and Lance, grew up with this manuscript in its various forms. In adulthood they made corrections and suggestions, found references, improved my writing, and taught me the computer. Their spouses, too, have had a hand in this book: Linda Thorne, Peter Lyman, Robert Brown, Joe Christy, and Carolee Winstein. To all of these my hearty thanks. I am deeply grateful, also, to Marlowe Thorne for help in describing the life and career of Wynne Thorne.

My support group, known as Friday, helped plot the women's movement in Utah and on our campus. We gave each other a leg up in our academic careers, shared joys and accomplishments, and stood by each other in difficult times. Current members are Charlotte Brennand, Patricia Gardner, Joan McFadden, Janice Pearce, and Jan Roush. Death claimed Betty Boeker and Dorothy Lewis. Today, Jane McCullough and Karen Morse live elsewhere but we keep in touch. Joan Shaw, who edited the *USU Status of Women News*; Idella Larson, who went with me to China; Bonita Wyse, who made possible my promotion to full professor; and Joyce Kinkead of the current USU administration have each been Friday members in the past. I am immensely grateful to all of Friday for their friendship and support throughout the past thirty years.

Ross Peterson of the USU history faculty recommended my manuscript for publication, and I am pleased that he has written the foreword. Pam Riley of sociology strongly urged publication. Thad Box, former dean of the College of Natural Resources, together with his wife Jenny, read the manuscript and recommended publication. Another couple, Don and Joyce Davis, have also given much support over the years. I appreciate the confidence these folks have placed in me.

I am also grateful to Jeff Simmonds, former director of USU Special Collections and Archives, now deceased, who urged me to put my papers there and who consistently encouraged me in the women's movement. Ann Buttars, current director of Special Collections and

Archives, continues that encouragement today. She read and improved some of my earlier writing, especially my study of women authors of Utah Agricultural Experiment Station bulletins.

Linda Sillitoe, an author whom I much admire, served as copy editor of my book and improved it immeasurably. To John Alley, executive editor of USU Press, I owe a special debt of gratitude for skill in editing and his ability to see important points that lay buried in the manuscript. He helped me bring them to the surface. To both editors, my deepest thanks. My thanks also to the two anonymous reviewers of the manuscript.

And finally, I wish to express special gratitude to Theodore W. Daniel for being a pillar of strength during the past four years. Our friendship reaches back to the 1940s.

Notes

Introduction

1. Laurie Sullivan Maddox, "Who Are You Calling a Liberal? Asks Demo," *The Salt Lake Tribune* (April 8, 1996).
2. Lewis Mumford, *The Conduct of Life* (New York: Harcourt, Brace & World, 1951), pp. 267–68.

CHAPTER 1: Growing Up in the 1920s

1. Dean Ava B. Milam's autobiography is the source of my description of Dr. Margaret Snell. Milam married after retirement and added her husband's name to her own. See Ava Milam Clark and J. Kenneth Munford, *Adventures of a Home Economist* (Corvallis, Oregon: Oregon State University Press, 1969), p. 39.
2. With few exceptions, home economists were unmarried across the country. See United States Office of Education, *Survey of Land-Grant Colleges and Universities Bulletin No. 9* (Washington D.C.: Government Printing Office, 1930), pp. 869–70 and 888. Quoted in Alison Comish Thorne, "Visible and Invisible Women in Land-Grant Colleges, 1890–1940" *72nd Faculty Honor Lecture* (Utah State University, October, 1985).
3. On Dr. Hedger, see Clark and Munford, 128.
4. John Watson was the behavioral psychologist who dominated child rearing advice in the 1920s. His ideas have come under much criticism. See Sheila M. Rothman, *Woman's Proper Place: A History of Changing Ideals and Practices, 1870 to the Present* (New York: Basic Books, 1978), pp. 210–13. Rothman also tells the story of the rise and fall of the Sheppard-Towner Act, pp. 136–53.
5. The quote is from p. 19 of the Newel Howland Comish autobiography, *A Life of Joy* (unpublished, 1959), with Alison Thorne papers in Special Collections, Utah State University Merrill Library. He describes his debating and the Ethical Society on pp. 21–26. See Utah Agricultural College yearbook, *The Buzzer* (1911), pp. 149–52, 193, 195.
6. S. George Ellsworth, ed., *Louisa Barnes Pratt: Mormon Missionary Widow and Pioneer* (Logan, Utah: Utah State University Press, 1998). S. George Ellsworth, ed., *The Journals of Addison Pratt* (Salt Lake City: University of Utah Press, 1990). May Hunt Larson, granddaughter of Louisa and Addison Pratt, was my mother's mother. May Hunt Larson, kept journals of happenings in Snowflake, which became six volumes of unpublished history (in LDS Church Archives).
7. Richard Hofstadter, introduction to *The Progressive Movement 1900–1915*, ed. Richard Hofstadter (Englewood Cliffs, N.J.: Prentice-Hall, 1963). For a

description of Newel Comish's graduate work at the University of Chicago and the University of Wisconsin, see his autobiography, pp. 39–50.

8. Karen J. Blair, *The Clubwoman as Feminist: True Womanhood Redefined, 1868–1914* (New York: Holmes and Meier, 1980). See also Molly Ladd-Taylor, *Raising a Baby the Government Way: Mothers' Letters to the Children's Bureau, 1915–1932* (New Brunswick: Rutgers University Press, 1986). These letters show that these mothers desperately needed and wanted government aid for their families. In Mormon communities the chief source of help was the Relief Society, which watched out for the welfare of the poor, the ill, and those in child birth. My grandmother, May Hunt Larson, was president of the Snowflake Relief Society all the years my mother was growing up. My mother's self-confidence as president of the Corvallis PTA and, later, president of faculty wives at the University of Oregon, came from watching her mother preside over Relief Society.

9. Louise Comish, *Family Record Book* (unpublished), pp. 65–66. (In possession of author.)

10. These pioneer books in consumption economics were Hazel Kyrk, *A Theory of Consumption* (Boston: Houghton Mifflin, 1923); Newel Howland Comish, *The Standard of Living: Elements of Consumption* (New York: Macmillan, 1923); and Elizabeth Ellis Hoyt, *The Consumption of Wealth* (New York: Macmillan, 1928). Consumer concerns received attention from the Progressive movement, but there was little academic writing on the subject until the 1920s.

11. Comish, *A Life of Joy*, describes the Cooperative Managers' Association, pp. 70–75.

12. See Ruth Barnes Moynihan, *Rebel for Rights, Abigail Scott Duniway* (New Haven: Yale University Press, 1983). On Benton County voting against woman suffrage see *Daily Gazette Times* (October 11, 1912), quoted in *The Society Record* 15, published by Benton County Historical Society (December 1992).

13. Alison Thorne, "Parents' Page," *Gifted Child Quarterly* (Summer 1967): 120 is my tribute to my mother's homemade fun with her children. She described her own childhood in "Snowflake Girl" (unpublished, 1960), an autobiography of her first twenty years. (With Alison Thorne papers in Special Collections, Utah State University Merrill Library.) An excerpt appears as "Snowflake Girl," in *Dialogue: A Journal of Mormon Thought* 6 (Summer, 1971): 101–10.

14. Marmee in Louisa May Alcott's *Little Women* held a daughter on her lap when she had something special to tell her, even when the daughters were grown.

15. Jessica B. Peixotto, *Getting and Spending at the Professional Standard of Living: A Study of the Costs of Living an Academic Life* (New York: Macmillan, 1927), pp. 39, 41–43.

16. Ibid., 100.

17. Ibid., 5, 138. In a study of Iowa State College faculty expenditures, Elizabeth Hoyt compared her findings with those of Peixotto. See Elizabeth E. Hoyt, *Consumption in Our Society* (New York: McGraw-Hill, 1938), pp. 311–12. For

further comment on Peixotto's work, see Daniel Horowitz, *The Morality of Spending: Attitudes Toward the Consumer Society in America, 1875–1940* (Baltimore: Johns Hopkins, 1985), 139–48. See also Mary E. Cookingham, "Social Economists and Reform: Berkeley, 1906–1961," *History of Political Economy* 19 (Spring 1987): 47–65.

18. Clarke A. Chambers, "Jessica Blanche Peixotto," in *Notable American Women, 1607–1950,* vol. 3, ed. Edward T. James, et al. (Cambridge: Harvard University Press, 1971), pp. 42–43.

CHAPTER 2: The Great Depression and College Years

1. Alison Comish, "Grandpa," *The Manuscript,* Oregon State College English Department (May 1931): 16–17.
2. See Alison Comish, "The Contract Plan in Retrospect," *School and Society* 34 (July 18, 1931): 95–96 and Alison Comish, "Buchholz Awakes the Educator," *Oregon Education Journal* 7 (October 1932): 16, 30–31.
3. I lived in the home of faculty member Guy C. Wilson and his wife, Melissa Stevens Wilson, together with their children who were also BYU students. They were a warm and hospitable family. I found the atmosphere of the entire university to be one of warmth. My father knew faculty member Lowry Nelson because they had been graduate students together at Wisconsin in 1914–15. In 1935–36 Nelson left BYU to become director of the Utah Agricultural Experiment Station at Logan, but he stayed only briefly. His long and distinguished professional career in sociology was at the University of Minnesota.
4. Elizabeth E. Hoyt, *Consumption in Our Society* (New York: McGraw-Hill, 1938), p. vi.
5. *The Iowa Stater* (June 1987): 2.
6. Elizabeth Ellis Hoyt, *Primitive Trade: Its Psychology and Economics* (London: Kegan Paul, Trench, Trubner, 1926); reprint (New York: Augustus M. Kelley, 1968).
7. Elizabeth E. Hoyt, *Choice and the Destiny of Nations* (New York: Philosophical Library, 1969), chap. 1. For a biography and listing of accomplishments of Elizabeth E. Hoyt, see my entry "Elizabeth Ellis Hoyt" in *The Biographical Dictionary of Women Economists,* ed. Robert W. Dimand, Mary Ann Dimand, and Evelyn L. Forget (Northampton, Maine: Edward Elgar, 2000), pp. 215–19.
8. Lionel Robbins, *An Essay on the Nature and Significance of Economic Science* (London: Macmillan, 1935). Robbins wrote in a terse, clear style, which Iowa State professors and graduate students admired.
9. Alison Comish, "Capacity to Consume," *American Economic Review* 26 (June 1936): 291–95.
10. Margaret G. Reid, *Economics of Household Production* (New York: Wiley, 1934). See especially p. 185 and Part VI, "The Future of Household Production."
11. Veronica Strong-Boag, "Pulling in Double Harness or Hauling a Double Load: Women, Work and Feminism on the Canadian Prairie," *Journal of Canadian Studies* 21 (Fall 1986): 32–52. See especially pp. 38, 42, 45, 47. A

woman who did identify herself as a feminist was Violet McNaughton, founder of the Saskatchewan Women Grain Growers and women's editor of the *Western Producer* from 1925 to 1951 (see p. 35). In 1928 a conference on home economics at the University of Saskatchewan brought together rural and urban groups, led by the president of the women's section of Saskatchewan's United Farmers. They proposed a far-reaching home economics extension department and that home economics be required for a teacher's certificate. Strong-Boag says of this conference, "In critical ways home economics was to have some of the same consciousness raising and research goals of the modern women's studies programmes. Above all it was to make women and their work a subject of serious study" (44–45).

12. Margaret G. Reid, "Status of Farm Housing in Iowa," *Iowa Agricultural Experiment Station Bulletin* 174 (1934): 288. (Sponsored by the Agricultural Economics and the Home Economics Sections of the Iowa Agricultural Experiment Station, in cooperation with the Iowa Extension Service and the Bureau of Home Economics of the USDA. Funds for collecting and tabulating data came from the federal Civil Works Administration.)

13. Letter from Theodore W. Schultz to Alison Comish Thorne, October 22, 1985.

14. Alison Comish, letter home, June 11, 1935. (Author's family letters are in Special Collections, Utah State University Merrill Library.)

15. Hazel Kyrk, *Economic Problems of the Family* (New York: Harper, 1929).

16. Christopher Lasch, "Sophonisba Preston Breckinridge," in *Notable American Women, 1607–1950*, vol. 1, ed. Edward T. James (Cambridge: Harvard University Press, 1971), p. 235.

17. Sophonisba Breckinridge, "University Women in the New Order," *AAUW Journal* 26 (June 1933): 198. Land grant colleges came under the National Economy Act, Section 213, which required, that in reducing personnel, a married person (living with husband or wife) should be dismissed before any other persons, if such was also in the service of the United States. This section was repealed in July 1937. See *AAUW Journal* 31 (October 1937): 45. Local and state governments, as well as school districts, had rulings against employment of married women, which continued long after the Depression.

18. See Richard J. Storr's biography of Marion Talbot in *Notable American Women*, vol. 3, pp. 423–24.

19. Lela B. Costin, *Two Sisters for Social Justice: A Biography of Grace and Edith Abbott* (Urbana: University of Illinois Press, 1983). *AAUW Journal* 29 (October 1935): 39, noted that Grace Abbott helped head off an anti-feminist movement at the International Labour Organization conference in 1934 in Budapest, where a resolution was adopted on women's right to work. The attempt had been made to exclude women from gainful employment in order to solve the unemployment problem.

The New Deal network of women was much concerned over the narrowing of women's sphere by fascism in Europe. According to Susan Ware, "Eleanor Roosevelt reported in a 1936 'My Day' column that in Germany highly trained scientific women were told that their minds were of no use to the country; they should concentrate on bearing children and managing homes." Susan Ware, *Beyond Suffrage: Women in the New Deal* (Cambridge: Harvard University Press, 1981), p. 11.

20. Ibid., 135.

21. Subsequently Eleanor Parkhurst pursued her major interest in social research and history by becoming editor-in-chief of a large suburban newspaper in Chelmsford, Massachusetts.

22. Fawn Brodie, *No Man Knows My History* (New York: Knopf, 1945).

23. I have told the story of my relationship with Hoyt, Reid, and Kyrk in Alison Comish Thorne, "Women Mentoring Women in Economics in the 1930s," in *Women of Value: Feminist Essays on the History of Women in Economics*, ed. Mary Ann Dimand, Robert W. Dimand, and Evelyn L. Forget (Aldershot, United Kingdom: Edward Elgar, 1995), pp. 60–70.

24. Margaret G. Reid, *Consumers and the Market* (New York: F. S. Crofts, 1938).

25. Winnifred Cannon, younger than I, combined journalism and home economics as an Iowa State student. After marrying Stuart Jardine, she moved to Utah and had a long career as food editor of the *Deseret News*.

26. Nancy Wolff and Jim Hayward, "The Historical Development of the Department of Economics at Iowa State, 1929 to 1985" (unpublished), p. 8.

CHAPTER 3: Producing Children and Books: The 1940s

1. For arguments that economic theory is not, and cannot be, value neutral, see Marianne A. Ferber and Julie A. Nelson, introduction to *Beyond Economic Man: Feminist Theory and Economics* (Chicago: University of Chicago Press, 1993), p. 7.

2. Luna and Duncan Brite were Presbyterians and therefore not bound by the Mormon insistence that the only real career for women should be as wives and mothers. Years later, Luna Brite earned an Ed.D. at USU, majoring in psychology, but she could not get a position on the faculty so she did volunteer tutoring of children.

3. See Annette B. Larsen, "Eighty Years of Faculty Women's League" (master's thesis, Utah State University, 1995), in Special Collections, Utah State University Merrill Library. Larsen shows that from its origin in 1910 through the 1950s the league was an avenue of legitimacy for faculty wives, who were denied employment at the university. Larsen names league projects benefitting the university, its students, and the community at large, and shows that the league was part of the vast network of women's clubs across the country, stemming from the Progressive era.

4. Inez Haynes Irwin, *Angels and Amazons: A Hundred Years of American Women* (New York: Doubleday Doran, 1933). This text is an impassioned history of the woman suffrage movement. See the biography of Irwin by Elaine Showalter in *Notable American Women, The Modern Period* (1980), pp. 368–70.

5. Ida Husted Harper, *The Life and Work of Susan B. Anthony* (Indianapolis: Hollenbeck). The first two volumes were published in 1898, and the third volume dealing with Anthony's later years was published in 1908. Our college library acquired these in 1920, the year the national woman suffrage amendment was ratified.

6. The Boston Women's Health Book Collective, *Our Bodies Ourselves* (New York: Simon and Schuster, 1971). Barrie, living in Boston, sent me an early newsprint version.

7. Frances Fitzgerald, *America Revised: History School Books in the Twentieth Century* (New York: Vantage, 1979), p. 152.

8. Ella M. Cushman, *Management in Homes* (New York: Macmillan, 1945), p. 20. Margaret W. Rossiter has written of Cornell's early attitude toward professionally trained women. See *Women Scientists in America: Struggles and Strategies to 1940* (Baltimore: Johns Hopkins University Press, 1982).

9. Mildred Weigley Wood, Ruth Lindquist, and Lucy A. Studley, *Managing the Home* (Boston: Houghton Mifflin, 1932), p. 44.

10. Bertha Damon, *Grandma Called It Carnal* (New York: Simon and Schuster, 1938), pp. 115–17.

11. Christine Herrick, *Housekeeping Made Easy* (New York: Harper, 1888), p. 85. Herrick was a daughter of Marion Harland, the famous writer on household advice. Almost a hundred years after Herrick's book, a history of household work finally appeared, and it was written by a woman. See Susan Strasser, *Never Done: A History of American Housework* (New York: Pantheon Books, 1982). For a more extensive history, see Suellen Hoy, *Chasing Dirt: The American Pursuit of Cleanliness* (New York: Oxford University Press, 1995).

12. George W. Norris, *Fighting Liberal: The Autobiography of George W. Norris* (New York: Macmillan, 1945), p. 24.

13. Robert Louis Stevenson, "A Good Play," in *A Child's Garden of Verse* (Boston: Scribners, original copyright 1909).

14. Marion Harland (Mary Virginia Hawes Terhune), *The Housekeeper's Week* (New York: Bobbs-Merrill, 1908), pp. 10–11. Harland says that she wrote this description of washing clothes thirty years earlier, which would be around 1878. My 1949 manuscript quoted her long paragraph just as she wrote it. In 1973 I treated it as found poetry and put it on library reserve for my students to read.

15. Caroline L. Hunt, *Home Problems From a New Standpoint* (Boston: Whitcomb & Barrows, 1908), pp. 76–77. Hunt, a home economist involved in causes of social justice, wrote this book while professor of home economics at the University of Wisconsin. She saw beyond the scientific management movement in her profession. See Glenna Matthews, *"Just a Housewife": The Rise and Fall of Domesticity in America* (New York: Oxford University Press, 1987), pp. 160–61.

16. Herrick, 306–07.

17. Ann Leighton, "The American Matron and the Lilies," *Harper's* (December 1946): 541–43. The dry bundle of sticks held aloft is on p. 542. Several magazines contained articles in 1946 on the woman question but rarely used the term "feminism." See Margaret Mead, "What Women Want," *Fortune* (December 1946): 172–75, 218–23.

18. Ferdinand Lundberg and Marynia Farnham, *Modern Woman the Lost Sex* (New York: Harper and Brothers, 1947).

19. Elsa Denison Voorhees, "Emotional Adjustment of Women in the Modern World and the Choice of Satisfactions," *Annals of American Academy of Political and Social Science* (May 1929): 369, 371, 373.

20. Edward A. Strecker, *Their Mothers' Sons: The Psychiatrist Examines an American Problem* (Philadelphia: J. B. Lippincott, 1946).

21. Leighton, 541.

22. Harland, 7.

23. Isabel Bevier and Susannah Usher, *The Home Economics Movement* (Boston: Whitcomb & Barrows, 1906), p. 14.

24. Elizabeth Hawes, *Why Women Cry: or Wenches with Wrenches* (New York: Reynal & Hitchcock, 1943), pp. 3, 5.

25. Charlotte Perkins Gilman, *Women and Economics* (Boston: Small, Maynard and Co., 1898), p. 244.

26. Lundberg and Farnham (1947). See also Philip Wylie, *Generation of Vipers* (New York: Holt, Rinehart and Winston, 1942). The Wisconsin Supreme Court decision is quoted in Inez Haynes Irwin, *Angels and Amazons: A Hundred Years of American Women* (New York: Doubleday Doran, 1933), p. 174.

27. Lynn White, Jr., *Educating Our Daughters* (New York: Harper, 1950). Susan M. Hartmann brings together the arguments of White, Taylor, and Horton in *American Women in the 1940s: On the Home Front and Beyond* (Boston: Twayne, 1982), pp. 111–16.

28. Dale Spender, *Women of Ideas and What Men Have Done to Them: From Aphra Behn to Adrienne Rich* (London: Routledge and Kegan Paul Ltd, 1982), p. 518.

CHAPTER 4: Search for Values

1. Alison Thorne, "Leave the Dishes in the Sink: An Inquiry into the Values Held by Wives and Mothers, and by the Advice-givers Who Influence Them" (unpublished, 1973).

2. Irma H. Gross and Elizabeth Walbert Crandall, *Management for Modern Families* (New York: Appleton-Century-Crofts, 1954), pp. 56–59.

3. Conversation with Ione (Daniel) Bennion, November 9, 1988. The title page of the typescript of the symposium, held November 1, 1950, includes this statement: "Four of Utah's successful, college-graduate women, holding positions of respect in their various communities, answer two questions: What has my college education meant to me? and What should college do for the woman of today?"

   Ione and Ted Daniel later divorced, and Ione returned to the name of her first husband, Wayne Bennion, who died in the early 1940s.

4. Ravenna Helson surveyed seven hundred Mills College alumnae, in five-year cohorts. See R. Helson, T. Elliott, and J. Leigh, "Adolescent Antecedents of Women's Work Patterns," in *Adolescence and Work: Influence of Social Structure, Labor Markets, and Culture*, ed. D. Eichorn and D. Stern (Hillsdale, New Jersey: Erlbaum, 1988), p. 50. I am indebted to Avril Thorne for this reference.

5. Lois W. Banner, *American Beauty* (New York: Knopf, 1983), p. 285.

6. Juanita Brooks, letter to Dale Morgan, April 5, 1942, quoted by Levi S. Peterson, *Juanita Brooks, Mormon Woman Historian* (Salt Lake City: University of Utah Press, 1988), p. 124.

7. William James, *The Varieties of Religious Experience: A Study of Human Nature* (Modern Library edition: Longmans, Green, 1902).

8. In the 1970s Luna and Duncan Brite built a large room at the back of their house to provide a meeting place for groups they cared about, including Thoughtless Thinkers, AAUW, the League of Women Voters, and the Presbyterian choir. When their health deteriorated in the early 1980s, the Brites sold the house and moved to their daughter's home in Pasadena. With their departure, Thoughtless Thinkers ceased to exist.

9. Sterling McMurrin was United States Commissioner of Education under President John F. Kennedy and then returned to the University of Utah. In the 1950s McMurrin was very nearly excommunicated from the Mormon Church for "heretical views," but intervention by David O. McKay, then president of the church, prevented it. In 1988 he received the first Governor's Award for the Humanities. See *The Salt Lake Tribune* (November 20, 1988).

10. Ralph Tyler Flewelling, *The Things That Matter Most: An Approach to the Problems of Human Values* (New York: Ronald Press, 1946). Nicolas Berdyaev, *Slavery and Freedom* (New York: Scribners, 1944), p. 21.

11. Wynne Thorne, talk for the funeral of Clara Nebeker Hulme, April 13, 1966. Ione Daniel read a beautiful tribute written by Edith Bowen.

12. Alison Thorne, journal (unpublished), 3:181, in Special Collections, Utah State University Merrill Library.

13. John Laird, *Idea of Value* (Cambridge: University Press, 1929).

14. Margaret L. Rhodes, *Ethical Dilemmas in Social Work Practice* (Boston: Routledge and Kegan Paul, 1986), pp. xi, 25–50. Margaret Rhodes was then on the faculty of the College of Public and Community Service, University of Massachusetts, Boston. I met her through Barrie. They were close friends as undergraduates at Stanford and later when they both lived in Boston.

15. Karen Horney, *Neurosis and Human Growth: The Struggle toward Self-realization* (New York: Norton, 1950); Gordon Allport, *Pattern and Growth in Personality* (New York: Holt, Rinehart and Winston, 1937, 1961). Extremely important is the test of values created by Allport, G. Lindzey and P. E. Vernon, *A Study of Values* (Boston: Houghton Mifflin, 1951). It resembles Elizabeth Hoyt's list of basic interests.

16. Howard Parsons later joined the faculty of Coe College in Iowa.

17. News clipping from the Knoxville *News-Sentinal* and enclosed in Alison Thorne family letter of April 29, 1954. The letter also says that Barrie and I attended the finals of Southern Appalachian district to see how LaVerne Weaver, the city winner, would do. She lost. The district included east Tennessee counties and three Kentucky counties in the mountains.

18. Barrie Thorne, letter to grandparents, April 3, 1954.

19. Alison Thorne, family letter, April 29, 1954.

20. Katharine Graham, publisher of *The Washington Post*, arrived as an undergraduate at the University of Chicago in the fall of 1936. I had left in June. In her memoirs she says that although she had friends who joined the

Young Communists, she herself was not persuaded. "[V]ery luckily for *The Washington Post* during the McCarthy era, when we were constantly being attacked as 'reds' by various constituencies, I never had been a member." Katharine Graham, *Personal History* (New York: Knopf, 1997), p. 84.

CHAPTER 5: Conformity and Creativity

1. Hoyt, *Consumption of Wealth* (1928), chap. 4.
2. Henry Steel Commager, "The Tests of a Free Society," *Utah Educational Review* (November 1955): 8, 24.
3. Hoyt, *Consumption in Our Society* (1938), pp. 272–76, 283–84.
4. William H. Whyte, Jr., "The Wives of Management," *Fortune* (October 1951): 86; Whyte, "The Corporation and the Wife," *Fortune* (November 1951). Even the editors found this demand for conformity excessive and wrote a piece in the November issue called "In Praise of the Ornery Wife," 75–76. Whyte's later book, *Organization Man*, was a full-scale indictment of excessive conformity and contained a fascinating appendix on how to cheat on psychology tests.
5. Alison Thorne, "Go Easy on Advice to Wives!" *American School Board Journal* (October 1963): 16, written in response to Jane and Clyde E. Blocker, "The School Executive's Wife," (May 1963): 12.
6. Alison C. Thorne, Frances G. Taylor, Rex L. Hurst, and Marjorie P. Bennion, *Space Required to Store Food in Western Farm Kitchens*, Utah Agricultural Experiment Station Bulletin 388 (July 1956). Marjorie Bennion, Marie Webster, Alison Thorne, and Frances G. Taylor, *Farm Kitchens*, Utah Agricultural Experiment Station Bulletin 389 (July 1956).
7. Almeda Perry Brown's Utah Agricultural Experiment Station Bulletins are numbers 213, 246, 257, and 266, published in 1929, 1934, 1935, and 1936. For greater detail see Alison C. Thorne, "Family and Community Studies from a Feminist Perspective" (Centennial Lecture: Utah State University, March 4, 1988), in Special Collections, Utah State University Merrill Library.
8. See Utah Agricultural Experiment Station Bulletins 369, 406, and 460, published in 1956, 1959, and 1966. For greater detail on Fredrickson see my Centennial Lecture, "Family and Community Studies from a Feminist Perspective."
9. *National 4-H News* (February 1956): 17. See also (April 1956): 16–17 and (May 1956): 17.
10. Pauline Udall Smith, assisted by Alison Comish Thorne, *Captain Jefferson Hunt of the Mormon Battalion* (Salt Lake City: Nicholas G. Morgan, Sr. Foundation, 1958). The drafts of this book, together with correspondence between Pauline Smith and Alison Thorne, are with the S. George Ellsworth and Maria Smith Ellsworth papers in Special Collections, Utah State University Merrill Library.
11. Alison Thorne, "Climate of Learning at Home," *Gifted Child Quarterly* 7 (Summer 1963): 47–50. Reprinted as "Suggestions for Mothering the Gifted to Encourage Curiosity, Learning and Creativity" in *Creativity: Its*

Educational Implications, ed. John Curtis Gowan, George D. Demos, and E. Paul Torrance (New York: Wiley, 1967), pp. 272–77.

12. My June 24, 1958 letter was a long one mailed to Wynne in Moscow. He brought it home with him.

13. Wynne Thorne, letter to Alison Thorne from Baghdad, June 2, 1958.

14. Alison Thorne, letter to Wynne Thorne, June 24, 1958.

15. A picture of the five Russians with the Chase family in the presidential living room is in Alice Chase, *The Story of a House: The President's Home, Utah State University* (n.d.).

16. Frank Barron, "Psychology of the Imagination," *Scientific American* (September 1958): 250–61.

17. I spoke to the Hyde Park Ladies' Literary Club in 1952. The mother's comment about girls is from my journal, 3: 30.

18. Ray Nelson's column "Thoughts and Things," in the *Herald Journal* (March 9 and 10, 1960), describes this organization in detail, naming as members Dr. Luna Brite, Dr. Sterling Taylor, Mrs. E. Milton Andersen, and many others.

19. Alison Thorne, "Suggestions for Mothering the Gifted," 272–74. Imagine our family's delight when we opened our November 1967 issue of *Scientific American* and found Kip S. Thorne, "Gravitational Collapse" on pp. 88–98.

20. Carl Rogers, "Toward a Theory of Creativity," in *Creativity and Its Cultivation,* ed. H. H. Anderson (New York: Harpers, 1959), pp. 75–76.

21. I told the story of the Indian Pavilion in Alison Thorne, "The Magic Carpet," *Gifted Child Quarterly* 9 (Autumn 1965): 141–42.

22. Solomon E. Asch, "Opinions and Social Pressure," *Scientific American* (November 1955): 107–11.

23. Jacob W. Getzels and Philip W. Jackson, *Creativity and Intelligence: Explorations with Gifted Students* (New York: Wiley, 1962), pp. 159, 183.

24. Wynne Thorne, "Education and Research," pp. 4–5. His paper, "Scholarship Plus," was given at the Phi Kappa Phi initiation on May 31, 1959 and published in the *Phi Kappa Phi Quarterly* 40 (Spring 1960) 1: 14–19. Ray Nelson of the *Herald Journal* printed excerpts in his column "Thoughts and Things" on June 30. Wynne's third paper, "Creative Process," was tied to the scientific method. He found Pareto's statement on fruitful error in Charles P. Curtis, Jr. and Ferris Greenslet, eds., *The Practical Cogitator, or The Thinker's Anthology* (Boston: Houghton Mifflin Company, 1945), p. 55.

    For Christmas 1966 Barrie gave Wynne a copy of Thomas S. Kuhn, *The Structure of Scientific Revolutions* (Chicago: University of Chicago Press, 1962), which contained a new and vital perspective on creativity in science.

25. Brewster Ghiselin, ed., *The Creative Process* (Berkeley: University of California Press, 1952), pp. 37, 44, 85, 226.

26. Alison Thorne, "Homemaking and the Idea of Creativity," *Proceedings of the Eleventh Conference of College Teachers of Clothing, Textiles, and Related Arts* (Utah State University, October 15, 16, 17, 1964). Norma Compton later became dean of home economics at Auburn and then at Purdue.

27. Dorothy Lee, "Discrepancies in the Teaching of American Culture," in *Education and Anthropology,* ed. George D. Spindler (1955), pp. 163–76.

28. Roy Heath, *The Reasonable Adventurer* (1964) reviewed by Daniel Yount in *Saturday Review* (August 15, 1964): 65–66.
29. Avril believes they wrote this bit of verse in May 1967, before she left home at age eighteen to live in Salt Lake City.

CHAPTER 6: Social Justice: The 1960s

1. Charles S. Peterson, "Changing Times: A View from Cache Valley, 1890–1915," *60th Faculty Honor Lecture* (Utah State University, November 1979), pp. 15, 19–20, 25.
2. The Fister episode and following ones including Kip, are from my family letter of November 2, 1961.
3. Cleon Skouson, a Mormon and an ardent fighter of communism, was Salt Lake City's former chief of police. Ernest Wilkinson, a wealthy and very conservative attorney, was president of Brigham Young University. Wilkinson ran for governor in 1964 and was defeated. Cache County gave him a higher proportion of "yes" votes than any other county, indicating to me how conservative our county was.
4. Alison Thorne, family letter, November 19, 1961. The recent meetings in Washington were those of the National Association of Land Grant Colleges and Universities.
5. Alison Thorne, family letters, February 7 and February 17, 1964.
6. Alison Thorne, family letter, February 6, 1962.
7. Corda Bauer and Dorothy Lewis were good friends of Wynne's and mine. Corda's husband, Norman Bauer, was a brilliant chemist who died young, but not before he made a mark in his profession and on campus. He tried valiantly to get United States nuclear testing stopped. Dorothy Lewis, originally from Ohio, taught child development at USU. Her children, Sherman and Carolyn, were the ages of Kip and Barrie. Dorothy became a Quaker and backed Bauer's view on nuclear testing.
   The year the Paulings visited Logan was the year that Linus Pauling received the Nobel Peace prize. He said the honor belonged as much to his wife as to him because they had given hundreds of speeches about world peace and avoiding nuclear war. Ava Helen Pauling was a feminist, peace activist, and social critic. See the *Oregon Stater* (June 1988).
8. Harden M. McConnell, "A Career Without Compromise," *Science* 2 (February 1996): 604.
9. Karen J. Blair, *The Clubwoman as Feminist: True Womanhood Redefined, 1868–1914* (New York: Holmes and Meier, 1980). The *Herald Journal* gave a full page spread to the Cache Women's Legislative Council on April 7, 1968, with four group pictures and a long list of delegates and the groups they represented. Because of its size, USU Faculty Women's League had three delegates. Carol Clay was council president in 1963–67, followed by Monna Judah in 1967–69.
   At this time the council had more power in dealing with Cache Valley issues than did the National Federation of Women's Clubs, an august body. The Faculty Women's League terminated its fifty-three year association

with the Federation in 1965. See Annette B. Larsen, "Eighty Years of Faculty Women's League: A History" (master's thesis, Utah State University, 1995), 72–73.

10. *Herald Journal* (December 4, 1962).

11. In my talks I was using Theodore Schultz's idea that education is not a cost. It is an investment. He had sent me some of his writing on this.

12. Bernarr Furse, quoted in *The Salt Lake Tribune* (September 23, 1989). Furse was on state Superintendent Ted Bell's staff in 1964 when the teachers "stayed out of school."

13. Alison Thorne, family letter, May 19, 1964.

14. Alison Thorne, family letters, April 23, July 9, and July 24, 1964. The municipal pool was dedicated November 23, 1965.

15. Wynne and I had our pictures on the front page of Section B of the *Deseret News* (January 27, 1965). I appeared as a new appointee to the Building Board. Wynne was shown with USU President Chase at the Ninth Annual Agriculture and Industry Conference, where Wynne spoke on contributions of scientists that more than pay back taxpayers' investment in higher education.

16. This description combines two unpublished accounts of the migrant school and OEO programs: Alison Thorne, "Community Work," chap. 10 in "Leave the Dishes in the Sink" (1973); and Alison Comish Thorne, "Leave the Dishes in the Sink: Women's Household and Community Work in Cache Valley," paper presented at the Mountain West Center for Regional Studies Symposium (Utah State University, May 14, 1992).

17. For articles and pictures about the migrant school see *The Salt Lake Tribune* (July 18, 1965) and *Herald Journal* (June 30, 1965, September 20, 1966, and August 6, 1969). My family letter of April 24, 1970, tells of the Cache school district taking over migrant education.

18. Alison Thorne, family letter, May 26, 1966. This letter also describes our receiving the NUCAP grant.

19. *Herald Journal* (January 22, 1971). NUCAP first vice president was Hyrum Olsen of Job Service.

20. It is interesting how things work out. Stanford Cazier of the USU history faculty was a member of our first CAP Board. When he left Logan to become president of Chico State in California, he recommended Marvin Fifield to replace him on the board. This was done and that's why Fifield was available to succeed me as board president. In 1979 Stanford Cazier became the twelfth president of Utah State University.

CHAPTER 7: Feminist Straws in the Wind

1. David A. Burgoyne was in the top administration of the Utah Agricultural Experiment Station. His wife, Allie, was my good friend in Faculty Women's League, Agronomy Wives, and civic projects. Dave's sister, Lucile Burgoyne, who had always lived with them, died of a sudden heart attack on May 20, 1963. She was a gifted teacher in the public schools and taught the first migrant school, which I described in chapter six.

2. Betty Friedan, *The Feminine Mystique* (New York: W. W. Norton, 1963), reprinted edition (Dell, 1974), p. 338.
3. "Straws in the Wind: The College Woman of the 'Sixties'" was the title of an article by Ruth Hill Useem in *Women's Education* 2 (September 1963) published by the AAUW Educational Foundation. Useem, who listed herself as research consultant in the Department of Sociology and Anthropology at Michigan State University, did not use the term "feminism"; it was still too early.
4. The program was recorded on December 8, 1961 in the large and drafty quonset hut that was USU's television and radio station. I have a carbon copy of the script. One observation made by family life faculty was that girls in college have scarcely begun to use their brains.
5. Alison Thorne, family letter, February 17, 1964.
6. *Deseret News* and *Herald Journal* (November 19, 1965). Alison Thorne, family letter, November 28, 1965. This letter also tells of the Governor's Conference on Education, planned by Sterling McMurrin. Wynne and I were each on subcommittees and appeared on separate panels.
7. Alison Thorne, family letter, February 23, 1963.
8. D. A. Broadbent, letter to D. Wynne Thorne, February 28, 1964. Filed in my papers under "Alison Thorne, Contracts."
9. See Susan Himmelweit, "The Discovery of 'Unpaid Work': The Social Consequences of the Expansion of 'Work'" *Feminist Economics* 1 (2, 1995): 1–19.
10. Don C. Carter, "Commitments in Marriage," *31st Faculty Honor Lecture* (Utah State University, 1965).
11. Although I helped plan it, I missed the first University of Utah conference on changing roles for women (September 7–8, 1962) because I was with Wynne on a quick trip to Venezuela. The next year, in March, at a planning meeting for the second conference, we heard Algie Ballif tell of the work of the President's Commission on Status of Women. She was a member of its committee on education, having been placed there by her sister, Esther Peterson. A distinguished Utah woman in her own right, Algie Ballif served in the Utah legislature and was former president of the Utah School Boards Association. Up to the time of her death, though living in highly conservative Provo, Ballif strongly advocated passage of the Equal Rights Amendment. See my family letter, March 24, 1963. My September 9, 1963 letter tells about the second University of Utah women's conference.
12. "Annual Leadership School for Women," (mimeographed, Utah State University, October 3–5, 1961). Esther Peterson, "Outlook for Women's Employment," talk given October 2. The remark about not being a feminist is on p. 7.
13. *American Women*, Report of the President's Commission on the Status of Women, 1963, had a separate supplement called "Report on Four Consultations," with six pages on "Portrayal of Women by the Mass Media" (March 19, 1963). Al Capp's remark is on p. 22 and Marya Mannes' on p. 25.
14. "The American Female," foreword, special supplement in *Harper's* (October 1962): 117.

15. Ibid., 153.
16. *Harper's* (July 1965): 37–43.
17. Among the organizations urging the governor to create a commission on status of women were the Utah Federation of Business and Professional Women's Clubs (BPW), the American Association of University Women (AAUW), the Utah Federation of Women's Clubs, the Women's Legislative Council (for the State and for Salt Lake City), the Young Women's Christian Association (YWCA), Utah Press Women, the Utah State Home Economics Association, the Utah Girl Scouts Council, the Women's Democratic Clubs, the Women's Republican Clubs, the Women's Division of the State Industrial Commission, the Women's Division of the Forest Service (USDA), and the Women's Auxiliaries of the American Legion, Disabled American Veterans, Elks, and AFL-CIO.
18. All subcommittee members were women except one. Members of my subcommittee on employment were a business entrepreneur, attorney, union organizer, two interviewers for Employment Security, and from USU, sociologist Carmen Fredrickson and Robert P. Collier, dean of business and social science, who was untroubled at being outnumbered. We had a hard time finding facts on employment of women in Utah. How I longed for the kind of information that Esther Peterson gave in her article "Working Women," *Daedalus* (Spring 1964): 671–99.
19. *Newsletter*, Utah Governor's Advisory Committee, vol. 1, no. 1 (September 1969). For a fuller description of the women on the committee and its work, see Alison C. Thorne, "Women and Higher Education," in *Higher Education: Dimensions and Directions*, ed. F. Robert Paulsen (Tucson; University of Arizona Press, 1970), p. 150–51.
20. *Progress and Prospects*, Report of the Second National Conference of Governors' Commissions on the Status of Women (Washington D.C., July 28–30, 1965).
21. The epilogue of Betty Friedan's *The Feminine Mystique*, reprint (New York: Dell, 1974), pp. 368–70, describes the formation of NOW. I had a very busy time on this trip east because I took Sandra, Avril, and Lance with me to see Washington, D.C. We also saw the New York World's Fair and visited Barrie in Boston.
22. Alison Thorne, family letter, June 24, 1968. For the program, see *1968: Time for Action, Highlights of the Fourth National Conference of Commissions on the Status of Women* (Washington, D.C., June 20–22, 1968). I accompanied Hilda Worthington Smith into the hall where Coretta Scott King spoke. We later exchanged letters, and I received a draft of her unpublished autobiography. Smith was an astounding woman. Susan Ware tells about her in *Beyond Suffrage: Women in the New Deal* (Cambridge: Harvard University Press, 1981).

   Gertrude Gronbech, with whom I stayed, was employed by USDA and worked with agricultural economists. I knew her when we were both graduate students under Hoyt and Reid. Much later, in 1985, I went with her to international agricultural economists' meetings in Spain. Soon afterwards she died of brain cancer, a great loss.

23. Alison Thorne, "Women and Higher Education," 153–55. At the PHT Degree Awards Program of June 2, 1967, I gave the salute to graduates. Dean of Women Helen Lundstrom conducted, and President Daryl Chase gave a welcome.

24. Ibid., 140–45.

25. Ibid., 148. Taken from National Institutes of Health, United States Department of Health, Education, and Welfare, *Special Report on Women and Graduate Study*, Resources for Medical Research Report No. 13 (Washington, D.C.: U.S. Government Printing Office, June 1968).

26. Diana E. Long review of Margaret W. Rossiter, *Women Scientists in America: Before Affirmative Action, 1940–1972*. (Baltimore, Maryland: Johns Hopkins University Press, 1995). The review appears in *Women's Review of Books* 13 (June 1996): 14–15.

27. The Logan hearing is in my family letter, October 9, 1964. The hearing in Price is in my letter of November 4, 1964, which also describes traveling from Salt Lake City toward Soldier Summit in a brown dust storm.

28. I wrote the NUCAP proposal in the Cache County Courthouse in the office of county extension agent, Ray Burtenshaw, with the help of Burtenshaw; William Farnsworth, also of extension; Sam Gordon of the Box Elder schools; and Ted Maughan, State Department of Employment Security.

29. My family letter of November 28, 1965, observes that the advisory council meets every two months, and I have become vice chairman. The letter of November 27, 1968, says the council no longer sits rigidly with labor on one side and employers on the other but is informal and there are now more women and representatives of disadvantaged groups. I became chair in 1975 and remained chair until 1982, when I resigned from the council because I was busy coordinating the Women and International Development program at USU.

30. Barrie Thorne to family, September 8, 1966.

31. Barrie Thorne to family, May 23, 1967; May 28, 1968; June 11, 1968.

32. Barrie Thorne to family, May 1969.

33. Barrie Thorne to Alison Thorne, November 20, 1989, after reading an early draft of this chapter.

34. Barrie Thorne to Sandra Thorne, September 16, 1969.

35. Alison Thorne, family letter, November 27, 1968.

36. Sandra Thorne-Brown to Alison Thorne, November 29, 1989, after reading an early draft of this chapter.

37. Avril Thorne to family, postmarked October 30, 1969. I knew Dr. Virginia Frobes because she co-chaired a subcommittee of the original Governor's Committee on the Status of Women. Trained in psychology, she was also a fluent speaker at the University of Utah women's conferences. It is noteworthy that she was dean of students, not dean of women. The University of Utah handled its student uprisings during this turbulent period with much wisdom, due in large part to Frobes' level-headedness.

38. Avril Thorne to family, February 1970.

Chapter 8: Activism in the 1970s

1. Avril Thorne, letter, postmarked February 10, 1970.
2. Avril Thorne, letter, November 17, 1970.
3. Alison Thorne, family letter, February 21, 1970.
4. *The Salt Lake Tribune* (May 3, 1970).
5. Alison Thorne, family letter, May 17, 1970.
6. Alison Thorne, letters, May 17 and June 23, 1970.
7. Kip's open letter to the *Herald Journal*, as quoted in Alison Thorne, family letter, May 26, 1970.
8. Anonymous letter to Alison Thorne, postmarked May 22, 1970. Copied into Alison Thorne, family letter, May 26, 1970.
9. Alison Thorne, letter, September 18, 1970.
10. Alison Thorne, letter, July 5, 1970.
11. Alison Thorne, letter, June 23, 1970, describes Sandra's work at the Bird Refuge.
12. Avril Thorne, letter, July 17, 1970, and enclosed news clipping from the Seattle *Post- Intelligencer* (n.d.).
13. Alison Thorne, letter, August 26, 1970, sent to relatives unable to attend the wedding.
14. Everett C. Hughes, Barrie Thorne, Agostino M. Baggis, Arnold Gurin, David Williams, *Education for the Professions of Medicine, Law, Theology, and Social Welfare*, A Report of the Carnegie Commission on Higher Education (New York: McGraw Hill, 1973), p. xvi.
15. Alison Thorne, letters, July 5 and October 25, 1970.
16. Alison Thorne, letter, November 7, 1970. Also see my folder on Utah preparation for the White House conference.
17. Alison Thorne, letter, January 23, 1970.
18. Alison Thorne, letter, April 24, 1970.
19. Austin and Alta Fife, eds., *Ballads of the Great West* (Palo Alto: American West Publishing, 1970). Wynne had known the Fifes from undergraduate days. When Austin joined the USU faculty in 1960, we became close friends.
20. Sandra Thorne-Brown, letter to Alison Thorne, November 29, 1989.
21. Sandra Thorne-Brown, letters, February 28 and April 13, 1973.
22. Sandra Thorne-Brown, letter, May 13, 1973.
23. Sandra Thorne-Brown, letter, July 7, 1973.
24. Sandra Thorne-Brown, letter, October 24, 1973.
25. Minutes of LWVCC meeting February 12, 1990, taken by Alison Thorne. This meeting celebrated twenty years of the league.
26. Jenny Box, "Cache County Mosquitoes," *LWVCC Voter* (May 1989): 4–5.
27. Joseph A. Geddes and Carmen D. Fredrickson, *Libraries as Social Institutions*, Utah Agricultural Experiment Station Bulletin 369 (1954). I commented on the attitude of the Cache County commissioners toward this study in my Centennial Lecture, "Family and Community Studies from a Feminist Perspective" (Utah State University, March 4, 1988): 11–12.

28. Kenneth W. Godfrey, "Warmth, Friendship, and Scholarship: The Life and Times of Virginia Hanson," *Utah Historical Quarterly* 60 (Fall 1992): 335–52. As laudatory as Godfrey's article is, he still does not do justice to Virginia.

29. Anne C. Hatch, "A History of the Library Servicing Cache County, Utah," booklet originally designed for Cache Public Library Board use (May 1973). "Library Study for Cache County," Cache County League of Women Voters (April 1974). Alexa West was chairman and members of her committee were Anne C. Hatch, Carmen Fredrickson, Judy MacMahon, and Marjory Stanley. When the library severed its tie with the county, Anne Hatch became chair of the new library board, with Marjory Stanley as a board member. Judy MacMahon, who had been a librarian in Ohio, became a librarian succeeding Virginia Hanson. Anne, Marjory, and Judy were LWVCC members.

30. I copied Newell Olsen's letter, my reply, the Holmgren letter, and Olsen's apology in my family letter of March 1, 1974. The Holmgren letter and Olsen's apology appeared in the *Herald Journal* (February 24, 1974). Art Holmgren was a distinguished botanist on the USU faculty. He and Doris were strong supporters of music and arts in the community.

31. The Committee of Five made its recommendations on July 29, 1976. These were acted upon as follows: On December 15, 1976, Cache County commissioners and Logan Mayor Desmond Anderson agreed to convey to the city total ownership of Cache Public Library after a period of seven years, during which time county residents could use the library free of charge. After seven years, county residents would be charged an annual fee of twenty-five dollars for a library card. However, in the 1990s, population growth and pressure on library resources forced the Logan Library to prohibit county residents from checking out books altogether, pending adequate library funding on the part of the county government.

32. Alison Thorne, family letter, November 17, 1974.

33. Sandy Hayes, "Local Profile: The League of Women Voters of Cache County," *League of Women Voters of Utah, Utah Voter* (Spring 1984).

Chapter 9: The Women's Movement at Utah State University

1. Minutes of Steering Committee meeting, October 26, 1972. Richard Swenson came to USU in 1971 from California State Polytechnic University in Pomona. His Ph.D. was from Iowa State in agronomy in 1957, and he had been on the faculty of Michigan State University.

2. In relation to the faculty I was a marginal woman, but this proved to be an advantage. On being an outsider while being a bridge, see Brenda R. Silver, "The Authority of Anger: *Three Guineas* as Case Study," *Signs* 16 (Winter 1991): 343–44.

3. Barrie Thorne, letter, February 28, 1972.

4. On equalization of faculty salaries, and on the secretaries organizing to get higher pay, see *USU Status of Women News* 1 (June 1973). The University of Utah paid clerk stenos $5,081; Idaho State, $4,727; and USU, $4,080.

5. Our green sheet was named "Sexism in the Classroom." See Alison Thorne file on the green sheet, which contains Michigan State University versions as well as the USU version. There is also a copy of Barrie Thorne's letter of May 26, 1981, explaining to the MSU provost why they are so similar and why "On Campus With Women" published USU's version.

6. Alison Thorne, family letter, November 18, 1973. Larzette Hale came to our women's studies course to speak on problems of racism. At USU she made the Accounting Department into a School of Accounting; she served on the Governor's Commission on the Status of Women; and in 1994 was on the state board of regents.

7. Alison Thorne, file on the USU Status of Women Committee.

8. Alvin Reiner, guest writer, *Student Life* (May 3, 1972).

9. Janet Osborne would be a moving force in making the old Whittier School into a Community Art Center. In 1976 the city put up four thousand dollars, and the rest of the funding came from grants and donations, which Janet helped secure. Alison Thorne, family letter, March 18, 1976. Janet also became codirector and later director of the USU Women's Center. She earned her Ed.D. in 1988.

10. Alison Thorne, family letter, June 1, 1973. This same letter said of the class, "Our activist group will stay together all summer and is trying to get the campus health center improved." I also wrote that Jeanne Young (of Huntsville, Texas) would come for commencement to receive her Ph.D. in sociology. I was on her doctoral committee and wrote to my family that no woman received a Ph.D. at commencement the year before, "and some of us are interested in having one go across the stand this year, by ginger."

11. Gail Casterline did a master's thesis in 1974 in the History Department, entitled "'In the Toils' or 'Onward to Zion': Images of the Mormon Woman, 1852–1890," showing that Mormon women defended, in print, their church and its teachings, in contrast to the popular image of polygamy as an oppression. I served on her thesis committee.

12. Alison Thorne, family letter, July 13, 1973.

13. *USU Status of Women News* 1 (October 1973). Jane Lott used such a leave, as did Pat Gardner and others. Their doctorates became stepping stones to advancement at USU. Bonita Wyse took the first leave and some years later became dean of the College of Family Life. Jane Lott (McCullough) became head of the Department of Home Economics and Consumer Education, and Pat Gardner became head of the English Department.

14. Judith M. Gappa and J. Nicholas Eastmond, Jr., "Gaining Support for a Women's Studies Program in a Conservative Institution" *Liberal Education* 64 (October 1978): 278–91.

15. Judith M. Gappa, "Women's Studies at USU, A Proposal," Prepared for the Instructional Development Division (Utah State University, March 1977). By then Ramona Moratz, Department of Family and Human Development, offered a graduate seminar "Women and Men." Pat Gardner and Shirlene Mason (Pope) in the English Department each offered a course on women in literature and women writers. Lynne Goodhart in the French Department taught a comparative literature course about women, offered through the

honors program. Marilynne Glatfelter taught personal assessment and assertiveness training. Soon Jane Post would teach a course about math anxiety, and Janice Pearce would teach "Women and Health."

16. Alison Thorne, letter to Wynne Thorne in Pakistan, March 18, 1976 and family letter, April 15, 1976. Three thousand residents of Cache county signed the petition. See *Herald Journal* (April 9, 1976). The controversy was still raging in August. See special edition of *Herald Journal* (August 17, 1976), which contains statements about Title IX by Joan Shaw, Judith Gappa, students, and the school superintendents. The students were tolerant of each others' views; it was parents who were polarized.

17. Alison Thorne, family letter, February 15, 1976. The Thorne and Henley book was published by Newbury House of Rowley, Massachusetts in 1975. In 1983 Barrie Thorne, Cheres Kramarae, and Nancy Henley edited a completely revised edition, also published by Newbury House. It is called *Language, Gender and Society* and dedicated to the editors' mothers and sisters.

18. Marilynne Glatfelter, "Panel on Nontraditional Students," in *Proceedings of the Centennial Centerpiece Closing Conference* (Utah State University, April 18–19, 1988): 79–82. This is a spirited discussion of reentry students, indicating their great value to the university and what they themselves learn.

Chapter 10: The Widening Reach of the Women's Movement

1. Jean Bickmore White, "Woman's Place Is in the Constitution: The Struggle for Equal Rights in Utah in 1895," *Utah Historical Quarterly* 42 (Fall 1974): 344–69.
2. *The Salt Lake Tribune* (October 1, 1970).
3. Jill Mulvay Derr, "Strength in Our Union: The Making of Mormon Sisterhood," in *Sisters in the Spirit: Mormon Women in Historical and Cultural Perspective*, ed. Maureen Ursenbach Beecher and Lavina Fielding Anderson (Urbana, Illinois: University of Illinois Press, 1987), pp. 194–95.
4. Alison Thorne, family letter, September 27, 1972.
5. Alison Thorne, family letter, December 30, 1972.
6. Alison Thorne, family letter, January 21, 1973.
7. Alison Thorne, family letters, September 16 and October 14, 1973.
8. Calvin L. Rampton, *As I Recall* (Salt Lake City: University of Utah Press, 1989), pp. 245–46.
9. Jean Christensen had already set up a volunteer program in the Cache County and Logan school districts that used many people's talents. See Edith Morgan, "Women Organize Volunteer Talent Pool," *Herald Journal* (January 17, 1977).
10. Emma Lou Thayne's talk was called "Ashtrays and Gum Wrappers." My notes are dated May 6, 1976, and are filed with my family letters.
11. Elaine Jarvik and George Buck, "Beyond Fascination, Toward Assertion," *Utah Holiday* 6 (May 1977): 14, 16.
12. For names of leaders of these ten groups see *Herald Journal* (July 24, 1977). An Inter-Faith Council was achieved but never had the power of the ministerial breakfasts. See Pamela Kipper, "Inter-Faith Council Brings Various Religions Together," *The Cache Citizen* (January 23, 1980). "Hands Across

the Valley" conferences were held twice more, but attendance dwindled and the USU Women's Center began to hold other types of conferences.

13. See my file on LDS and non-LDS women's group meetings.

14. Alison Thorne, family letter, July 3, 1977.

15. Linda Sillitoe, "Inside the IWY Conference: Women Scorned," *Utah Holiday* (August 1977): 26–28, 63–69; Dixie Snow Huefner, "Church and Politics at the Utah IWY Conference," *Dialogue, A Journal of Mormon Thought* (Spring 1978): 58–75.

16. Emma Lou Thayne column, "My View," with headline "Women need to reach across the valley, try again," *Deseret News* (September 13, 1977). I have found very little written historically about efforts of Mormon and non-Mormon women to work together. A notable exception is Carol Cornwall Madsen, "Decade of Détente: The Mormon-Gentile Female Relationship in Nineteenth Century Utah" *Utah Historical Quarterly* 63 (Fall 1995): 298–319.

17. My family letter, August 20, 1977, describes the state Democratic convention and contains a copy of my letter to the editor of *The Salt Lake Tribune*, which appeared August 13, the same day as the convention. My *Tribune* letter told of the United States Supreme Court decision. I said women in Utah are second class citizens, and I urged ratification of the ERA.

18. A description of my efforts to wrest two observer passes from Gunn McKay is in my family letters of October 30 and November 12, 1977. He sent only one.

19. *Herald Journal* (November 18, 1977).

20. Gloria Steinem, *Outrageous Acts and Everyday Rebellions* (New York: Holt, Rinehart, and Winston, 1983), p. 1.

21. Much of this description of the conference is from Alison Thorne, "The National Women's Conference, Houston, November 1977," A Report to the Utah Division of AAUW, p. 9. (A copy is in my IWY folder.)

22. Gail Sheehy, "Women in Passage," *Redbook* (April 1978).

23. Alison Thorne, family letter, October 8, 1979.

24. The complete text of the National Plan of Action is in Caroline Bird, *What Women Want: The National Women's Conference* (New York: Simon and Schuster 1979). On Marjorie Bell Chambers' talk, see my family letter, May 16, 1979.

25. Anne Hatch, Becky Canning, and I attended a Women's Educational Equity Act proposal-writing workshop at Idaho State College in Pocatello on May 2, 1978. It was for novices, and we certainly qualified. Alison Thorne, family letter, May 15, 1978.

26. Alison Thorne, family letter, April 29, 1979.

27. Judith M. Gappa and Janice Pearce, *Sex and Gender in the Social Sciences: Reassessing the Introductory Course*, Women's Educational Equity Act Program (United States Department of Education, December 1980).

28. American Sociological Association Committee on the Status of Women in Sociology, "How to Recognize and Avoid Sexist Biases in Sociological Research," American Sociological Association, *Footnotes* (January 1979). American Psychological Association, *Guidelines for Nonsexist Language in APA Journals* (Washington, D.C. 1977). The Committee for Race and

Gender Balance in the Economics Profession, *Guidelines for Recognizing and Avoiding Racist and Sexist Biases in Economics* (1990). Summary in *Newsletter of the Committee on Status of Women in the Economics Profession, American Economic Association* (June 1991): 2.

29. These guidelines heralded the emergence of a strong movement in feminist economics. See Marianne A. Ferber and Julie A. Nelson, eds., *Beyond Economic Man: Feminist Theory and Economics* (Chicago: University of Chicago Press, 1993) and the journal *Feminist Economics* 1 (Spring 1995).

30. Sonia Johnson, *From Housewife to Heretic* (New York: Doubleday, 1981), p. 394. Of all the LDS chapels I have been in, during my long life, only our Logan First Ward pictured a woman so prominently. The artist, Everett Thorpe, was on the USU faculty.

31. Alison Thorne, family letter, August 7, 1979.

32. I copied the wording of the advertisement into my family letter of December 2, 1979.

33. Alison Thorne, family letter, December 2, 1979. This is also the date of the *The Salt Lake Tribune* story about the rally where Esther Landa spoke.

34. Linda Sillitoe and Paul Swenson, "A Moral Issue," *Utah Holiday* 9 (January 1980): 18–34.

35. Alison Thorne, family letter, October 12, 1980.

36. Logan High School *Grizzly* 57 (October 15, 1980).

37. Alison Thorne, family letter, April 28, 1984.

38. The ERA's original seven year term for ratification expired in October 1978, but Congress gave it a thirty-nine month extension, which ended June 30, 1982 with three states still needed for ratification.

39. Barrie Thorne with Marilyn Yalom, eds., *Rethinking the Family: Some Feminist Questions* (New York: Longman, 1982).

40. George D. Smith, ed., *Religion, Feminism, and Freedom of Conscience: A Mormon- Humanist Dialogue* (Salt Lake City: Signature Books, 1994). Bryan Watterman and Brian Kagel, *The Lord's University: Freedom and Authority at BYU* (Salt Lake City: Signature Books, 1998).

41. *Herald Journal* (November 15, 2000).

Chapter 11: The University, Women, and History

1. Helping plan this workshop were Mimi Gaudreau, a French-speaking doctoral candidate in agronomy who had served three years in the Peace Corps in Zaire; Nancy O'Rourke, who with her family had lived in Morocco and Tanzania for nearly five years; Jane McCullough of HECE and Dean Joan McFadden. We consulted with Boyd Wennergren, director of International Programs; Clark Ballard, vice president for Extension; Dean Thad Box of Natural Resources; Dean William Lye of HASS; and Glen Taggart, former USU president who was with BIFAD (Board for International Food and Agricultural Development), which linked universities with U.S. AID.

2. These international women were Alaz Rufael of Ethiopia, Chileshe Gowon of Zambia, Latita Srinivasan of India, and Rosa Marie Garcia-Jaurequie of

Mexico. We had two outside distinguished speakers, Arvonne Frazier with U.S. AID and Kathleen Cloud of the Women and Communication Network, based in Boston.

Later, when the regional Consortium for International Development (CID), headquartered in Tucson, created CID/WID, Kate Cloud was placed in charge. I attended CID/WID meetings in Tucson and wrote proposals for CID/WID funding for our WID projects. Another source of our funding was Title XII of the Foreign Assistance Act, under U.S. AID.

3. Alison Thorne, family letter, January 17, 1981.
4. Jack Keller, project director of Water Management Synthesis II, was a vigorous supporter of our WID. At his invitation, Nancy O'Rourke and I regularly attended his water management seminars.
5. Alison Thorne, family letters, May 16, September 12, and October 2, 1982. The description of students in the class is from my two-page report filed with course materials of HECE 235.
6. No longer WID coordinator, I took a three weeks' tour to China, led by Ed Glatfelter in political science, following which my companion, Idella Larson, and I went on to Nepal where Marlowe Thorne, my brother-in-law, showed us Kathmandu and the Terai, where he directed the U.S. AID project in agricultural education.
7. Judy B. Rollins, "Foreign Students' Wives Go to School Too," Lifestyle Section, *The Salt Lake Tribune* (December 9, 1984).
8. *Staff News* (February 1, 1985).
9. See pp. 35 and 67 of International Association of Agricultural Economists, *Members Bulletin No. 8* (Oxford England: Institute of Agricultural Economics, February 1987). See also Irene Tinker's pioneering article, "The Adverse Impact of Development on Women," in her book, edited with Michele Bo Bramsen, *Women and World Development* (Washington, D.C.: Overseas Development Council, 1976). A family letter, September 14, 1985, describes my trip to Spain.
10. Conversation with Afton Tew, director of International Student Services, February 10, 1996.
11. Alison Thorne, family letter, July 29, 1984.
12. Alison Thorne letter of February 2, 1984 to Tom Peterson, head of HECE, and Pam Riley, head of Sociology. By fall, Jane McCullough was head of HECE and Brian Pitcher was head of Sociology.
13. Letter of appreciation from Alison Thorne to Jon Moris, December 20, 1984.
14. Alison Thorne, family letter, November 25, 1984.
15. Alison Thorne, family letter, October 12, 1985. Barrie's reference was to Carol Gilligan, *In a Different Voice* (Cambridge: Harvard University Press, 1982). Avril's reference was to her own doctoral dissertation at the University of California, Berkeley, "Disposition as Interpersonal Constraint: A Study of Conversations Between Introverts and Extraverts" (1983).
16. Alison Comish Thorne, "Women in the History of Utah's Land-Grant College," paper prepared for Utah State University Faculty Women's League in commemoration of its 75th year (presented on March 7, 1986). Allie Burgoyne's paper was "Our University as I Know It" (talk prepared

by Mrs. David A. Burgoyne for the Utah State University Faculty Women's League program, November 7, 1958). Copies of these two unpublished papers are in Special Collections, Utah State University Merrill Library.

17. Levi S. Peterson, using Juanita Brooks' papers, describes her receiving the honorary degree, in *Juanita Brooks, Mormon Woman Historian* (Salt Lake City: University of Utah Press, 1988), p. 305.

18. Alison Thorne, family letter, June 13, 1982.

19. *Herald Journal*, June 9, 1985. My letter to Duncan Brite, dated June 9, 1985, is filed with my family letter of June 15, 1985. Peterson's eighty-fifth birthday party was December 9, 1991 at the Red Lion Hotel in Salt Lake City.

20. May Swenson received an honorary doctorate of letters and was commencement speaker on June 6, 1987.

21. The Tom Emery correspondence is in the folder labeled "D. Wynne Thorne Research Awards." A copy is also with my family letters. Tom Emery died at age sixty on April 25, 1992, of a heart attack while playing tennis. The obituary reads, "He left this earth the way he wanted: 'I'll go with a bang on the tennis courts.'"

22. *Utah Journal* (July 31, 1889), quoted by Joel Edward Ricks, *The Utah State Agricultural College, A History of Fifty Years 1888–1938* (Salt Lake City: Deseret News Press, 1938), p. 24.

23. On Aaron DeWitt, see Ian Craig Breaden, "Poetry, Polity, and the Cache Valley Pioneer: Polemics in the Journal of Aaron DeWitt, 1869–96," *Utah Historical Quarterly* (Fall 1993): 323–38.

24. A. J. Simmonds, "Looking Back," *Herald Journal* (March 22, 1987): 5. Simmonds quotes extensively from Sarah Eddy's speech. For Eddy's ranking as professor of history see *Annual Catalogue of the Agricultural College of Utah, 1894–95*. Ricks demoted her to instructor in his *Fifty-Year History*, p. 165.

25. Ricks, *Fifty-Year History*, pp. 121–125. Ricks does not name Fogelberg's mother but simply reports that her mother was the first student to enroll. He is strangely blind to women, failing to include Almeda Perry Brown in his list of faculty of 1890–1938.

26. "Program of Events. Semi-Centennial Celebration. Utah State Agricultural College. June 3 to 7, 1938." Dr. Paul Popenoe was director of the Institute of Family Relations, Los Angeles. Elder Stephen L. Richards was an apostle of the LDS Church. Anne Carroll Moore, distinguished writer and librarian in New York, was a close friend of the president's family. See Mrs. E. G. Peterson, *Remembering E. G. Peterson: His Life and Our Story*, pp. 125–28.

27. See biography of Abby Lillian Marlatt in *Notable American Women*, vol. 2, pp. 495–97.

28. Alison Thorne, letter to Karen Morse, Bonita Wyse, and Women and Gender Research Institute, April 17, 1987. Leonard J. Arrington, "Celebration of a Century of Accomplishments," *Proceedings Centennial Centerpiece Opening Conference* (April 14–16, 1987): 47–52. Dean F. Peterson, "An Assessment for the Future," *Proceedings*: 79–83. John M. Neuhold, "Summary and Conclusions," *Proceedings*: 70–78. Neuhold's remark about grass roots is not in the printed text. Maxine Stutler helped direct our WID program. Marilyn Noyes was associate director of the extension service.

29. Marilynne Glatfelter, "What Responsibilities Has Utah State University to the Nontraditional Student?" *Proceedings Centennial Centerpiece Closing Conference* (April 18–19, 1988): 79–82.
30. Karen Morse later became provost but left USU the summer of 1993 to become president of Western Washington University at Bellingham.
31. On reasons why Faculty Women's League thrived for decades and then died, see Annette B. Larsen, "Eighty Years of Faculty Women's League: A History" (master's thesis, Utah State University, 1995).
32. Karen Shepherd was not reelected in 1994 during the Republican sweep; she lost to Republican Enid Greene Waldholtz, who lasted only one term because of financial scandal.
33. The Women and Gender Research Institute (WGRI) was formed in 1984 with a twelve member steering committee. Leaflet (n.d.).
34. Alison C. Thorne, "Family and Community Studies from a Feminist Perspective" (Centennial Lecture: Utah State University, March 4, 1988). Sponsored by Department of Home Economics and Consumer Education; Department of Sociology, Social Work and Anthropology; and the Women and Gender Research Institute. The quotation, taken from p. 9 of my lecture, refers to Almeda Perry Brown's Utah Agricultural Experiment Station Bulletin 266 (1936).

Chapter 12: Gathering up Loose Ends

1. David McCullough, *Truman* (New York: Simon and Schuster, 1992), p. 915.
2. *Washington Spectator* (March 15, 1996): 2.
3. C. Haynes, scholar in residence of The Freedom Forum First Amendment Center, spoke at Utah State University April 11, 1996 as part of a two-day symposium on "Values and Liberty: An American Crisis," sponsored by the College of Humanities, Arts, and Social Sciences and funded by the O. C. Tanner Foundation.
4. Ruth Rosen, "Hillary Clinton's Current Confrontations Reflect Nation's Ongoing Gender Clash," *The Salt Lake Tribune* (February 6, 1996): A9; written for the *Los Angeles Times*. Rosen is professor of history at the University of California, Davis.
5. Alice S. Rossi, "Equality Between the Sexes: An Immodest Proposal," *Daedalus* (Spring 1964): 607–52. Rossi's change of mind is shown in "A Biosocial Perspective on Parenting," *Daedalus* (Spring 1977): *1-31*. See also Carol Gilligan, *In a Different Voice* (Cambridge: Harvard University Press, 1982).
6. *Cache Citizen* (February 13, 1985).
7. Alison Thorne, family letter, February 18, 1985. The battered women's shelter is sponsored by CAPSA, now known as Citizens Against Parental and Spouse Abuse.
8. Barrie and I inquired into the relation between feminism and home economics, or family studies, as it is often called. We spoke on the subject at Minnesota, May 14, 1987. Alison C. Thorne and Barrie Thorne, "Feminism and Family Studies, Past and Present." Biester-Young

Lecture, Department of Family Social Science, University of Minnesota (unpublished).

At USU when Dean Bonita Wyse asked the board of regents for permission to start a Ph.D. program in the College of Family Life, I wrote the historical part of the proposal, carefully writing "home economics/family life," because early Utah legislation gave home economics to the Utah Agricultural College, not to the University of Utah.

9. Alison Comish Thorne, "Women Mentoring Women in Economics in the 1930s," in *Women of Value: Feminist Essays on the History of Women in Economics*, ed. Mary Ann Dimand, Robert W. Dimand, and Evelyn L. Forget (Aldershot, United Kingdom: Edward Elgar, 1995), pp. 60–70. See also review by Deborah A. Redman in *Feminist Economics* 2 (Fall 1996): 159–67.

10. Sandra Harding, "Can Feminist Thought Make Economics More Objective?" *Feminist Economics* (Spring 1995): 27–28.

11. Julie A. Nelson, "The Study of Choice or the Study of Provisioning," in *Beyond Economic Man: Feminist Theory and Economics*, ed. Marianne Ferber and Julie A. Nelson (Chicago: University of Chicago Press), pp. 23–36.

12. *Feminist Economics* 2, special issue in honor of Margaret Reid (Fall 1996).

13. Robert Irion, "The Shaman of Space and Time," *Science* (24 November, 2000): 1488.

Appendix: Life and Career of Wynne Thorne

1. Marlowe Driggs Thorne, ed., "The Life and Times of Ida Vilate Young Thorne, October 24, 1882–December 16, 1969," unpublished excerpts from diaries and journals (1988), pp. 58, 68, 89, 162 (Harold B. Lee Library, Brigham Young University Library Archives). A further portrayal of the Milton Thorne family is in Marlowe Driggs Thorne, "The Life and Times of Marlowe Driggs Thorne" (unpublished, 1993). In possession of author.

2. A blue carbon copy of the Barbarians' constitution lies inside Wynne's *The Buzzer*, the USAC yearbook. Barbarians were also called Independents. They had a long history at Oregon State, and my father was one of their advisors. When I was a student at Oregon State in 1930–32, I joined Phrateries, the women's division of Independents. The USAC Barbs' constitution also lists Phrateries.

3. Kip Thorne also went from a bachelor of science degree to Ph.D. in three years, at Princeton.

4. The Second International Symposium on Iron Nutrition and Interaction in Plants was held at USU in early August 1983.

5. Walter Hale Gardner, "Flow of Soil Moisture in the Unsaturated State" (Ph.D. diss., Utah State Agricultural College, June 2, 1950). The other Ph.D. was awarded to U Than Mynt in animal nutrition and biochemistry. Mynt was from Burma. We knew him well. I am indebted to James Shaver, dean of the School of Graduate Studies, for hunting up the facts about these two first Ph.D.s.

6. Wynne appended a list of his technical publications to his *Faculty Research Lecture* in 1951. His vita for 1972 lists his publications 1951–72. These and

other bibliographic materials are with his papers in Special Collections, Utah State University Merrill Library.

7. Wynne Thorne, ed., *Land and Water Use* (American Association for the Advancement of Science Publication 73: Washington D.C., 1963). Wynne chaired Section O of the AAAS when these papers were drawn together.

8. Kenneth W. Hill was director of the Utah Agricultural Experiment Station from 1966–71, and then became head of the Plant Science Department when Wynne Thorne became station director, 1972–74. Upon Wynne's retirement, Doyle J. Matthews, who was dean of agriculture, became director of the experiment station as well. Kenneth W. Hill, *History of the Experiment Station: Science Serves the Citizens, 1938–1978*, Utah State University: Utah Agricultural Experiment Station Bulletin 507.

9. D. Wynne Thorne, "Research: The Third Dimension," *USU Bulletin* 69 (December 1969): 13–16. Adapted and published in *Agricultural Science Review* 8 (2nd and 3rd quarters, 1970): 27–30. Research administrators of Ohio State University and Oregon State University wrote Wynne saying it was an extremely important article, as did others. Wynne served on the editorial board of the *Review* from its inception.

10. Utah State University, Division of Research, *Biennial Report July 1, 1972–June 30, 1974*: 24–25, 20–21. See bound volume *Utah State University Research 1955–1974*, containing reports of all those years. Incoming vice president for research, Dean F. Peterson, presented this volume to Wynne Thorne as indicating "the contributions you have made to a truly amazing program."

11. Letter to Wynne Thorne from Eastman N. Hatch, dean of graduate studies, March 19, 1975, in bound volume of *Letters of Tribute Presented to Dr. Wynne Thorne*, Utah State University, 1975.

12. Family letters, June 9, July 18, and July 24, 1960.

13. Family letter, November 25, 1960.

14. My family letter of July 15, 1976, describes our stay in London. The Swindales came to Logan November 2, 1979, to present a posthumous award honoring Wynne. Alison Thorne, family letter, November 3, 1979.

15. Alison Thorne, family letter, March 28, 1975.

16. Wynne Thorne and Alison C. Thorne, "Land Resources and Quality of Life," in *Renewable Resource Management for Forestry and Agriculture*, ed. James S. Bethel and Martin A. Massengale (Seattle: University of Washington Press, 1978), pp. 17–34.

17. D. Wynne Thorne and Marlowe D. Thorne, *Soil, Water, and Crop Production* (Westport, Conn.: AVI Publishing, 1979). Marlowe spent four years helping develop agricultural universities under U.S. AID. Two of these years were in Utter Pradesh, India, and two in Nepal. He did shorter term service (one to three months) in Sri Lanka, Pakistan, Brazil, Peru, and Niger.

18. R. S. Albrechtsen, "New Grain Varieties for Utah: Wynne, a New, Hard Red, Semi-dwarf Spring Wheat," *Utah Science* 45 (Spring 1984): 14–17. Marlowe Thorne drew my attention to researchers at Ohio State University who very early developed a Thorne Wheat named for a noted plant breeder there. Marlowe Thorne, letter to Alison Thorne, December 19, 1994.

Index

Abbott, Edith, 34–35, 38
Abbott, Grace, 34–35, 38
abortion, 138, 172, 178, 186, 192–93, 219–20
Abzug, Bella, 194
Addams, Jane, 33–34, 222
advertising, 50–51, 61–62, 66–67, 90, 135, 145
affirmative action, 33, 164–68, 175, 195
Agricultural Experiment Stations, 29, 31, 44, 92, 110, 162, 167, 220–21, 232–33, 235–37, 239–40, 242–43
Agronomy Wives, 75–77
American Association of University Women (AAUW), 33–34, 38, 45–46, 50, 68, 77, 92–93, 113, 156, 174, 194, 207–8
Committee on the Economic and Legal Status of Women, 30, 36
Ames, Iowa, 37, 210
Anthony, Susan B., 48, 180, 192
anti-nepotism, 43–45, 48, 82–83, 92, 126, 131–32, 223
antiwar movement, 35–36, 124–25, 145–51, 223
Armstrong, Barbara, 19
Arrington, Leonard, 81, 187, 217
Asch, Solomon, 104
Associated Women Students (AWS), 23, 77, 131

Barron, Frank, 101, 104, 106
Bennion, Ione, 145, 151, 158, 176, 191, 242
Bennion, Vera Weiler, 78
birth control, 30, 39
Breckinridge, Sophonisba, 33–35, 38, 77, 222

Brigham Young University, 22–23, 39, 157
Brite, Duncan, 45, 212
Brite, Luna, 45
Britton, Virginia, 37–38
Brodie, Fawn McKay, 36–37
Brookings Institution, 29
Brooks, Juanita, 77–78, 80, 170, 211, 214, 223
Brown, Almeda Perry, 92, 207, 220–21
Brown, Ida Stewart, 78–79
Brown, Robert, 146, 245
Bruce, Dorothy Hart, 18
Buchholz, H. E., 22
Burgoyne, Allie Peterson, 44, 113, 210–11

Cache Valley, Utah, xi, 6, 50, 98, 108–10, 112–15, 122–24, 172–74, 181–84, 188
California Institute of Technology (Caltech), 95, 151–52, 156, 229
California State Civil Service Commission, 19
Cannon, Clawson Y., 38, 41
Cannon, Winnifred Morrell, 38, 41
Carter, Bertha Fietz, 26
Cell 16, 145
Chase, Alice, 131
Chase, Daryl, 100, 108, 131–32, 140, 235
Chicago, Illinois, 34
child care, 30, 47, 66, 93, 158, 166, 172, 178, 226
child development, 5, 8, 30, 54, 57, 62–63, 74, 85, 92, 101–5, 220, 223
Colorado State College, 37, 203–4
Comish, Elaine, 1–2, 4–6, 9–17, 20, 87, 117, 211